THE COMPLETE IDIOT'S GUIDE TO

Economics

Second Edition

by Tom Gorman

ALPHA

A member of Penguin Group (USA) Inc.

ALPHA BOOKS

Published by the Penguin Group

Penguin Group (USA) Inc., 375 Hudson Street, New York, New York 10014, USA

Penguin Group (Canada), 90 Eglinton Avenue East, Suite 700, Toronto, Ontario M4P 2Y3, Canada (a division of Pearson Penguin Canada Inc.)

Penguin Books Ltd., 80 Strand, London WC2R 0RL, England

Penguin Ireland, 25 St. Stephen's Green, Dublin 2, Ireland (a division of Penguin Books Ltd.)

Penguin Group (Australia), 250 Camberwell Road, Camberwell, Victoria 3124, Australia (a division of Pearson Australia Group Pty. Ltd.)

Penguin Books India Pvt. Ltd., 11 Community Centre, Panchsheel Park, New Delhi—110 017, India

Penguin Group (NZ), 67 Apollo Drive, Rosedale, North Shore, Auckland 1311, New Zealand (a division of Pearson New Zealand Ltd.)

Penguin Books (South Africa) (Pty.) Ltd., 24 Sturdee Avenue, Rosebank, Johannesburg 2196, South Africa

Penguin Books Ltd., Registered Offices: 80 Strand, London WC2R 0RL, England

Copyright © 2011 by Tom Gorman

International Standard Book Number: 978-1-59257-981-5
Library of Congress Catalog Card Number: 2010908788

13 12 11   8 7 6 5 4 3 2 1

Interpretation of the printing code: The rightmost number of the first series of numbers is the year of the book's printing; the rightmost number of the second series of numbers is the number of the book's printing. For example, a printing code of 11-1 shows that the first printing occurred in 2011.

Printed in the United States of America

Most Alpha books are available at special quantity discounts for bulk purchases for sales promotions, premiums, fund-raising, or educational use. Special books, or book excerpts, can also be created to fit specific needs.

For details, write: Special Markets, Alpha Books, 375 Hudson Street, New York, NY 10014.

Publisher: *Marie Butler-Knight*

Associate Publisher: *Mike Sanders*

Senior Managing Editor: *Billy Fields*

Senior Acquisitions Editor: *Paul Dinas*

Senior Development Editor: *Phil Kitchel*

Senior Production Editor: *Janette Lynn*

Copy Editor: *Jaime Julian Wagner*

Cover Designer: *William Thomas*

Book Designers: *William Thomas, Rebecca Batchelor*

Indexer: *Angie Bess*

Layout: *Ayanna Lacey*

Proofreader: *Laura Caddell*

Contents

Introduction

Economics touches every part of our lives. Our jobs and livelihoods, our purchase and investment decisions, our choice of where and in what to live, even the way we vote—all depend to some extent on economics. The economy—the system that we as a society use to decide what to produce and who gets what—is a powerful force in our lives.

Yet few of us truly understand how our economy works. We may have conventional wisdom of the type summed up in old sayings: The rich get richer, and the poor get poorer. Money comes to money. The best things in life are free. There is even some truth to these sayings when you look at income patterns, returns on investment, and certain quality-of-life issues. But despite their truth, those sayings don't provide enough information, insight, or inspiration to guide us in our economic lives. They are substitutes for understanding economics, a subject many people find mysterious.

There are several reasons for the mystery that shrouds economics, but I believe the main reason is that most people think the whole subject is way too complicated. Part of this has to do with language. Just like medicine, auto repair, and other fields, economics has its own words for things. The words that describe economic activity may be unfamiliar, but they're still only words. Those words all refer to concepts and phenomena that you'll probably recognize, and once you understand what they mean, much of the mystery drops away.

Many people also think that economics is full of mathematics. Although there can be a lot of numbers in economics, the most important concepts can be explained in plain English. Also, except in specialized areas such as economic forecasting, the arithmetic that does pop up is very basic.

Economics is a social science. Like the other social sciences, such as psychology, it explains human behavior. Economics explains people's behavior in the marketplace. Why do people buy what they buy? How do merchants decide what prices to charge? Why can't everyone have what they want? How do the owners of a business decide what to make and how much to pay workers? What, if anything, can the government do to help poor people become better off? Economics answers these questions—and answers most of them without mathematics.

Sometimes economists make economics seem complicated. Economists are the highly educated experts who study economics deeply, conduct research, formulate theories, and teach in colleges and universities. They also advise business and political leaders about the economy. Economists can play an important role in society, but like all experts, they create many of the complexities of their subject. This book simplifies the complexities and serves as your guide to economics and the workings of our economy.

If you are a business person, professional, investor, or just a citizen with a vote you don't want to waste, *The Complete Idiot's Guide to Economics, Second Edition*, will help you make better decisions. If you are a student, this book will give you a clearer explanation of many economic concepts than textbooks or lectures often supply. No matter what roles you play in our economy—and we all play multiple roles, as workers, employers, buyers, sellers, lenders, borrowers, and so on—this book will explain that role and show you how to play it better.

Why a second edition of *The Complete Idiot's Guide to Economics*? Like everything else, economics and the economies it studies keep developing. Although the law of supply and demand and the workings of the marketplace have not changed, there have been a few developments. First, certain areas of economics, particularly health care and energy, have grown in importance since the first edition. Second, we have seen the wrenching end of a business cycle and the start of a new one—as well as potentially larger changes in the U.S. and global economic landscape. Third, the government has taken a more active role in the management of the economy, and people in general have become more interested in economic policy. Finally, more people than ever realize that their quality of life depends in large part on the performance of the economy in which they live and work. They've seen first-hand how economic events that once seemed remote can affect their daily lives.

Also, while virtually all of the basic material from the first edition has been retained, it has been streamlined in spots and explained more fully (and clearly) in others. New chapters cover the economic cycle, as well as health care, energy and sustainability, and the impact of policies. Most parts and many chapters have been reorganized to present the material in more accessible ways and to add more examples and references. And, of course, charts, graphs, and other data-driven features have been updated.

Like the first edition, this is not a book about economic theories, although it covers the major ones. It is a book about economic realities—so it is geared to the needs of the student, business person, worker, investor, and voter. I point out the effects of economics on businesses, consumers, lenders, borrowers, various segments of society, and our global neighbors. I will also, when appropriate, suggest steps you can take to protect yourself or benefit from economic realities.

Although economics can be fraught with politics, I have no political agenda in writing this book. When an author writing about economics has an ideological ax to grind or fails to stay politically neutral, then he's not just discussing economics. He's presenting political viewpoints. Staying politically neutral when discussing economics can be difficult, but it means, for example, pointing out both management's and labor's view of an issue, such as unions, or the right's and the left's arguments for and against deficit spending.

Viewpoints are fine and, like everyone, I have mine. However, I want to give you a clear understanding of economics and leave you free to develop your own viewpoint. So I've kept my political beliefs out of this book and presented the views of supporters and opponents when it comes to economic issues.

Here's the approach we'll take:

Part 1, Economics Explains It All, gives you an overview of economics, the U.S. economy, and some basic tools of economics. It also presents the concepts of supply and demand and shows you how prices are determined in the marketplace.

Part 2, Capitalism at Work, examines the ways in which consumers and businesses make decisions, the dynamics of income and spending, and the distribution of income and wealth, particularly in the United States.

Part 3, The Government and the Economy, covers the determinants of economic growth and patterns of expansion and contraction. It also examines taxes, government spending, and fiscal policy, and thus the role of the government in the economy and its occasional attempts to stimulate it through spending.

Part 4, Money, the Banking System, and Policy, explains the roles that money, credit, the Federal Reserve, and the banking system play in our economy. This chapter also explains monetary policy, which is the other way (aside from fiscal policy) that the government tries to keep the economy stable and growing.

Part 5, The Global Economy, takes you beyond U.S. borders and into the workings of the global economy. Here we examine imports and exports, international trade policy, the foreign exchange system, and the issues facing developing nations.

Part 6, Situational Economics, delves into health care, an important economic issue for many U.S. citizens, and into energy and the issue of sustainable growth, which depends on energy sources, population growth, and lifestyles. This part also shows how to monitor the economy yourself and then wraps up with ways of dealing with economic developments in your daily life.

In the tradition of the *Complete Idiot's Guides* series, *The Complete Idiot's Guide to Economics, Second Edition,* takes a complex subject and makes it clear and, I hope, fun to learn about. As you read this book, either straight through or when a part or chapter will help you understand something going on in the world (or in class), keep in mind that economics is affecting you every day, whether you know it or not. If you look around, listen to the news, and watch what people do, you will see every aspect of economics at work in the real world.

Yet the real value of your reading will come when you see the workings of economics—supply and demand, expansion and recession, monetary and fiscal policy—in your daily life: in your paycheck, wallet, pocketbook, credit card statement, bank account, and investment portfolio. The more you know about the economics of a situation, the better you'll be able to understand the situation and know what action to take.

Some "Economic Indicators"

Throughout the book, you will find the following features that will clarify certain points, add to your knowledge, and keep it real.

ECONOTALK

These boxes explain economic concepts and technical terms in plain English.

ECONOTIP

These boxes warn you about potential points of confusion and help you apply the concepts and analytical tools to everyday life.

THE REAL WORLD

These boxes show aspects of economics at work in history, business, and the news.

Acknowledgements

Thank you to everyone who helped make this book possible: Marie Butler-Knight, publisher at Alpha Books and the entire editorial team: Paul Dinas, editor; Phil Kitchel, development editor; Janette Lynn, production editor; and Jaime Julian Wagner, copy editor. I also want to thank Mike Snell, my agent; my wife Phyllis and my sons Daniel and Matthew; my professors and instructors at New York University's Stern School of Business; and my past employers and colleagues, particularly those at the economic forecasting and consulting firm DRI/McGraw-Hill (now IHS Global Insight Inc.), where I worked as the managing editor from 1991 to 1996.

Trademarks

Economics Explains It All

How does economics "explain it all"? By recording, analyzing, and studying the way people behave in markets, with the knowledge that most human behavior occurs in markets of some kind. Thus economics explains where people live and work, what they need and want, what they earn and buy, and how they make most decisions. Economics studies people in all of their roles as economic actors: in government, private industry, households, and nations. In its way, economics includes aspects of psychology, sociology, philosophy, history, and mathematics. So even though it's an imperfect science, economics at least *tries* to explain it all.

This first part of the book will introduce you to key concepts and tools, with an overview of economics and a look at the players in the U.S. economy—consumers, businesses, the government, and importers and exporters.

Economists typically think in terms of markets. An economy contains thousands and thousands of markets. That would be pretty overwhelming if they didn't all work the same fundamental way. All markets operate by the law of supply and demand and use prices to match supply and demand in a way that works for both buyers and sellers. So Part 1 will also show you how markets work, how prices behave, and how certain external forces can affect a market.

Let's get started.

Who Gets What, and How?

In This Chapter

- Why economics matters
- How societies make decisions
- Major economic theories

Let's face it: if there's one fundamental principle guiding life on Earth, it's scarcity. There simply aren't enough beachfront houses, luxury cars, and seats at the theater for everyone who wants one! And, on a more serious note, there's not enough food, clothing, and medical care for everyone who needs it.

The entire discipline of economics—and all economic activity—arises from a scarcity of goods and services in comparison to human wants and needs. If there is not enough of something for everyone who wants or needs it, society faces a serious problem: how do we decide who gets that something and who goes without it?

Throughout history there have always been people who obtained what they wanted or needed by force. The barbarians who sacked Rome practiced this form of economic activity, and in modern times, it is practiced by armed robbers. But a society worthy of the name requires an orderly system of producing and distributing the necessities and luxuries of life. Such a system is essential to a stable society. Economics is the study of systems of production and distribution—which are called economies—and of their fundamentals, dynamics, and results.

This chapter introduces the science of economics and examines various ways in which societies organize their economies. It also introduces several important economists and explains their ideas, which lead to major schools of economic thought.

What Is Economics and Who Cares?

Economics is the study, description, and analysis of the ways in which societies produce and distribute *goods and services*. Economics can be applied to ancient civilizations—the Greeks and Phoenicians had economies—and to modern societies at the national, state, and local levels. For instance, California has the largest economy of any state, while New York City has the largest of any U.S. city. Even a household has an economy (although this book does not cover home economics). Any system for deciding what is produced, how it is produced, and who gets to consume it—whether it is the system of an entire planet (as in the global economy) or a defined segment of society—is an economy and can be understood in economic terms.

ECONOTALK

Economics is the study, description, and analysis of the ways in which a society produces and distributes goods and services. In economics, the term **goods and services** refers to everything that is produced in the economy—all products and services, including government services, such as national defense and the prison system.

An Inexact Science?

Economics is one of the social (as opposed to natural or physical) sciences, like psychology and anthropology. Social sciences examine and explain human behavior and interaction. Because of this, the findings and knowledge produced by a social science generally cannot be as exact or predictable as those of a physical science, such as physics or chemistry.

For instance, if you put water in a saucepan on a stove, you can be certain that it will boil when it reaches 212° Fahrenheit. But if you are the governor of a state and you raise the sales tax, you cannot be certain about the effect it will have, nor will you be able to answer any of the following basic questions: How much money will the tax raise? To avoid the tax, will people take more of their business across the state line? Will companies in the state experience lower sales and generate lower corporate income taxes as a result?

Economics deals with these kinds of questions, but it seldom produces totally precise explanations or predictions. Human behavior in the economic realm is as complex and mysterious as it is in any other sphere of life.

It's Not Perfect, but It Helps!

The good news is that economics can tell us the *likely* results of a sales tax. In addition, as a scientific discipline, economics provides useful analytical tools and frameworks for understanding human behavior when it comes to getting and spending money, which (let's face it) occupies the majority of most people's waking hours.

Economics deals with fundamental, often life-or-death, issues. That is why economics is important. Its challenge lies in its mysteries: we don't know when the next expansion or recession will arrive. We don't know if a federal tax cut will help the economy grow. We don't know which new technologies should be encouraged and which ones won't pan out. And, tragically, we don't know how to overcome poverty, hunger, crime, and other evils rooted in economic reality. But economics is the branch of the social sciences most concerned with these matters, and it does help us deal with them.

Economics helps you understand government policies, business developments, and consumer behavior here and abroad. It provides a rich context for making decisions in your business, professional, and financial life. The economy is to business as the ocean is to fish. It is the environment in which business operates. The more you know about this environment, the better you will function as a manager, employee, consumer, voter, and all-around decision-maker.

Macroeconomics and Microeconomics

Economics has two main branches: macroeconomics and microeconomics.

Macroeconomics (*macro* means *large*) focuses on the study of whole systems of production and distribution—that is, whole economies and the forces that determine their short- and long-term growth. Macroeconomics focuses on broad levels of economic activity, such as overall income and production, relationships among sectors of the economy, and an economy's cycles of expansion and contraction. Macroeconomics also examines issues of employment, inflation, and living standards. In general, macroeconomic techniques study interactions between sectors of the economy, which include the private and the public sector, or between broad phenomena such as interest rates and economic growth.

We'll talk about sectors of the economy in more detail in Chapter 2 but, broadly, most economies contain a public sector—local, state (or provincial), and federal governments—and a private sector, which includes consumers, businesses, and non-profit and nongovernmental organizations.

Microeconomics, as the name indicates, concerns itself with smaller portions of the economy. Microeconomics focuses on individual economic entities, such as businesses or households, or on specific economic activities or phenomena, such as supply and demand in a market and how prices are set. In general, microeconomic techniques study the behavior and decisions of individual consumers, households, and businesses in the economy and the effects of their behavior and decisions.

ECONOTALK

Macroeconomics focuses on whole economies and large sectors of economies and on broad levels of economic activity, economic cycles, issues of long-term growth, and interactions among sectors of the economy. **Microeconomics** focuses on individual economic entities, such as a single business or household, or on specific economic activities or phenomena, such as employment or prices.

One other aspect of economics warrants mention: econometrics. (*Metrics* is just another word for measures.) The discipline of econometrics uses statistical methods to analyze economic behavior and problems. Much of econometrics focuses on forecasting economic activity, such as next year's auto sales or interest rates, or when the next expansion or recession will begin. Economic forecasts are notoriously inaccurate, but then so are weather forecasts. Like most views of the future, economic forecasts should be used to describe different potential scenarios and their possible effects.

Applying Economics

As a social science, economics has most of the characteristics of other sciences. Economists observe behavior and outcomes, systematically catalog those observations (by collecting data), and identify patterns and trends. Then they develop and test theories to explain the behavior, outcomes, patterns, and trends they have seen. Although economists can rarely test their theories in controlled experiments, they do seek practical applications of their theories. This application often takes the form of *economic policies* implemented by local, state, and federal governments. Economic policies also affect major decisions by large corporations and financial institutions. We'll discuss economic policies in greater depth in Parts 3 and 4.

ECONOTALK

Economic policies are actions that a government takes to help stabilize or grow its economy. Tools of economic policy include increasing or decreasing government spending and borrowing, adjusting certain interest rates, and increasing or decreasing taxes. They can also include direct government assistance to households, businesses, and banks, as seen in the 2008–2009 recession.

For example, economists have formulated theories about the relationship between interest rates and the amount of money businesses and consumers borrow. These theories help the government develop policies that affect how easily people can borrow money—that is, use credit. The availability of credit affects the level of people's spending, which in turn affects the level of production, which affects the rate of economic growth.

Economists and economics play an important role in addressing many of the world's most pressing problems. Many high-ranking public finance officials hold degrees in economics or are economists. The Council of Economic Advisors helps the president address economic issues.

Virtually every state, many cities, and some regions of the United States have established economic development agencies that create programs to maintain and improve the economic health of the area. Their goals include attracting and retaining businesses and jobs, fostering development of new technologies, and educating the area's workforce.

On a larger scale, U.S. and international organizations, such as the World Bank, build programs to develop and stabilize economies of less-developed nations around the world. The International Monetary Fund monitors national economies, trade activity, and the value of the world's various currencies.

The U.S. economy and even state and local economies cannot be completely controlled by the government or any other entity. They are too large and people's behavior is too complex to fully understand, let alone control. However, economic theory helps government efforts to stabilize and grow economies and temper the effects of recessions.

Many people see economics as a theoretical ivory tower pursuit. That's far from the truth. All of the world's major investment and commercial banks—and many major manufacturers—have staff economists monitoring the impact of consumer, business, and government decisions on the markets and on their customers.

A Firm Base

Let's look at a few basic concepts that underlie the discipline of economics.

First, economics assumes that people make rational choices in the face of scarcity. It assumes that people can and will rationally decide what they need and what they can do without. At times, this assumption may seem odd. Are economists saying that people deliberately choose jobs with low pay? Are they saying that people choose poorly made products over high-quality ones?

Well, in a way, yes. Although individuals may have limited choices or make bad choices, they do make choices. Economics aims to explain and predict people's financial and economic decisions and the ways in which conditions affect their decisions. Almost by necessity, economists generally assume that people are making rational, rather than irrational, economic decisions. However, a relatively new specialty—behavioral economics—recognizes that social, emotional, and psychological factors can affect people's decisions and explain some of their irrational behavior, particularly in the financial markets.

Second, economics assumes that people have preferences that underlie their economic decisions. This resembles the idea of rational choice but focuses more on the trade-offs people are willing to make among their likes and dislikes. The assumption is that people know what they prefer and make choices that reflect these preferences.

Third, people's choices and preferences—their decisions—take the form of transactions in the marketplace. With these transactions they buy and sell labor, products, and services in exchange for money. Furthermore, these transactions collectively amount to economic activity. For example, someone who decides to work at a certain job in a certain place for a certain salary has engaged in a transaction. When we sum up all of the work-related transactions that people in an economy have made, the result is employment activity, which can be quantified, described, and studied.

Fourth, economic activity occurs in *markets*. A market is a place where goods and services and the factors of production—raw materials, labor, and plant and equipment—are bought and sold. Although most of us think of a market as a physical place, economists define markets more broadly. The market for financial securities, for example, is located not only on Wall Street but also in cyberspace, where online brokerage services enable people to buy and sell securities. Economics delves deeply into markets—how they function and how people function within them.

ECONOTALK

Markets are organized mechanisms or systems for exchanging money for goods and services (or, in a barter system, goods and services for goods and services). They may be physical places, such as the New York Stock Exchange, or they may be located in cyberspace, like the international currency market. A market enables buyers and sellers to engage in transactions.

Finally, some mechanism of exchange is required for a market to function properly. That mechanism used is usually the price mechanism, and prices are expressed in money. (Bet you were wondering when we would get around to money.) In all modern economies, money is recognized as the medium of exchange. A medium of exchange is something people within an economy have agreed to use as a standard of value. Certain Native American tribes reportedly used wampum, the purple parts of clamshells, as money. Other forms of money have included gold, furs, and huge round stones—all of which make about as much sense as using pieces of paper displaying pictures of deceased leaders. Essentially, money is anything that people agree to use as a medium of exchange on a large scale.

These concepts—people making rational choices and expressing preferences in marketplace transactions valued in money—form the basis of all that follows in economics. Keep these concepts in mind as we examine matters like the law of supply and demand in Chapter 4.

Also, bear in mind that markets, like governments, can be inefficient in delivering goods and services—and, as demonstrated in the 2000s, at allocating capital. Markets are considered most inefficient at delivering public goods. Essentially, a public good is something that everyone wants, such as clean air or a well-educated populace, but no one wants to pay for individually. Although the United States is experimenting with market incentives to obtain these goods—for instance, tradable exemptions from emissions controls and school voucher programs—markets have a generally poor record of delivering public goods. For instance, if you see health care as a public good, then the U.S. health-care system is an example of this, in that it delivers great care—and poor care—depending on people's ability to pay.

Getting Organized: Command, Market, and Mixed Economies

Not all economies are organized in the same way. The three major ways they can be organized are as a *market economy*, a *command economy*, or a *mixed economy*.

In a market economy, consumers and producers decide what they want to purchase and produce by voting with their dollars in the marketplace. Purchasers decide what to buy based on their preferences and the prices of goods and services. Producers decide what to produce based upon their sales and the prices they get for their goods and services. In a pure market economy, also known as a *laissez-faire* economy (from the French *allow to do*), the government plays a very limited role. The government does not direct, and may even lack the power to direct, the private sector to purchase or produce specific goods and services.

ECONOTALK

In a **market economy,** the private-sector businesses and consumers decide what they will produce and purchase with little government intervention. A **laissez-faire** economy is a "pure market economy," in which the government plays a very limited role. In a **command economy,** also known as a planned economy, the government largely determines what is produced and in what amounts. In a **mixed economy,** both market forces and government decisions determine which goods and services are produced and how they are distributed.

In a command economy, also known as a planned economy, the government largely determines what is produced and in what amounts. It directs producers to make and deliver goods and services in specified amounts. In practice, command economies are associated with socialism and communism, two closely related forms of government. Socialism and communism are characterized by collective ownership of the means of production and central planning functions that try to produce what people want and need, in the quantities and at the time required. The underlying philosophy of socialism is: "From each according to his abilities, to each according to his needs."

In command economies, the people (in the form of the state) own the means of production. The state, which is seen to embody the will of the people, decides what will be produced according to a plan based upon what the state calculates to be people's need and desire for various goods and services. The state also plays an important role in determining how goods and services are distributed—that is, in deciding who gets how much of what.

In a mixed economy, both market forces and government decisions determine which goods and services are produced and how they are distributed. In general, market forces prevail in mixed economies. The government does not direct the private sector to produce certain goods and services in certain quantities at certain times. However, the government's influence in the economy stems from the amount of money (raised in the form of taxes and borrowings from the private sector) that it spends (on defense, for example) and, through various forms of *welfare* and *entitlement programs*, redistributes.

ECONOTALK

Welfare refers to government efforts to provide for people's basic needs. Also known as public assistance, these are usually payments made by the government to support basic needs of those who cannot afford them. The Supplemental Nutrition Assistance Program (formerly known as food stamps) and Temporary Assistance for Needy Families are both forms of welfare.

Entitlement programs, such as Social Security, are also efforts to provide for basic needs, but people pay taxes specifically to support those programs and are thus entitled to them (though they must qualify by age or specific conditions, such as disability).

Today, the economies of most industrial countries are mixed economies. In Western European nations, the government usually plays a larger role in the economy than in North America. Since the fall of the Soviet Union in 1991, the only two major planned economies are those of North Korea and the People's Republic of China. However, China has begun to incorporate market mechanisms, such as competition, into its economy.

Although many people characterize the U.S. economy as a free-market economy, it is clearly a mixed economy. The federal government alone accounts for about 20 percent of the U.S. economy (depending on what forms of government spending are counted). Adding state and local governments brings the public sector share up to about 28 percent. With that kind of economic clout, government at various levels has a lot to say about what is produced in our society and who gets what. Nevertheless, the United States relies on markets to a larger degree than any other major industrial nation in the world.

Three Key Economists and Their Theories

The three most important economists were Adam Smith, Karl Marx, and John Maynard Keynes (pronounced *canes*). Each was a highly original thinker who developed economic theories that were put into practice and affected the world's economies for generations.

Adam Smith and His Invisible Hand of Capitalism

Adam Smith, a Scot and a philosopher who lived from 1723 to 1790, is considered the founder of modern economics. In Smith's time, philosophy was an all-encompassing study of human society. In examining the world of business, Smith concluded that the individuals in society, each acting in his or her own self-interest, collectively manage to produce and purchase the goods and services that they as a society require. He called the mechanism by which this self-regulation occurs "the invisible hand" in his groundbreaking book, *The Wealth of Nations*, which was published in 1776, the year of America's Declaration of Independence.

Although Smith couldn't prove the existence of this hand (it was, after all, invisible), he presented many instances of its working in society. Essentially, the butcher, the baker, and the candlestick maker individually go about their business. Each produces the amount of meat, bread, and candlesticks he judges to be correct. Each buys the amount of meat, bread, and candlesticks that his household needs. All of this happens without their consulting one another and without all the king's men telling them how much to produce. It's the free market economy in action.

In making this discovery, Smith founded what is known as classical economics. The key doctrine of classical economics is that a laissez-faire attitude by government toward the marketplace will allow the invisible hand to guide everyone to create the greatest good for the greatest number of people and generate economic growth. Smith also delved into the dynamics of the labor market, wealth accumulation, and productivity growth and gave generations of economists plenty to think about and build on.

Karl Marx: It's Exploitation!

Karl Marx, a German economist and political scientist who lived from 1818 to 1883, looked at capitalism from a more pessimistic and revolutionary viewpoint. Where Adam Smith saw harmony and growth, Marx saw instability, struggle, and decline. Marx believed that once the capitalist (the person with the money and the organizational skills to build a factory) has set up the means of production, all value is created by the labor involved in producing whatever is being produced. In Marx's view, presented in his 1867 tome *Das Kapital* (*Capital*), a capitalist's profits come from exploiting labor—that is, from paying workers less than the value they are actually creating. Thus, Marx opposed the notion of a profit-oriented organization.

This situation of management exploiting labor underlies the class struggle that Marx saw at the heart of capitalism, and he predicted that this struggle would ultimately destroy capitalism. To Marx, class struggle is inherent in the system and intensifies over time. It intensifies as businesses become larger and larger, due to the inherent efficiency of larger operations and their ability to withstand cyclical economic crises. Ultimately, in Marx's view, society moves to a two-class system of a few wealthy capitalists and a mass of underpaid, underprivileged workers.

Marx predicted the fall of capitalism and movement of society toward communism, in which the people (that is, the workers) own the means of production and thus have no need to exploit labor for profit. Marx's thinking had a tremendous impact on many societies, particularly on the USSR (Union of Soviet Socialist Republics) in the twentieth century.

In practice, however, two events have undermined Marx's theories. First, socialist, centrally planned economies have proven far less efficient at producing and delivering goods and services than capitalist systems. Second, workers' incomes have generally risen over time in capitalist economies, undercutting the theory that labor is exploited for profit. If workers' incomes are rising, they are sharing in the profits and in the growth of the economy.

On the other hand, large companies do tend to get larger and do tend to exploit their market power. In capitalist economies, a good amount of government intervention—ranging from anti-trust laws that can be used to break up large companies to minimum-wage laws to rules about workplace safety—are required to prevent gross exploitation of workers.

So although Marx's theories have been largely discredited, they are fascinating and worth understanding. They even say something about weaknesses in capitalism. For instance, large companies have certain advantages over small ones and can absorb or undercut them, as shown by examples as old as Standard Oil (now ExxonMobil) and as recent as Microsoft, and by the family farm giving way to major agricultural companies such as ConAgra. In addition, as we will see in Chapter 10, highly competitive, U.S.-style capitalism tends to create a two-tiered class system of haves and have-nots.

Karl Marx was a true revolutionary and philosopher. Of Jewish descent but baptized and raised as a Lutheran, he coined the phrase "Religion is the opiate of the people," thus contributing to the rise of "godless Communism."

Marx's philosophy was based on a materialistic conception of history. This was in sharp contrast to the then-popular idea that God was shaping human affairs. Essentially, Marx believed that the prevailing economic system at a given time determines the way people think. He also believed that history is a process of the evolution of economies, which proceed from pre-capitalism, to capitalism, to communism.

Even before he wrote *Capital,* Marx wrote *The Communist Manifesto* with his fellow philosopher Frederick Engels, which posited the idea of a classless society. There was clearly more than a little idealism in Marx, despite his notorious irritability and arrogance.

Marx made his often meager living as a journalist. In 1849, after pretty much being thrown off the continent for revolutionary activities, he settled in London, where he spent the rest of his life and is buried.

Keynes: The Government Should Help Out the Economy

John Maynard Keynes, a British economist and financial genius who lived from 1883 to 1946, also examined capitalism and came up with some extremely influential views. They were, however, quite different from those of Karl Marx and Adam Smith. In 1936, he published his *General Theory of Employment, Interest, and Money.* We will examine Keynes's theories later in this book. They mainly involve people's propensity to spend or to save their additional money as their incomes rise, and the effects of increases in spending on the economy as a whole.

The larger significance of Keynes's work lies in his view of the role of government in a capitalist economy. Keynes was writing during the Great Depression. We will look at the Great Depression in Chapter 11, but it's worth noting now that, in the 1930s, U.S. unemployment reached about 25 percent and millions of people had lost their life savings. Moreover, there was no clear path out of the depression, which led people to question whether Smith's invisible hand was still guiding things. Was this worldwide collapse of economic activity the end of capitalism?

Keynes believed that there was only one way out: the government had to start spending in order to put money into private-sector pockets and get demand for goods and services up and running again. As it turns out, President Franklin D. Roosevelt gave this remedy a try when he started a massive public-works program to employ a portion of the idle workforce. However, the U.S. entry into World War II rendered this a less-than-pure experiment in government spending. The war effort boosted production to extremely high levels (to make guns, ammunition, planes, trucks, and other equipment) while taking millions of men (and women) out of the civilian workforce and putting them into uniform.

The validity and desirability of Keynes's prescription for a sluggish economy—using government spending to prime the pump—are still debated today. Indeed, President Obama's stimulus bill to combat the recession in 2009 represents the most recent major debate. Many on the political left felt that the roughly $775 billion package should have been larger, while many on the right felt it should have been smaller. Again, we will look at the theory and practice of what came to be known as *Keynesian economics* later in this book.

ECONOTALK

Keynesian economics is an approach to economic policy that favors using the government's power to spend, tax, and borrow to keep the economy stable and growing. A Keynesian is an economist or other believer in Keynesian economics.

Many other economists of note advanced theories and otherwise added to the body of knowledge in the science. We will look at their ideas as they arise in our examination of economics. However, Adam Smith, Karl Marx, and John Maynard Keynes (later Lord Keynes) are widely recognized as the most influential—Smith because he founded and formalized the science of economics, Marx because he challenged capitalism and had so much impact on society and politics, and Keynes because he prompted new practices as well as new theories of economic policy. Keynes also played a key role in the founding of the International Monetary Fund and in other political economic measures at the end of World War II.

The Dismal Science?

Thomas Malthus, a British clergyman and professor who lived from 1766 to 1843, developed the theory that orderly society was doomed because population growth would eventually outstrip the food supply. The Reverend Malthus believed that the resulting war, famine, and disease would periodically wipe out significant portions of the population in most countries.

He presented his theory, supported by mathematical proof, in 1798 in his *Essay on the Principle of Population*. When the Scottish historian Thomas Carlyle read the piece, he pronounced economics "the dismal science," and the name has stuck. The idea behind Malthusian economics—that the scarcity or exhaustibility of resources breeds catastrophe—has also stuck with many people. Many today believe that overpopulation will ruin the planet and that the finite nature of fossil fuel, and even timber, may lead to catastrophe.

They may have a point, but optimistic economists point to countervailing forces. These forces include ever-increasing efficiency in food production, natural tendencies to limit population growth, and people's ability to develop substitutes for finite resources. Also, we are, as pointed out in Chapter 21, now becoming more focused on adopting sustainable energy usage and business practices.

Still, the dismal science tag has stuck, and economics is, after all, the science of scarcity. Moreover, life can be dismal for people who don't have everything they want, and it is downright desperate for those who don't have everything they need.

Yet economics is also the science of plentitude. At its best, the discipline aims to further our understanding of how to keep society stable and economies growing. That way, the proverbial pie grows larger and everyone has what they want and need, including productive work, basic necessities, some luxuries, and peace and prosperity.

The Least You Need to Know

* A stable society needs an orderly system of producing and distributing goods and services. Economics is the study of these systems and of people's individual and collective behavior within those systems.

* Macroeconomics focuses on the study of whole systems of production and distribution—that is, whole economies—and large sectors within an economy. Microeconomics focuses on individual economic entities—such as a business or household—or on specific economic activities or phenomena—such as employment or prices.

* Economics generally assumes that people make rational choices and express preferences by engaging in transactions in the marketplace, which employs prices—valued in money—as its exchange mechanism.

- Basically, a nation's economy can be characterized as a market, command, or mixed economy, depending on the role the government plays in decisions about what is produced and how it is distributed.

- Adam Smith, Karl Marx, and John Maynard Keynes are history's most influential economists. Smith founded the science of economics and formulated the basic theory of capitalism. Marx challenged capitalism and had a wide impact on the political world. Keynes developed new practices and theories, the key one being the idea that government spending can stimulate the economy.

GDP and the Players Three

In This Chapter

- Major sectors of the U.S. economy
- The role of consumers, business, and government
- Drivers of economic growth

You may know the answer to the question, "How do you eat an elephant?"

"One bite at a time."

That's the approach to take when you are trying to understand the U.S. economy, which is the largest in the world. In this chapter, we start by carving this elephant into some fairly large parts, or sectors, as economists call them.

As we learn about these sectors, keep in mind that each one is made up of human beings. Actual people, in households, businesses, and government, decide how much of which goods and services to produce, what to purchase, and how much to pay for them. When dealing with trillions of dollars and entities like government and business, it's easy to forget this. But when we lose sight of the people in the economy, we can also lose sight of the fact that we, and not some malevolent machine or faceless bureaucracy, *are* the economy.

All Together Now: C + I + G

Consumption by consumers, investment by businesses, and government spending are the three major parts of our economy and of most economies. (Foreign trade, conducted by exporters and importers, is the remaining sector, which I'll discuss soon.)

The size of a nation's economy is the total value of the goods and services produced in the nation in a year. This production can be measured either by the total spending that occurs in the economy or by the total cost of the goods sold, which would equal total income. You arrive at the same number whether you add up the spending on the goods and services produced or the cost of producing them (the wages, profits, interest, and rent paid to workers, companies, lenders, and property owners). The first method is called the flow-of-product approach, and the second is called the earnings or cost approach.

In either case, when you add up all of these transactions—including the value of foreign trade—the result is *gross domestic product,* or GDP. The formula for GDP is:

$$GDP = C + I + G + (Ex - Im)$$

The parts of the formula are simple:

C = total spending by consumers

I = total investment (spending on goods and services) by businesses

G = total spending by government (federal, state, and local)

(Ex – Im) = net exports (exports – imports)

In 2009, C + I + G + (Ex – Im) equaled over $14 trillion in the United States. That means the United States produces more than $14 trillion of goods and services within its borders *every year.*

 ECONOTALK

Gross domestic product is the total value of the goods and services produced in a nation's economy in a year. The formula for GDP is: GDP = C + I + G + (Ex – Im), where *C* equals spending by consumers, *I* equals investment by businesses, *G* equals government spending, and *(Ex – Im)* equals net exports—that is, the value of exports minus imports. Net exports may be negative.

You should know several things about GDP. Spending by consumers, which economists call consumption or consumption expenditure, is by far the largest part of the U.S. GDP. In the mid-2000s, it accounted for about 70 percent of GDP in the United States. In the years following the 2008–2009 recession, consumers may spend less because they are expected to save more and to use less credit. This would signal a return to their more traditional role of accounting for two thirds of the U.S. economy.

Business investment is the total amount of spending by businesses on plant and equipment, and it accounted for about 17 percent of total GDP in the mid-2000s. This might seem to be a relatively small portion of GDP for business, but it's an extremely important one. Businesses invest in productive equipment, and that equipment typically creates jobs as well as goods and services. Note that wages and salaries are not counted as businesses investment (I). That money is already counted in consumption (C) because that is the money that households are spending. Investment (I) includes only spending by businesses on goods and services, including raw materials, vehicles, offices and factories, computers, furniture, and machinery.

Government spending on goods and services averages about 19 percent, or one fifth, of total GDP. The government takes in an amount equal to more than one fifth of GDP in taxes, but a portion of that money, equal to about 10 percent of GDP, goes to transfer payments rather than expenditures on goods and services. Transfer payments include Social Security, Medicare, unemployment insurance, welfare programs, and *subsidies*. These are not included in GDP, because they are not payments for goods or services, but rather means of allocating money to achieve social ends. By the way, although Social Security and Medicare represent transfer payments, they are not welfare; they are programs the participants have paid into to be entitled to the benefits. That's why they're called entitlement programs.

ECONOTALK

Subsidies are transfer payments to assist industries that benefit the public but might not survive or remain stable if operated for profit without subsidies. Farm products and rail transportation are subsidized in most modern economies.

Net exports for the United States are typically negative, usually about 6 percent. Yes, the United States exports a tremendous amount of goods, but it imports even more.

So the composition of GDP breaks down roughly as follows:

Consumption	70%
Investment	17%
Government	19%
Net Exports	-6%
	100%

Each component of GDP is important. In this chapter, we examine the role and contribution of each component.

ECONOTIP

You may have heard the term Gross National Product, or GNP. Economists now usually use GDP—gross domestic product—rather than GNP to measure the economy. Here's why: GDP includes all goods and services produced *within* a nation's borders. GNP includes all goods and services produced *by* a nation, including those produced overseas by that nation's companies.

For example, given the number of foreign companies, such as car manufacturers, now operating in the United States, most economists see GDP as the better measure of U.S. economic activity. U.S. companies have operations in foreign nations, but that does not create goods, services, jobs, or income in the United States.

GDP Is "The Economy"

When people refer to "the economy," they are generally referring to GDP. If a newsperson says, "The economy grew by 3.5 percent last year," it means that GDP grew by 3.5 percent during the year (compared with the previous year's GDP). Incidentally, a growing economy (also called increasing output) characterizes an expansion, also known as a recovery. A contracting economy (or decreasing output) characterizes a recession. We will examine the cycle of recession and recovery—that is, the business cycle—in detail in Chapter 11. For now, it's important to know that a society benefits greatly from a stable, growing economy.

ECONOTIP

Economists also refer to GDP—total spending on goods and services—as total demand. In other words, the amount of goods and services accounted for in GDP is also approximately the amount demanded by households, businesses, and the government.

A growing economy generates increasing amounts of jobs, incomes, and goods and services for its citizens. All of these are good things, of course. In a contracting economy, jobs and incomes are lost and the amount of goods and services produced shrinks. This puts people out of work and means that there are fewer goods and services to go around. A stagnant economy—one that is neither growing nor contracting—isn't much better than one that's contracting. The population is always growing, so more people need jobs and goods and services, and a stagnant economy doesn't produce them.

If you look at the formula for GDP, you'll see that if any one component increases, then total GDP increases (assuming that the other components remain unchanged). For example:

- If consumer spending grows—if people buy more clothing and cars and homes—then the economy grows.

- If business investment grows—if companies invest in new buildings and equipment and buy more raw materials—then the economy grows.

- If government spending grows—if money is poured into the space program, defense, roads, and police forces—then the economy grows.

By the same token, if any one component of GDP decreases, then total GDP decreases, unless another component of GDP increases enough to make up for the loss.

Consumers: Buyers, Buyers Everywhere

As you have surely noticed, Americans are avid consumers. In a sense, the U.S. economy has been built on high household consumption. The advertising, credit card, banking, and retail industries have created an environment in which people spend freely on the things they want and need. In contrast, the Japanese put a higher percentage of their incomes into savings, and both Asians and Europeans make much less use of credit cards. Consumer demand in the United States has fueled the nation's continual economic growth.

THE REAL WORLD

In the recession of 2001, the media pointed out that consumers continued spending, despite concerns about job security and economic conditions. Indeed, consumer spending held up well while business investment contracted. Businesses cut their spending because of worries over the growth prospects of the economy and downward pressure on profits.

In the 2008–2009 recession, however, the consumer ran out of steam due to reduced availability of credit and high unemployment, and the financial insecurity those bring. Going into that recession, the U.S. savings rate stood at an all-time low and household debt stood at an all-time high. With baby boomers soon starting to retire, higher savings will probably prevail as they build their nest eggs. Also, the conspicuous consumption in vogue from the 1980s until the 2008–2009 recession may go out of favor, and credit will probably not be as available.

In general, several fundamental factors drive consumer spending in the United States and other nations. The most important of these are:

- Population growth and household formation
- Employment
- Incomes
- Interest rates and taxes

Let's examine each of these drivers individually.

Population Growth and Household Formation

Population growth and household formation tend to drive one another as well as consumer spending. This occurred in the post–World War II years, when returning servicemen married and started families. The individuals born during the baby boom years of 1946 to 1965 have a well-documented record of consumption. By the same token, a decrease in population—or a lower growth rate—will generate lower consumer spending.

The post–World War II years were a time of high rates of household formation. When people (usually two) form a household, a whole series of purchases becomes necessary. First, there's the housing itself. Economists keep a close eye on housing starts—the number of single-family houses and multifamily dwellings on which construction began in a period—because a home is the largest purchase that most families ever make. Second, people then need to buy a huge number of items for the house or apartment—furniture, televisions, carpeting, appliances, pots, pans, dishes, and so on. Finally, in most households, sooner or later one plus one equals three, which brings us back to population growth.

Economists look at population growth, as well as the age patterns within the population, to gauge long-term economic growth. However, the growth rate of the population is a very long-term *indicator* of economic growth. Short-term indicators of economic growth include household formation and housing starts. When housing starts fall—or when home construction and sales nosedive, as they did in the 2008–2009 recession—economic activity decreases.

ECONOTALK

Economic indicators are measures of economic activity, such as growth rates, levels of income and spending, and percentages (such as the unemployment rate) that point to what is going on in the economy and, at times, forecast future trends.

Let's Work: Employment

As we will see in Chapter 6, the more money people have, the more they spend. But to spend money, you must make money, which is why employment and growth in employment are so important. Moreover, people need jobs not only so they can take care of their needs but also to occupy themselves productively. High unemployment, a common result of a recession, is associated with increased crime and political instability, as well as with poverty.

Economists look at employment in terms of economic indicators, with some of the most important being the following:

- **Employment** is the percentage of the workforce that is either employed or self-employed. This may also be the reported number of people employed (rather than, or in addition to, the employment rate). This is usually expressed as nonfarm employment to focus the number on nonseasonal jobs, and it excludes the armed services.

- **The unemployment rate** is the percentage of the workforce that is out of work but looking for, and willing to, work. The unemployment rate is reported more commonly than employment; it is a bit more accurate because people file claims for unemployment insurance.

- **"New jobs"** is (as you surely suspected) the number of new jobs generated by the economy in a period, usually a calendar month, quarter, or year. The number of new jobs is commonly reported in the business news.

- **"Jobs lost"** is also just what it sounds like—the number of jobs eliminated in the economy in the period being considered.

- **"Net new jobs"** is the number of new jobs minus the number of jobs lost. Jobs lost and net new jobs are also reported in the business news.

These employment and job data all indicate the health of the economy. The larger the portion of the workforce that is employed, the better. A growing economy creates jobs, which is one reason that governments want to keep their economies growing. Political questions surround the government's role in ensuring *full employment*, and we will examine ways in which the government attempts to do that in Parts 3 and 4.

ECONOTALK

Full employment occurs when every person in the economy who is willing and able to work has a job. In the United States, economists consider full employment to have been achieved when the unemployment rate falls to about 4 percent. That 4 percent is considered frictional unemployment—mainly people who just entered or re-entered the workforce or who are between jobs.

Income and Income Growth

Income is the total amount of money that households receive for supplying labor and capital in the economy: salaries, wages, bonuses, tips, benefits, interest, dividends, and so on. Rising incomes give people more money to spend and save. That increases demand and fuels economic growth.

Households can do only one of two things with their *disposable income:* spend it or save it. Which they choose has a profound effect on the economy, and we'll examine that effect in Chapter 7. For now, it's enough to know that higher incomes (or lower taxes) put more money into consumers' pockets. When they spend it, they are increasing consumption—the *C* in the GDP formula. Yet even when they save it, they are fueling GDP growth, albeit longer-term GDP growth. Some of that savings goes into bank accounts or investments that put money into the hands of businesses, which in turn invest that money and boost the *I* in the GDP formula and the economy's longer-term productive capacity.

ECONOTALK

Disposable income is household income minus taxes. Disposable income is either spent, and thus boosts consumption, or saved, which makes it available for investment by businesses.

Another way of looking at income is national income, which is the total of all of the money and benefits (such as health insurance premiums and pension benefits) that are paid to workers, landlords, and investors in a period. It includes wages, salaries, tips, benefits, and royalties; dividends and interest; corporate profits and other money earned by business owners; and rents paid to landlords, less their expenses.

Here's another way to think of the economy. We all go out to work every day and create things of value—a huge pile of goods and services. But instead of attacking that pile and fighting over it, we accept income for our efforts and use that income to purchase the goods and services that we want and need in the amounts that we prefer (and can afford).

Interest Rates and Taxes

The other main drivers of consumption are interest rates and taxes. U.S. consumers are the world's greatest users of credit. When interest rates are low, people will borrow and spend more money. This is particularly true with regard to interest rates on home mortgages and auto loans. When lower taxes increase people's disposable income, they dispose of it, either by spending it and boosting consumption, or by saving it, which makes it available for investment. Higher taxes, which nobody really wants, take money away from households and thus lower consumption expenditure. Yet higher taxes do not *necessarily* reduce GDP. If the government purchases goods and services with all the money raised through higher taxes, then total demand and GDP remain unchanged. Also, if the government spends tax dollars on investments in public infrastructure, such as roads, water treatment, and power generation, then the long-term productive capacity of the economy increases, which increases long-term economic growth.

I mention interest rates and taxes together because they are two of the three major levers that the federal government uses to implement economic policy. The other lever is government spending, and we will cover them all in Parts 3 and 4.

Let's turn to the role of business investment in the economy.

Investment: Business Buys as Well as Sells

The word investment can mean several things: a purchase of stock by an individual investor, the government's program to restore the Everglades, a college student's investment in herself in the form of tuition, or a company's investment in a new factory or a new fleet of trucks. Only the last of these would be counted as investment in the formula for GDP. Investment refers to business investment—money spent by businesses to expand or maintain their capacity.

ECONOTIP

Keep in mind that wages and salaries paid by companies are not included in investment. Doing so would double count wages and salaries in GDP, because that money is already included in consumption expenditures.

By definition, a capitalist economy is one in which people in the private sector can raise capital, invest it in businesses, produce goods and services, and attempt to sell them in the market at a profit. Several forces drive business investment, and the most important of these are:

- Interest rates and taxes

- Availability of capital

- Availability of opportunities

Interest Rates and Taxes, Again

Why would interest rates and taxes be listed first for business investment but last for consumption? Because, compared with consumption, business investment is more sensitive to interest rates and taxes. Of course, people are people, and people are making decisions to spend money whether they are part of a household or a business. However, people making business investment decisions usually (but not always) make them in a more disciplined and analytical manner than people making household spending decisions. A business tends to look more closely at the cost of money and at the tax implications of decisions.

A business analyzes the amount of money it will earn on a new factory or piece of equipment and expresses it as a percentage of the money invested. That percentage is the investment's *rate of return*. The analysis compares the rate of return on an investment with the interest rate to be paid on the money that will finance the investment. If the rate of return on the investment is higher than the interest rate, the business will typically make the investment. For example, if a piece of equipment that costs $100,000 a year to lease and operate will annually produce goods that can be sold for a profit of $10,000, then the rate of return on the investment is 10 percent. ($100,000 ÷ $10,000 = 10 percent) If the business pays an interest rate of, say, 7 percent on the money for the investment, then the investment would probably be considered attractive.

ECONOTALK

The **rate of return** on an investment is the amount of profit earned on the investment—that is, the amount of money earned after subtracting the expenses from the revenue brought in by the investment—expressed as a percentage of the investment.

Lower interest rates mean that more projects become attractive to businesses, because more lower return projects become viable when rates fall. For instance, projects with a rate of return of 8 percent are not attractive to a company that has to pay 10 percent interest. But if it has to pay only 5 percent interest, then the investment that pays 8 percent becomes worthwhile. So when rates fall, businesses will make more investments.

Taxes on business, such as the corporate income tax and the capital gains tax, also affect business investment. This is a politically charged issue, as are most taxes. Those who favor taxes (or higher taxes) on business believe a business benefits from government services, such as national defense, and should therefore pay its fair share of the cost. Those who favor no taxes (or lower taxes) on business believe that everyone who works for, invests in, or profits from a business already pays personal income taxes. They also believe that taxes discourage business investment, and thus employment growth, by taking money away from businesses and lowering the amount of money—the return—that the company realizes on an investment.

Although lower taxes can boost business investment, other factors—particularly interest rates—are usually more important drivers than taxes.

Availability of Capital

The availability of investment capital—that is, money—drives interest rates, but for the sake of clarity I discuss it separately from interest rates. Investment capital comes from households, through the banking system and the financial markets. People save their money in banks, buy insurance policies, and invest in stocks, bonds, and vehicles such as 401(k) accounts and mutual funds. A good portion of that money flows through financial intermediaries, such as banks and investment funds, to businesses that invest it in plant and equipment.

As I mentioned earlier, U.S. households have a relatively low savings rate. But the U.S. economy has a record of such productivity, growth, and stability that many foreign financial institutions, which channel the savings of foreign households into investments, quite willingly invest in the United States. This foreign investment increases the supply of capital in the states beyond what it would be if U.S. businesses relied solely on the savings of U.S. citizens. That said, the recession of 2008–2009 and high levels of U.S. government and household debt could reduce the flow of funds into the United States.

The government also borrows from households through the financial markets to finance *budget deficits.* When the government borrows truly large sums of money relative to the available capital, a phenomenon known as *crowding out* occurs. Crowding out refers to the fact that the government can borrow enough funds to crowd businesses out of the market for investment capital. In other words, if the government borrows enough money, it can curtail the availability of funds to other borrowers.

ECONOTALK

Budget deficits occur when a government of a nation, state, or city spends more than it acquires in tax revenue during the period under consideration. The government borrows money from households and businesses to cover the spending that is not covered by taxes. A budget surplus occurs when the government takes in more tax money than it spends in a period.

Available Opportunities

The major determinant of business investment may be the one least subject to economic analysis: the number of good investment opportunities available to businesses. It's true that lower interest rates can make low-return investments more attractive and that lower taxes and plentiful capital can spur investment. But unless businesses see good opportunities, they will hold onto their cash or distribute it to their stockholders as dividends.

The business cycle of expansion and recession affects the number of opportunities for better or worse. Business formation—the number of businesses being established in a period—also affects the level of business investment.

For instance, business investment remained relatively low throughout 2001 and 2002. In that relatively mild recession, consumers did their part to hold the economy up by continuing to spend. Also, during 2001 and 2002, interest rates remained at 30-year lows. However, when businesses didn't see opportunities, they certainly weren't about to invest. In the 2008–2009 recession, not only did business investment and bank lending to businesses plummet but consumers also dramatically pulled back their spending. That is why the government had to undertake stimulus spending to boost demand and keep the economy from going even deeper into recession—or even depression. (See *The Complete Idiot's Guide to the Great Recession*, which I also wrote, for a thorough account.)

Government: He's Your Uncle, Not Your Dad

As we've seen, the U.S. government—Uncle Sam—spends money on goods and services, thus boosting GDP. The government also makes transfer payments, which are not counted in the government's contribution to GDP. Transfer payments can, however, contribute to consumption expenditure if they wind up in the hands of households who will spend that money, which they often do. But that's part of C, and we are now discussing G.

The government's money comes from only two sources: taxes and borrowing. The government levies taxes on and borrows funds from the private sector. This is true of government at the federal, state, and local levels. (Yes, government agencies do charge fees, for instance at national and state parks, and states and cities assess fines for criminal and traffic violations. Technically, these are not taxes, but economists lump them in with tax revenue.)

The role of the government in an economy is large and complex, and there are various views of how the government should play it. In most modern, capitalist economies, however, the role of the government is to create and maintain conditions that will ensure a stable, orderly (but free) society.

The most basic of these conditions are a sound currency, low unemployment, and sustained economic growth. A sound currency maintains its buying power because the economy undergoes minimal *inflation*. We'll talk about inflation in Part 3.

ECONOTALK

Inflation refers to price increases that erode the value of currency.

The government uses economic policy to help ensure a sound currency, low unemployment, and sustained growth. Economic policy falls into two broad areas: fiscal policy and monetary policy. Fiscal policy, which we take up in Part 3, has to do with budgetary matters, such as taxes, spending, and borrowing. Monetary policy, covered in Part 4, has to do with interest rates and the amount of money in the economy.

Imports and Exports

When a country exports goods, it sells them to a foreign market—that is, to consumers, businesses, or governments in another country. Those exports bring money into the country, which increases the exporting nation's GDP. When a country imports goods, it buys them from foreign producers. The money spent on imports leaves the economy, and that decreases the importing nation's GDP.

Net exports can be either positive or negative. When exports are greater than imports, net exports are positive. When exports are lower than imports, net exports are negative. If a nation exports, say, $100 billion worth of goods and imports $80 billion, it has net exports of $20 billion. That amount gets added to the country's GDP. If a nation exports $80 billion of goods and imports $100 billion, it has net exports of minus $20 billion, and that amount is subtracted from the nation's GDP. (Conceivably, net exports could be zero, with exports equal to imports, and in fact this does occasionally happen.)

If net exports are positive, the nation has a positive balance of trade. If they are negative, the nation has a negative trade balance. Virtually every nation in the world wants its economy to be bigger rather than smaller. That means that no nation wants a negative trade balance.

Because no nation wants a negative trade balance, some countries try to protect their own markets. This policy, called (logically enough) *protectionism*, uses barriers to keep out imports. These barriers include high *tariffs*—taxes or surcharges on imported goods—and strict rules about what products can be imported.

Despite some nations' attempts at protectionism, *free trade*—trade unencumbered by barriers—has recently been the overall trend (if not a complete reality) for most countries. For instance, in 1999, the European Union did away with most trade barriers among its member nations. Economists usually favor free trade because it tends to give consumers the greatest choice of products at the lowest prices. That occurs because some nations are better at producing certain products than others.

ECONOTALK

Protectionism refers to government policies designed to restrict imports from coming into the nation. A **tariff,** also called a duty, is a tax on imports as they come into the country. **Free trade** means international trade that is unrestricted by tariffs or other forms of protectionism.

Part 5 covers trade policy and the drivers of international trade in detail. In general, however, the more goods a nation exports, the better for that nation's GDP.

THE REAL WORLD

A nation's balance of trade is calculated for a country in relation to the rest of the world and in relation to other individual nations. It can even be calculated for a specific industry.

For example, since 1976, the United States has run a negative balance of trade with the rest of the world. That means the United States imports more than it exports. (U.S. dependence on imported oil is a major reason for this.)

The United States also has a negative balance of trade with Japan. The United States imports more from Japan than it exports to Japan. However, the United States exports more fruits, grain, and vegetables to Japan than it imports from Japan. So the United States has a positive agricultural trade balance with Japan.

It All Adds Up

The U.S. economy is a multi-trillion dollar system of production and consumption, but it can be broken down and analyzed. The major players—consumers, businesses, and government—constantly interact with one another. Each interaction, whether it is a purchase or sale, investment or paycheck, tax or loan, constitutes a transaction and a form of economic activity.

It is that economic activity—and the millions of decisions that underlie that activity—that add up to our economy. The same is true of the economies of other nations. Economics is the study of the interactions of these various players, and of the motivation behind and the effects of these interactions.

The Least You Need to Know

- Consumption by consumers, investment by businesses, spending by government, and foreign trade all add up to the economy, which is measured by gross domestic product, or GDP.

- The formula for GDP is C + I + G + (Ex – Im). *C* is consumption. *I* is business investment. *G* is government spending on goods and services and does not include transfer payments. *(Ex – Im)* is exports minus imports, or net exports, which may be either positive or negative.

- The most important forces driving consumption are population growth and household formation, employment, incomes, interest rates, and taxes.

- The most important forces driving business investment are interest rates, availability of capital, and availability of investment opportunities.

- Government spending accounts for almost 20 percent of GDP, but government economic policies regarding taxes and the money supply also play a large role in the economy.

- Exports increase GDP, while imports decrease GDP. Therefore most nations want their exports to be higher than their imports, and many use some form of protectionism to try to ensure that this occurs.

The Economist's Toolbox

In This Chapter

- Understanding economic data
- How to read charts and graphs
- Pitfalls to avoid in the economic news

Virtually all aspects of economic activity can be measured, and most of them are. As you've seen, consumer spending, business investment, government expenditures, exports, and imports are all counted. So are the number of houses under construction, automobiles sold, people looking for work, and people who already have work. Economists monitor the levels of income, debt, and prices, and even the way consumers feel about the future of the economy.

All of this information helps people understand the economy—even people who aren't economists. For instance, say you want to buy a house and need a mortgage, but you would be happy to keep your present house for another 6 to 12 months if it would benefit you financially. If you have a good idea of the direction in which interest rates are moving, you can better decide whether to buy that house now or nine months from now. To have a good idea of interest rate movements, however, you must understand current and recent levels of interest rates and the forces that affect rates.

Even then, you might be wrong. Heaven knows the interest rate forecasts of highly paid economists are often incorrect. (In fairness, they are trying to be quite precise, and they usually do get the direction of interest rate movements right.) The point is that if you understand interest rates—or whatever economic activity might affect you or your business—you will be right more often than wrong.

This chapter introduces some concepts and tools that economists use to understand economic developments. These concepts and tools will help you more quickly grasp the rest of this book and the economic and business news. That way, you will improve your ability to form sound opinions and use economic information to make your own decisions.

Numbers Please: Economic Data

In this book and in the business media, you will read economic data. Often these data are called economic indicators, because they indicate the level of activity or future activity in some area of the economy. I will explain economic data and indicators as they arise in this book, but first I want to introduce you to some tools that economists use to organize and present data. These tools—various types of tables and charts—portray relationships between data and help you understand the nature and degree of the economic activity that the data represent.

Reading Tables

Much of the economic data you will encounter will be presented in tables. To orient you to tables of economic data, we're going to work with actual gross domestic product (GDP) data. Table 3.1 shows annual GDP for the years 1999 to 2009 in two different ways and with two different growth rates.

Table 3.1   Gross Domestic Product (1999–2009)

(1) Year	(2) GDP in Billions of Nominal Dollars	(3) Percent Change Based on Nominal Dollars	(4) GDP in Billions of Real Dollars*	(5) Percent Change Based on Real Dollars*
1999	9,354	6.4	10,780	4.8
2000	9,952	6.4	11,226	4.1
2001	10,286	3.4	11,347	1.1
2002	10,642	3.5	11,553	1.8
2003	11,142	4.7	11,841	2.5
2004	11,868	6.5	12,264	3.6
2005	12,638	6.5	12,638	3.1
2006	13,399	6.0	12,976	2.7
2007	14,078	5.1	13,254	2.1

(1) Year	(2) GDP in Billions of Nominal Dollars	(3) Percent Change Based on Nominal Dollars	(4) GDP in Billions of Real Dollars*	(5) Percent Change Based on Real Dollars*
2008	14,441	2.6	13,312	0.4
2009	14,256	-1.3	12,987	-2.4

*2005 dollars

Source: Bureau of Economic Analysis

When you look at a table, be sure to read the title of the table and all the headings for the columns and rows carefully. It's easy to plunge into the numbers without really reading the words, but the words tell you what numbers you are looking at. There are a lot of numbers here, and some unfamiliar terms in the column headings, so let's take this piece by piece.

The title of the table indicates that it covers gross domestic product for an 11-year period from 1999 to 2009. (These are all actual values from the Bureau of Economic Analysis website, www.bea.gov.) I've numbered the columns 1 through 5 for easy reference as I walk you through the table. The column headings describe the data in the column.

Taking each column in its turn, Column 1 indicates the year for the data in that row. (So far, so good.) The other columns require a bit more explanation.

Nominal vs. Real Dollars

Column 2 is GDP in billions of *nominal dollars*. These dollar values are expressed in billions, meaning that you should imagine that each dollar figure in the table is followed by nine (yes, nine) zeros. So GDP for 2009 is $14,256,000,000,000, or fourteen trillion, two hundred and fifty-six billion dollars. Another way of writing this would be $14.256 trillion.

Nominal dollars, also known as current dollars, are dollar values that have *not* been adjusted for inflation. They are dollars counted the way everyone counted them in the corresponding year, with the effect of inflation *included*. Again, we will learn about inflation in Part 3, but you know that inflation causes money to lose its value. If the general rate of inflation is 3 percent a year, then the average item that cost $100 on January 1 of that year would cost $103 by December 31. The price is inflated because the dollar lost some of its value—that is, some of its purchasing power.

Economists want to be able to look at what's going on in the economy without the effect of inflation. They want to know that GDP or exports or incomes are really growing, not just being inflated by a currency losing its value. So to get rid of the effect of inflation, they convert current dollars into *real dollars*, which are also known as inflation-adjusted dollars. In Table 3.1 they do this by converting all of the values in Column 2 into the 2005 dollar values you see in Column 4. I won't bother you with the calculations economists use to do this, but they do it. Also, they could have pegged the real value to the value of the dollar in another year—for instance, 1996. The key thing is to convert the value of GDP across all years to the value of the currency in one base year. That way, you are comparing year-to-year growth in real GDP, not nominal GDP.

ECONOTALK

Values expressed in **nominal dollars,** also known as current dollars, have not been adjusted for the effect of inflation. They are values reported in the dollars of each year being examined. Values expressed in **real dollars,** also known as inflation-adjusted dollars, are free of the effect of inflation. Economists use real dollars in many analyses because they want to understand economic activity without the distortions introduced by inflation. If nominal incomes are rising, but real incomes are falling, consumers are actually worse off, even though they are making more money.

To see the results of their calculations, let's jump over to Column 4. In Column 4, GDP is valued in billions of real dollars. As a result, we see that some of the value of our $14 trillion economy is indeed due to inflation. In fact, the real, inflation-adjusted value of the 2009 GDP in 2005 dollars is *only* $12.987 trillion.

So now when you hear a newscaster say, "Real GDP grew by 2.5 percent last year," you'll know what it means. In fact, GDP growth rates reported in the business news usually are based on real, inflation-adjusted values.

The use of 2005 as the base year for converting nominal to real dollars creates an issue that will help you understand the nature of real dollars. You may have noticed that in the year 2005 both nominal and real dollar values are the same: $12.638 trillion. Before the year 2005, the real dollar values for GDP are higher than the nominal dollar values. After 2005, the real dollar values are lower. That's because *after* 2005, the conversion from nominal to real dollars deflates the nominal GDP number. However, *before* 2005, the nominal values inflate GDP to the value of the dollar in 2005, which was higher. (This would not have occurred if real dollars valued in a base year before 1999 had been used. All of the real dollar values would be lower than the nominal dollar values, because some inflation occurred in every year.)

Knowing that in, say, 2007 GDP grew by 5.1 percent in nominal terms but by only 2.1 percent in real terms tells me a lot. It tells me that inflation was at or about 3 percent. I say "at or about" because the official 2007 inflation rate as measured by the Consumer Price Index—which is one, but not the only, measure of inflation—was 2.85 percent.

Keep on Growing

Columns 3 and 5 tell us about the rate of GDP growth. The point of using real, rather than nominal, dollars becomes really clear when you look at growth over the years. For instance, in 2008 nominal GDP grew by 2.6 percent. But real GDP grew by a paltry 0.4 percent, a little over zero. That was the first year of the recession of 2008–2009, and in 2008 the economy grew by only 0.4 percent. Meanwhile, nominal growth was 2.6 percent. In 2009 nominal GDP fell by 1.3 percent but real GDP fell by 2.4 percent. The rate of growth of real GDP is telling a much more accurate story than the rate of growth for nominal GDP.

Here's another interesting way of looking at GDP growth. (It's a good idea to refer to Table 3.1 during this discussion.) Nominal GDP grew from over $9 trillion back in 1999 to more than $14 trillion in 2009. That means that GDP grew by a total of 52 percent in the 11 years from 1999 to 2009 in nominal terms (14,256 – 9,354 = 4,902 and 4,902 ÷ 9,354 = 0.524 or 52%). However, real GDP grew by only 21 percent in the same period (12,987 – 10,780 = 2,207 and 2,207 ÷ 10,780 = 0.205 or 21%). That's well under half the rate of nominal growth!

ECONOTIP

Over the long term, meaning 20 years and longer, U.S. GDP grows at an average of about 3 percent in real terms. In 1990 to 2001, a period of advances in technology, healthy levels of consumer spending and business investment, relatively low inflation, and good management of the economy by the government, real GDP still grew at an average rate of only 2.85 percent.

In the 2000s, a decade characterized by an expanded use of debt and a massive housing bubble, real growth averaged only 1.9 percent. Granted, that includes the four consecutive quarters of contraction in the last half of 2008 and the first half of 2009, but even leaving out 2009, real growth averaged only 2.4 percent—still under the 2.85 percent of the 1990s.

Even though tables are kept in a handy place in the economist's toolbox, charts are every bit as important.

How to Construct and Read a Chart

If one picture is worth a thousand words, one chart may be worth a thousand numbers. Charts or graphs enable economists to see things they are always looking for: trends in data and economic activity, and relationships between two or more economic concepts or activities.

A chart almost always consists of two lines, each called an axis—one horizontal and one vertical. (Some charts feature one horizontal and two vertical axes, but we won't get into them here.) A point is plotted on a chart by using the axes as coordinates that define the spot where the point goes.

For example, the following chart relates the quantity of baloney sold to the price of baloney at a fictitious supermarket chain. The manager of the chain has only four pieces of data: when the price of baloney is $3, they sell 2,000 pounds per month, and when the price is $1.50, they sell 7,000 pounds per month.

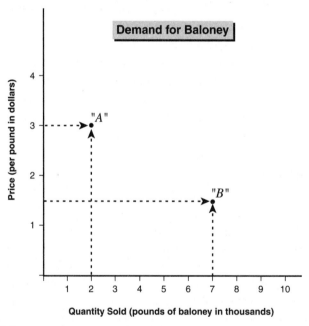

Figure 3.1

You plot a point on this chart by going along the vertical (price) axis to find the $3 mark and along the horizontal (quantity) axis to find the 2,000 pound mark. Those are your coordinates for the first point to be plotted, which I've labeled point A. You do the same for the next two pieces of data: the price of $1.50 and the quantity of 7,000 pounds. Those coordinates yield point B.

Notice that charts should be properly labeled, as this one is. The title of the chart, "Demand for Baloney," is clear, and each axis is labeled for the data that it represents. Also, the measure—whether it is dollars or pounds of baloney—is mentioned in parentheses. To understand a chart, you must have this information.

Now the two points on a chart can be connected, like in Figure 3.2.

When we connect two or more data points, the result is a curve. Figure 3.2 relates the price of baloney to the quantity sold—it tells us about the demand for baloney at these prices. Even if they are not actually curved, they are called curves. Some of the curves in this book would normally be drawn as actual curves, but I have generally used straight lines to keep the data simple and the explanations clear.

Economists also call a curve like this—in which two variables are related—a function. That's because the quantity of baloney sold—the demand for baloney—is a function of its price. The two variables in the function are price and quantity. Of course, other variables may affect the demand for baloney, such as the time of year or the price of ham. But those are left out of this particular function so that the economist can isolate the relationship between price and quantity.

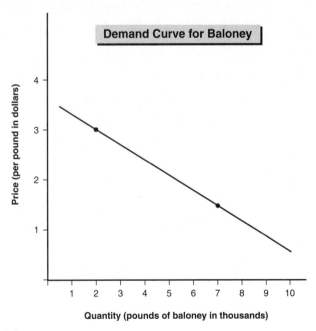

Figure 3.2

Incidentally, the relationship between the price of baloney and the demand for it is *inverse.* That means that the higher the price, the lower the quantity sold, and the lower the price, the higher the quantity sold. Variables can also be in a *positive* relationship, meaning that as one variable increases, the other increases, and as one decreases, the other decreases.

ECONOTALK

The relationship between two related variables may be **positive** or **inverse.** In a positive relationship, as one variable increases, the other increases, and as one decreases, the other decreases. In an inverse relationship, when one variable increases, the other decreases, and when one decreases, the other increases.

Figure 3.3, "Household Income and Spending on Clothing" depicts a positive relationship between two variables. This chart needs no numbers to illustrate the positive relationship between income and spending on clothing: the higher the income, the higher the amount spent on clothing; the lower the income, the lower the amount spent on clothing.

Two more points about charts are important. First, when economists, managers, or analysts plot data points on a chart, those points don't line up so that you can connect the dots and have a nice smooth curve in the way I do here. For instance consider the data points shown in Figure 3.4, which, again, relate spending on clothing to annual household income.

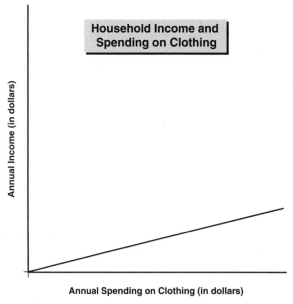

Figure 3.3

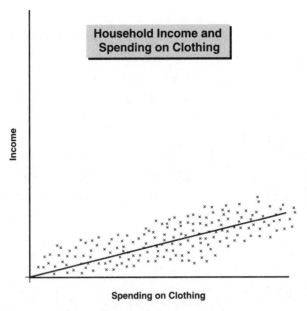

Figure 3.4

The points all over the lower part of Figure 3.4 resemble the kind of pattern that often results when the data on two related variables are plotted on a chart. This is called a *scatter diagram* for the obvious reason that the data points are scattered over the chart. Data points that represent variables that are related will cluster into a pattern, but they certainly won't fall neatly into a line or curve.

Then what's that curve doing in there? It's called the *line of best fit*. This is a line that is plotted through a set of data so that the relationship between the two variables becomes clearer. The line of best fit is calculated mathematically by computer in such a way that the distances between all of the variables and the line is minimized. In other words, the line of best fit is the line that is as close as possible to all of the data points. (That's why it's called the line of best fit—it's the line that best fits into the pattern of the data points on the chart.)

ECONOTALK

A **scatter diagram** shows the various data points plotted onto a chart. If the variables are related, the plotted points on a chart will tend to cluster into a pattern. The **line of best fit** is a line plotted through a scatter diagram that represents the relationship between the two variables.

Again we will be dealing with simple curves in this book. However, I want you to know that in reality, the data, the curves, and the functions are not always that simple.

Finally, what happens in situations where there is no relationship between two variables? Suppose you were to plot average annual temperature in the United States over the past 50 years against each year's growth in real GDP. You might wind up with a chart that looked very much like the one in Figure 3.5.

Here there is no relationship between the variables, and no meaningful line of best fit or function to be developed. There is no discernable pattern to help us relate GDP growth to average temperature. GDP growth and average temperature might, however, be related variables when considering the GDP of a single state. (Yes, each state has its own GDP.) For instance, unusually warm years might hurt the GDP of a state such as Vermont or Idaho, where ski resorts bring in significant sums of money from other states.

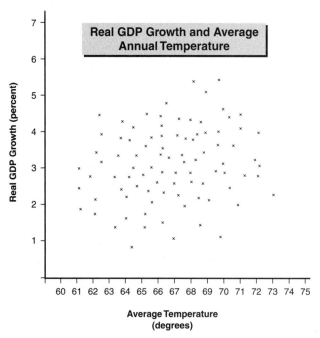

Figure 3.5

Charting GDP

In addition to helping us clarify relationships between variables, charts give us a way to visually depict trends over time by relating a value on one axis, usually the vertical, to a point in time, usually on the horizontal axis.

> **ECONOTIP**
>
> It is up to the economist, analyst, or manager reviewing the data to think through relationships and their meaning. No computer—or any other tool—can do that for us.

For example, let's return to the nominal and real GDP data we examined earlier and look at the trend in GDP over that 11-year period. Trends are best seen in line charts, which plot the values of a variable over time.

Figure 3.6 (on the next page) is a line chart of the values for nominal and real GDP from Table 3.1. The solid line represents nominal GDP, and the dotted line represents real GDP.

The chart is saying that annual GDP grew significantly in both nominal and real terms. The chart shows that nominal GDP grew faster than real GDP because the solid (nominal GDP) line is steeper than the dotted (real GDP) line. The chart also shows the recession of 2008 and 2009 in nominal and real terms.

Line charts are widely used in the investment profession to track the performance of various stocks. In finance, they are used to track sales, expenses, and other numbers. In economics, they are used mainly to see the trend of a variable such as GDP, income, and specific types of spending and production over time.

Also with a line chart and its underlying mathematical function, economists try to forecast the future performance of GDP, income, spending, production, and other variables. The mathematical functions—called equations—that represent the line are quite complex and not covered in this book. But essentially, in economic forecasting and econometrics (which I mentioned in Chapter 1), an economist plots a line that represents the relationship among multiple variables and attempts to gauge the future path of that line, and thus the future value of whatever is being forecasted.

A bar chart is another tool that helps us make comparisons between variables over time. For example, again, going back to Table 3.1, the bar chart in Figure 3.7 shows the growth rates for both real and nominal GDP from 1999 to 2009.

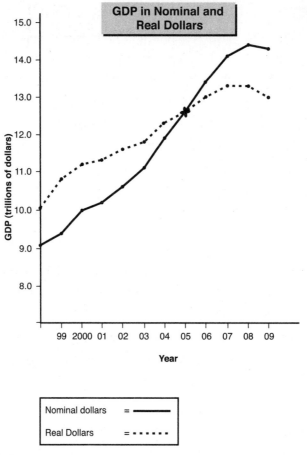

Figure 3.6

Figure 3.7 clearly shows that real GDP growth was substantially less than nominal growth throughout the 11-year period.

In economics, in business, and in this book, tables and charts are the two main tools for organizing, presenting, and analyzing data.

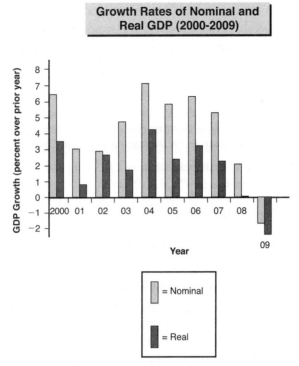

Figure 3.7

Watch Out!

When you are considering economic data and other numbers—for example, financial data—watch out for the following ways of misinterpreting information.

Correlation Is Not Causality

Just because two variables seem related, one is not necessarily causing the other to occur. For example, suppose in our earlier example of the average U.S. temperature and growth in GDP, we found that the higher the average temperature, the higher the growth rate in GDP.

It would be premature to assume that the higher average temperatures were causing the higher growth simply because high temperature and high growth were correlated. (Correlated is a mathematical term meaning that two variables move together, in either an inverse or positive relationship, in a consistent manner.)

Household	Income
A	$94,000
B	$41,000
C	$40,000
D	$39,000
E	$38,000
F	$37,000
G	$37,000

The average household income is about $46,600 (which equals the total of the seven incomes, $326,000, divided by 7). The mean is not representative of the level of income among these seven households. It is well above six of the seven incomes. That, of course, is because the mean is being pulled up by the income of $94,000.

The *median* is the central value—the value in the center when all of the values are arrayed from highest to lowest or lowest to highest. In our example here, the median value of $39,000 is far more representative of the level of income of most of the households in the group.

Although I have obviously constructed this sample to make the point about the median being preferable to the mean, the fact is that, in economics, income figures (among many others) usually are reported, presented, and analyzed as median values rather than averages. Beware of averages when you hear them quoted, and use them carefully when you do use them.

"Holding everything else constant."

Actually there is nothing wrong with using this phrase, which is used often by economists and throughout this book. It indicates that you are going to be isolating the effect of a change in one variable, such as interest rates, on another variable, such as borrowing. The phrase—which is often rendered in the Latin *ceteris paribus* and which also can be translated as *holding all else equal*—means that the analysis assumes that nothing changes except the variable being analyzed.

Economists know that this is not the way things work in the real world, and you should, too. But for the purposes of understanding a single variable, it is a useful and widely used convention.

The Least You Need to Know

- Data is the lifeblood of the economics profession—and of anyone who wants to understand and keep up with economic developments. Tables and charts are the two main tools for handling economic data.
- The distinction between nominal and real growth in GDP, incomes, spending, production, or other aspects of economic activity is a crucial one. Nominal dollars are dollars as they were valued in the year they relate to. Real dollars are dollars valued in a base year, chosen by the economist or analyst, in order to eliminate the effect of inflation.
- Be aware that the way economic information is presented and discussed can affect your understanding of economic events.

Supply, Demand, and the Invisible Hand

In This Chapter

- The dynamics of supply and demand
- How free markets function
- What makes a monopoly

Transactions occur because various consumers, businesses, and government agencies have various wants and needs. In Chapter 2, you learned that these transactions all add up to gross domestic product, or GDP. Economists also refer to GDP as total demand. Economists analyze not only total demand but also demand for specific goods and services. The demand for a specific item depends on many factors, including its uses and importance, the size and age of the population, the prevailing fashions and tastes, and, of course, its price.

In a market economy, if there is demand for something, there will surely be people willing to supply it. In that sense, supply is the flip side of demand. Economists think and talk in terms of the supply of, and demand for, cars and housing, the supply of labor and materials, and so on. The supply of a product or service depends on many things, including the resources and productive capacity devoted to producing it and, again, its price.

In a market economy, the interaction of supply—resources and productive capacity—and demand—wants and needs—largely determine what is produced and how it is allocated. Those interactions occur in markets and are mediated by the prices of goods and services.

This chapter examines the dynamics of supply and demand and the interaction of these two essential market forces. It also shows how these forces determine prices in a market.

Demand: Wants, Needs, and Red Meat

In a market economy, everything has a price, and buyers—those with the demand—always want the price to be lower. Meanwhile, sellers—those with the supply—want the price to be higher.

In general, the lower the price of a given product or service, the greater the quantity that people will be willing to buy. The higher the price of the product or service, the lower the quantity that people will be willing to buy. People buy more hamburgers than caviar, more costume jewelry than diamonds, more Chevrolets than Cadillacs.

Let's assume that a large supermarket chain sells beef (a fairly safe assumption). Let's further assume that it has experimented with various prices and has gathered the following data, here arranged into what economists call a *demand schedule*.

Table 4.1   The Demand Schedule

Price per pound	Pounds of beef sold
$10.00	20,000
$8.00	40,000
$6.00	60,000
$4.00	80,000
$2.00	100,000

The demand schedule shows the quantity of a product that people will buy (demand) at a series of specific prices. *Holding all other things equal*, the lower the price, the greater the quantity of beef people will buy. Conversely, the higher the price, the lower the quantity of beef people will buy.

ECONOTALK

A **demand schedule** shows the quantity of a product that people will buy (or demand) at a series of specific prices. A demand curve shows the same information in graphic form.

I emphasize *holding all other things equal* for two reasons. First, we are assuming that the price of beef is rising or falling and that the prices of all other goods are not. That is, we are assuming that the price of beef is rising or falling *relative* to the price of other goods. We make this assumption because if, say, the price of chicken were rising or falling, this might not be the demand schedule for beef. (I'll explain why in a moment.)

Second, we are assuming that no factors other than price are affecting demand. There have been no reports of mad cow disease in Kansas, which would surely lower demand for beef. There are no new scientific studies telling us to eat more beef because it is rich in iron and makes us healthier, which would increase demand. Assuming that all other things remain equal may be unrealistic (actually, it *is* unrealistic), but it lets us analyze the effect of price on demand.

If we plot the data—prices and quantities—from the demand schedule on a chart, we get a picture of the demand for beef as shown in Figure 4.1. The demand curve slopes downward because, as the price increases, the quantity of beef demanded decreases. A downward sloping demand curve holds true for most—but not all—types of products and services. There's an inverse relationship between price and demand: the higher the price, the lower the quantity demanded. The lower the price, the higher the quantity demanded.

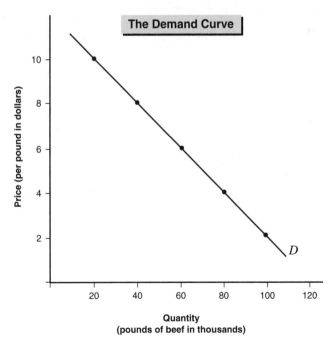

Figure 4.1

It may seem obvious that people will buy more of a product when the price decreases and less when the price increases. However, they do so for two reasons. First, many people who never buy a product because it is too expensive will buy it if the price falls far enough. For instance, many seafood lovers never buy lobster because it's just out of their price range. If the price of lobster fell substantially, they would start buying it. Second, many people who already buy a product will buy more of it if the price decreases. If the price of lobster fell substantially, affluent lobster lovers would buy it more often.

Demand Change!

Okay, let's stop holding everything else equal. Aside from movements in prices, what factors might cause a change in the demand for a product such as beef?

Overall demand can change, moving upward or downward, because of changes in:

- Preferences
- Population
- Prices of other goods and services
- Incomes
- Perceptions of future prices

Preferences

In Chapter 1, I mentioned that people express their preferences in the transactions they enter into. Some people like beef and some don't. Moreover, people's preferences can, and usually do, change over time. For instance, demand for beef can increase or decrease because of social trends—say, toward or away from steakhouse dining or vegetarianism—and health concerns—beef is high in cholesterol but also rich in iron.

Population

In Chapter 2, I noted that population growth affects consumption (consumer demand). That's also true for the demand for a specific product. Imagine that Argentina's economy collapses (which it did in 2002) and hundreds of thousands of Argentines immigrate to the United States (which they did not). The people of

Argentina are great beef eaters, and a huge number of Argentines entering the U.S. population could conceivably increase the demand for beef. Usually, however, population growth occurs slowly over time, exerting gentle, long-term pressure on demand.

THE REAL WORLD

When a product or brand appeals only to older people, the manufacturer often becomes concerned over future demand. For instance, the average age of Cadillac and Lincoln buyers is over 55. Those brands are working hard to develop products that appeal to younger buyers. Similarly, so-called brown liquors, such as bourbon and scotch, are consumed more by older people, while young adults favor white liquors, such as vodka and rum. Therefore makers of bourbon (Jim Beam) and scotch (Dewars) use advertising to appeal to young adults. Producers hate it when demand for their product dies off.

The more important reasons for a change in demand, however, involve factors other than preferences or population. Key among these is the price of other goods and people's incomes.

Prices of Other Goods

If the price of beef remained the same while the price of chicken fell dramatically, what do you think the effect on the demand for beef would be?

THE REAL WORLD

The world of information and entertainment technology provides many examples of economic reality. Not only are most of us familiar with these technologies, but the markets for them change so fast. It's the economic equivalent of the geneticist studying fruit flies because a new generation comes along every three days.

A mass market for an entertainment product cannot develop until the product falls to a price where people will use it as a substitute for another product. Expensive substitutes are not going to find a large market. For instance, video on demand devices, such as TiVo, and personal digital assistants (PDAs), such as BlackBerry, had to reach prices where people saw the products as reasonable substitutes for movie tickets or cell phones, or just doing without them.

Demand for beef would *decrease*. Why? Because chicken is a *substitute* for beef. A substitute is a product or service that people use *in place of* another product or service. When shoppers in supermarkets see that the price of chicken has plummeted while the price of beef has stayed the same, they'll substitute chicken for beef in their diets. They may not eliminate beef, but they will certainly start eating more chicken and less beef. This would also happen at fast-food restaurants—more Kentucky Fried Chicken and fewer Big Macs would be sold. Other examples of substitutes include rice and potatoes, bus rides and train rides, and (to the horror of the music industry) compact discs and music shared over the Internet.

Sometimes the price of a *complement* to a product can affect demand for the product. A complement is a product or service that people use *with* another product or service. For example, if the price of hamburger rolls were to increase dramatically, we could expect demand for hamburger meat to decrease. Other examples of complements include DVD players and DVD disks, turkey and stuffing, rods and reels, gin and vermouth.

ECONOTALK

A **substitute** is a product or service that people use in place of another product or service. A **complement** is a product or service that people use with another product or service.

Income

Changes in income can also change overall demand for a product or service. As people's incomes rise, they demand more goods and services. They also demand better goods and services—the good things in life.

Many people still rate red meat among those good things, and indeed more red meat is consumed in wealthy nations than in poorer nations. Similarly, when people's incomes fall, they demand fewer goods and services—and fewer of the good things in life. Therefore, if incomes increase, we would expect demand for red meat to increase. If people's incomes were to decrease, we would also expect a decrease in the demand for beef.

However, this leaves aside cultural developments that can affect consumption. For example, concerns about health, weight gain, and animal rights have tended to lower red-meat consumption, especially in higher-income groups.

Incidentally, this assumes that beef is among what economists call *normal goods.* Normal goods are those for which demand increases as incomes rise, which includes many products and services. Products and services that see decreased demand when incomes rise are called *inferior goods*. Porgies—a bland, bony, but inexpensive fish—are a good example of such a product. Subway rides are such a service. As incomes rise, people substitute salmon for porgies and taxi rides for subway rides.

> **ECONOTALK**
>
> **Normal goods** are those for which demand increases as people's incomes increase. **Inferior goods** are those for which demand decreases as income increases.

Perception of Future Prices

Yet another factor can shift demand for a product: the price people expect to pay for it in the future. If people suddenly learned that beef prices were going to double next month, they would probably stock up their freezers with steaks, roasts, and hamburgers this month. People buy and hoard products when they believe sharp price increases lay ahead.

Notice that this factor does not affect services as much. You might have dental work done or have your house painted right now if you knew the price of those services was going to increase soon. But you could not have two haircuts or make two visits to your doctor now in the hope of not needing another one in the near future.

Back to the Curve

A change in overall demand represents a *shift* in demand, upward or downward. That means that one or more of the factors I just discussed can cause the entire demand curve to shift to the right (upward) or to the left (downward), as shown in Figure 4.2 (on the next page).

A shift in demand is different from a change in the quantity demanded because of a change in the price. If the supermarket chain lowers the price of beef from $8 to $6 and sees its sales increase from 40,000 to 60,000 pounds, the price change caused a change in the quantity demanded. That change represents movement *along the demand curve*—that is, along the curve D, the middle curve of the three curves in Figure 4.2.

A shift in demand occurs when the whole relationship between price and quantity changes. The new demand schedule (Table 4.2 on the next page) provides the values that correspond to all three demand curves in Figure 4.2.

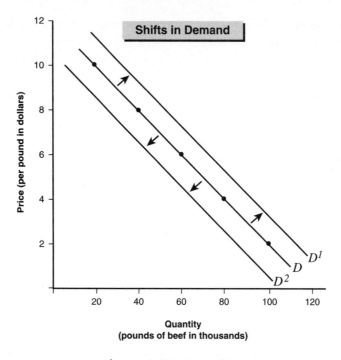

Figure 4.2

Table 4.2   Shifts in Demand

	Old demand schedule (D)	New higher demand schedule (D¹)	New lower demand schedule (D²)
Price per pound	*Pounds of beef*	*Pounds of beef*	*Pounds of beef*
$10.00	20,000	30,000	10,000
$8.00	40,000	50,000	30,000
$6.00	60,000	70,000	50,000
$4.00	80,000	90,000	70,000
$2.00	100,000	110,000	90,000

The whole relationship between price and quantity changes when a shift in demand occurs. For example, the new, higher demand curve shows that at the $6 price, people will now buy 70,000 pounds of beef. Perhaps the price of chicken has increased to the point where people figure they may as well buy beef. Or maybe incomes in the region have increased to the point where people now have more money to spend on beef. Or perhaps concerns about health, weight, and animal rights have somehow been addressed. If that's the case, at the $6 price—and at any price along the new demand curve—they will buy more of it.

Similarly, along the new, lower demand curve, people collectively will buy only 50,000, rather than 60,000, pounds of beef at $6. This type of shift also usually occurs for one of the reasons I just discussed. For instance, the price of chicken may have fallen sharply or people's incomes may have decreased due to layoffs in the region.

As I mentioned at the start of this chapter, when there is demand for a product in a market economy, someone will supply it. Let's move to the other side of the transaction and examine the dynamics of supply.

Supply: You Want It, We Got It

Just as there is a quantity that consumers will demand at a given price, there is a quantity that producers will supply at a given price. The demand schedule depicts the relationship between the price of a good and the quantity consumers will buy. Similarly, the supply schedule depicts the relationship between the price of a good and the quantity that producers will make.

As you may imagine, the relationship between price and quantity supplied differs from that between price and the quantity demanded. Table 4.3 below depicts this relationship.

Table 4.3   The Supply Schedule

Price per pound	Pounds of beef produced
$10.00	120,000
$8.00	90,000
$6.00	60,000
$4.00	30,000
$2.00	0

The supply schedule shows the quantity of a product that producers will produce (supply) at a series of specific prices. Holding all other things constant, the higher the price, the greater the quantity of beef producers will supply, and the lower the price, the lower the quantity of beef people will supply.

Notice the positive relationship between price and quantity supplied: the higher the price, the higher the quantity supplied. This stands in contrast to the inverse relationship between price and quantity demanded. When the data are plotted on a chart, they generate a very different curve.

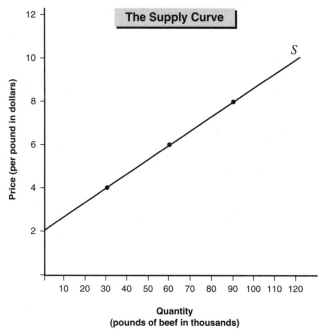

Figure 4.3

The supply curve depicts the quantities that producers will make at a series of given prices. As you can see, the quantities supplied at the various prices generally differ from those that consumers are willing to purchase at those prices. We'll see how this is resolved later in this chapter.

The supply curve can apply to a single supplier or to all suppliers as a whole, and it holds true for virtually every product or service produced for profit in a market economy. Also in holding all other things constant, the supply schedule and supply curve leave certain realities out of the analysis in order to focus solely on price. Those other things can change the overall relationship between price and quantity supplied, so let's look at them just as we did for demand.

Change Supply!

A change in the overall quantity supplied can occur because of changes in any of the following areas:

- Capacity and technology
- Cost structure
- Prices of substitutes and complements
- Perceptions of future prices

Capacity and Technology

From time to time you may have heard that there is too much capacity in an industry. This was the case in the North American auto industry, which at the end of 2008 had the capacity to make about 7 million more cars than the market was demanding, according to *BusinessWeek*. The magazine also reported that the worldwide industry had the capacity to make about 94 million vehicles, or about 34 million more than were demanded.

When overcapacity occurs in an industry, the entire supply of that industry's product increases. When that happens, producers are willing to deliver a greater quantity of goods and services for the same price. Why shouldn't they? They have more capacity than they can use, so they may as well use as much as they can, at any price (well, almost any price). If demand for the product is simply low and remains there, however, the industry will have to reduce capacity.

THE REAL WORLD

Shifts in supply and demand usually occur over a long time. For example, the U.S. auto industry lost market share to foreign manufacturers very gradually. In 1950 the Big Three (General Motors, Ford, and Chrysler) had 87 percent of the U.S. market. In 1980 it had 74 percent, and even in 1990 it still had 72 percent. But by 2000 that share had dropped to 66 percent, and by 2008, to 48 percent. Oil prices, quality issues, and changing tastes in vehicles have affected U.S. manufacturers for better and worse—but mainly for worse over the long term.

An increase in supply also occurs if there are numerous producers for a product or service. With the success of foreign automakers in the United States, the nation wound up with too many suppliers. As a result, in the late 2000s recession, General Motors and Chrysler seriously downsized, reducing their number of models, dealers, and workers. Finally, technological developments can lead to a shift in supply. Returning to our beef example, suppose the industry develops better methods of feeding cattle or controlling disease, or suppose more efficient processing and shipping technologies come along. Under those circumstances, the quantity supplied for a given price would increase.

The converse of these factors also holds true. Too little capacity, a paucity of producers, or lack of technological innovation will decrease the supply.

Cost Structure

If the cost of any factor of production—labor, raw materials, equipment—decreases, the quantity that producers are willing (and able) to supply at a given price increases. Producers with lower costs will always be able to supply more of a product at a given price than those with higher costs. Therefore, a decrease in producers' costs will increase the supply.

Conversely, if production costs increase, the quantity supplied at a given price will decrease—again, holding other things equal. Higher costs mean that producers will have to produce less to be able sell a product at a given price. If you're thinking, "Why don't they just raise their prices when their costs go up?" you're asking a good question. Essentially, consumers will resist the higher prices and may move to substitutes, do without the product, or buy from a more efficient producer.

Prices of Substitutes and Complements

A producer sees substitutes and complements differently than consumers do. To a producer, a substitute is another product he can make instead. Suppose a major meat producer can devote feed, feedlots, transportation, and other resources to raising either cattle or sheep. That makes cattle and sheep *substitutes in production*.

ECONOTALK

Substitutes in production are two or more products or services that a producer can make or deliver in place of one another. For instance, a farmer may be able to grow either corn or soybeans, a manufacturer may be able to produce either men's or women's clothing, or an arena may be able to host either sports events or concerts. A producer or service provider who can supply substitutes in production has the flexibility to offer whichever good is in greater demand.

If the meat producer has the flexibility to choose to raise cattle or sheep, and the price of lamb rises dramatically, what do you think she will do? She will devote more resources to raising sheep and fewer to raising cattle. In general, if the price of a substitute in production (lamb) rises relative to its related product (beef), then the supply of the related product (beef) will decrease. If a producer can produce either of two products, she's going to produce the one that fetches the higher price.

The reverse is also true. If the price of a substitute in production falls, then the supply of the related product will increase. If the price of lamb nosedives, the outfit will devote fewer resources to sheep and more to cattle. As a result, the supply of beef will increase.

Complements in production are products that are created along with one another. Cowhide and beef are complements in production. (Wool, of course, can be obtained by shearing sheep, rather than slaughtering the poor things.) If the price of a complement (cowhide) rises, so will the supply of the related product (beef).

ECONOTALK

Complements in production are products created with one another. Often one is a by-product of another, that is, a product created in the course of making another product. For instance, certain lubricants and other petroleum products are by-products of making gasoline from crude oil.

Why? If the cattle producer makes more money off the cowhide, he can afford to sell the beef at a lower price. If he increases his cowhide production when its price rises, his supply of beef is going to automatically increase as well. That means more beef will be available at a given price, which increases the supply of beef. Conversely, if the price of cowhide falls far enough, so might the supply of beef.

Perception of Future Prices

Finally, if a producer believes she can get a better price in the future, she will hold off production or delivery and sell when the price has risen. Thus if higher prices for beef are expected four months from now, producers will decrease the quantity they are now supplying. Conversely, if producers can get a better price now than they can expect in four months, they will produce more now, which increases the supply.

Notice that the effect of perceptions of future prices on supply are the opposite of their effect on demand. Higher prices in the future increase current demand but decrease current supply. Lower prices in the future decrease current demand but increase current supply. Stated another way, higher prices in the future shift demand into the present and supply into the future. Lower prices in the future shift demand into the future and supply into the present.

As Figure 4.4 shows, if supply increases for any reason, the supply curve shifts to the right because producers are willing to supply more beef at a given price. Conversely, if supply decreases, the supply curve shifts to the left because producers will supply less beef at a given price.

Thus the dynamics of supply and demand tend to work at cross-purposes. But that's why we have markets, where these forces working at cross-purposes start working together. Let's turn to the market and see what happens—especially to prices—when demand and supply interact.

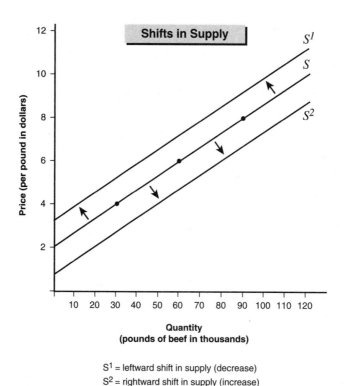

Figure 4.4

ECONOTIP

Think of the supply curve as shifting to the left (for decreased supply) or to the right (for increased supply) rather than thinking of the curve shifting *up* or *down*. It's potentially confusing because an *upward* movement of the curve—to the left—actually depicts a decrease in supply and a *downward* movement—to the right—is signaling an increase. Instead, think rightward is an increase in supply and leftward is a decrease.

Equilibrium: Mr. Demand, Meet Mr. Supply

The beauty of the market is that the competing motivations of consumers and producers interact to arrive at a price and quantity for a product that's determined by impersonal market forces. You've heard the expression *market price* (or seen it written on menus next to the word *lobster*). The market price for a product is the price at which the quantity demanded is equal to the quantity supplied. Figure 4.5 shows how this occurs.

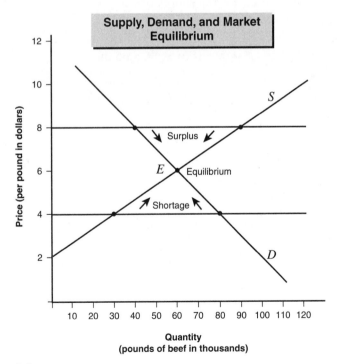

Figure 4.5

The arrows along the supply and demand curves in this chart indicate the pressures at work in the market for beef (or any market, for that matter). To understand how the price and quantity reach the equilibrium point, let's first examine the area above that point. Above the equilibrium point—say, at the $8 price where I have drawn a line—producers would be supplying more beef (90,000 pounds) than consumers would be demanding (40,000 pounds). That price results in a surplus of beef on the market—supply would be greater than demand because consumers won't buy enough of it at the $8 price.

If supply is greater than demand, then there are meat lockers full of unsold beef across a region. What are the suppliers of that beef going to do? They will cut the price until consumers start buying it. In this way, a surplus of a product puts downward pressure on its price.

It also puts downward pressure on its supply. If beef is not selling briskly—if there's a surplus of it on the market—what are producers going to do? They are going to raise fewer cattle. They'll shift the resources to raising sheep or maybe hogs. Maybe some ranchers will get out of the business. Whatever it takes, that surplus quantity of beef will be taken off the market for the simple reason that consumers don't want to buy that quantity of beef at the price suppliers want for it. The excess supply will dwindle until the quantity supplied equals the quantity demanded—at a price both consumers and producers can live with—in this case, $6 a pound.

So surplus quantity puts downward pressure on the price and the supply of the product. That pressure is exerted by market forces until the quantity supplied equals the quantity demanded.

Let's turn to the area *below* the equilibrium point. There we have a shortage of beef. At that $4 price, the market is demanding more beef (80,000 pounds) than the quantity that producers are supplying (30,000 pounds). That results in a shortage, which puts upward pressure on prices.

How? When sellers see that they are constantly running out of beef before the next delivery, they know they can raise the price of the stuff. Consumers, in effect, are bidding up the price. When the price starts increasing (from the $4 mark), producers start producing more beef. They send their cattle to market sooner, and they move resources away from raising sheep and into raising cattle. If it's a long-term trend, more people may take up cattle ranching.

Again, whatever it takes, that shortage of beef will disappear as the price rises and the higher prices bring more beef to market. How much more beef will come to market? Enough to bring the quantity supplied equal to the quantity demanded—in this case, 60,000 pounds—again, at a price both consumers and producers can live with—in this case, again, $6.

Market Forces Are the Invisible Hand

The market forces described here, working through the price mechanism, are the essence of Adam Smith's "invisible hand" (see Chapter 1). The beauty of a market is that supply and demand come into balance without central planning, mandates, boycotts, raids, or wars, as each consumer and producer responds to the price of the product. The price sums up, contains, and channels the forces of the market—the motives and desires of consumers and producers.

This is not to say that markets do away with pain and loss for consumers and producers. Market forces generate tremendous amounts of pain and loss. People go without beef, suffer protein deficiencies, and even go hungry. They see people eating sirloin steak and prime rib and feel terrible that they can't afford it. Producers get stuck with beef they can't sell. Some meat may be sold at a loss or go to waste. Some ranchers and meat wholesalers go out of business and lose their livelihoods.

Markets can be inefficient and even cruel. However, the pain and loss that occur in the market arise largely from decisions—good and bad decisions—made freely by consumers and producers. Therefore, most Americans prefer the inefficiencies and cruelties of the market to those of a command economy.

What About Shifts in Demand or Supply?

Finally, let's return to those overall shifts in demand or supply. What effect do they have?

Essentially, they shift the equilibrium point up or down. Two pictures will be worth 2,000 words. First, let's look at the effect of a shift in demand as illustrated in Figure 4.6 (on the next page).

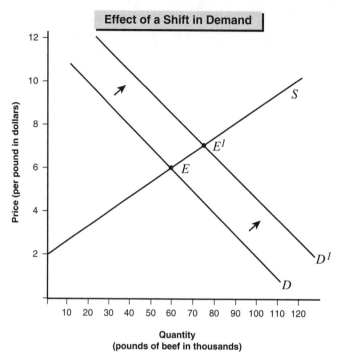

Figure 4.6

As the chart shows, an increase in demand raises the quantity demanded at a given price. This results in a new, higher market price, and producers will be more than happy to supply that higher quantity, which is 75,000 pounds, at that higher market price, which is $7. Thus, when demand shifts upward, the equilibrium point rises.

To see the effect of a decrease in demand, simply reverse the situation and pretend that the curves in the chart are reversed (that D is the new curve and D¹ is the original one). A shift to lower demand decreases the quantity demanded at a given price. Producers will (not quite so happily) meet that lower demand at a new, lower market price. This generates a new, lower equilibrium point.

Turning to a shift in supply, as depicted in Figure 4.7, an increase in supply—which shifts the curve to the right—lowers the market price to $5 and raises quantity supplied from 60,000 to 70,000. That is why overcapacity or numerous competitors in an industry will cause the price to decrease. There's more supply than people demand.

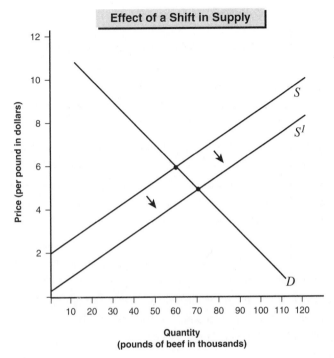

Figure 4.7

However, a decrease in supply—which shifts the curve to the left—has the opposite effect, as you can see by pretending that S¹ is the original curve and S is the new one. The decrease in supply *increases* the market price. That's because demand now exceeds the quantity supplied, and in that circumstance consumers bid up the price.

It's Not Just a Good Idea, It's "The Law"

All of this boils down to the law of supply and demand. The greater the demand for a given supply of a product, the higher the market price. The lower the demand, the lower the price. Likewise, the greater the supply of a product given a certain level of demand, the lower the price of that product. The lower the supply—the scarcer it is—the higher the price.

You knew that was the case. But now you know why. You also understand how markets work, how market forces are channeled into prices, and what can cause overall demand or supply for a product to shift.

The Least You Need to Know

- A demand schedule and demand curve for a product show the quantity of the product that consumers will purchase at a range of prices.

- Overall demand for a product can shift upward or downward because of changes in preferences, population, prices of related products, incomes, and consumers' perceptions of future prices.

- A supply schedule and supply curve for a product show the quantity of the product that producers will make available at a range of prices.

- The overall supply of a product can shift upward or downward because of changes in productive capacity or technology, producers' costs, prices of related goods, and producers' perceptions of future prices.

- Market dynamics move the price and quantity of a product to an equilibrium point. At that point, producers are supplying the quantity that consumers are demanding (and vice versa) at a price both parties can live with.

- While markets represent an orderly and efficient way of determining how much of which goods and services are produced for whom, they are neither painless nor perfect for all goods and services.

Look at These Prices!

In This Chapter

- Factors that affect prices
- All about elasticity
- How a sales tax affects supply and demand
- The effects of rent control and a minimum wage

As the saying goes, "Everything has a price." The question for anyone trying to understand an economy is, "Why that particular price?"

In Chapter 4 we saw how supply and demand interact in the market so that the right amount of goods and services is produced. Chapter 4 also introduced the price mechanism and its role in determining supply and demand. In this chapter, we learn how the consumer's need for a product affects demand and how market interventions, such as sales taxes and rent control, affect supply, demand, and prices.

Let's Stretch: Elasticity of Demand

Anyone who has set foot in a discount store knows that some sellers try to increase the quantity of goods they sell by lowering their prices. From what we saw about supply and demand, that should work. However, in reality, it may or it may not. Moreover, the seller may or may not bring in more money even if he does sell more goods at the lower price.

If a seller reduces his prices, will demand always increase? (Hint: never say "always" in economics.) The more important question is, "How much should he reduce his prices?" In other words, how much will demand rise in response to a price reduction?

The answers to these questions depend on the buyer's situation and his need or desire for the product, as well as on the seller's situation. That is, the answers depend on the *elasticity of demand* for the product or service.

Don't be alarmed by the technical term *elasticity*. It's really a snap. (Sorry, I couldn't resist.) Elasticity of demand refers to the change in demand for a product or service that occurs when its price changes. Specifically, it is the degree to which an increase or decrease in price will change the quantity demanded.

ECONOTALK

Elasticity of demand refers to the change in demand for a good or service that occurs in response to a change in its price. Specifically, it is the degree to which an increase or decrease in price will change the quantity demanded. It is a way economists have of nailing down the relationship between price and demand more precisely.

First, I'll discuss the three degrees of elasticity: *unitary elasticity, elasticity,* and *inelasticity.* Then we'll look at the factors that contribute to the elasticity of demand of a product.

If you drive a car, you need gasoline. If the price of gasoline was cut in half starting next week, would you start buying twice as many gallons of it per week? If the price rose by 100 percent, would you buy half as much per week? Let's say that, in both cases, you would.

Let's put some numbers to this example. We'll start with gasoline at $2.50 per gallon and with you using 100 gallons a week. (Ever think of shortening your commute?) This example will show how changes in the price affect your demand and flow through to affect the revenue that the gas station receives from you. Revenue, also known as total sales, equals price multiplied by quantity: $R = P \times Q$.

Table 5.1 shows the changes in price, quantity, and revenue in the example I'm presenting here.

Table 5.1 Unitary Elasticity of Demand for Gasoline

	P	×	Q	=	R
Original situation	$2.50	×	100 gals.	=	$250
Price drops 50%	$1.25	×	200 gals.	=	$250
Price doubles	$5.00	×	50 gals.	=	$250

In this admittedly fanciful example, your demand for gasoline is characterized by unitary elasticity. Unitary elasticity occurs when the quantity of a product demanded changes in response to price changes in a way that leaves total revenue the same. Here, regardless of price increase or decrease, revenue remains at $250.

With unitary elasticity, the percentage increase in price results in an offsetting decrease in demand. If the seller doubles his price, he sells half as much. Similarly, a percentage decrease in price results in an offsetting increase in demand. If he halves his price, he sells twice as much. Either way, the seller brings in the same revenue. (His profit—the amount he makes after subtracting his costs from his revenue—may vary, but that's another story, told in Chapter 8.)

 ECONOTALK

Unitary elasticity occurs when the quantity of a product demanded changes in response to price changes in a way that leaves total revenue unchanged. **Elasticity** occurs when a reduction in price increases the quantity demanded so that the seller's revenue increases. **Inelasticity** occurs when a reduction in price increases the quantity demanded by more than zero but less than unity. (Unity refers to the proportional change in quantity sold and revenue that occurs under unitary elasticity.)

Figure 5.1 illustrates the unitary elasticity relationship.

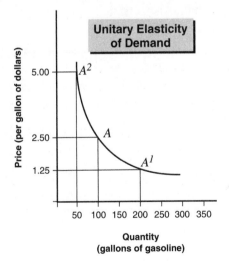

Figure 5.1

Figure 5.1 is saying that when the price decreases from $2.50 (point A) to $1.25 (point A¹), total revenue equals $250 in both cases (100 gallons at $2.50 a gallon equals $250, and so does 200 gallons at $1.25).

This chart is also saying that the price increase from $2.50 to $5.00 leaves revenue unchanged because the demand for gasoline falls to 50 gallons (50 gallons at $5.00 a gallon equals $250).

When a producer or seller faces unitary elasticity of demand, she can't increase revenue by increasing or decreasing her price. Why? Because the quantity demanded will exactly offset the effect of any change in price. However, that is rarely the case in the real world.

Selling More by Charging Less

Sticking with our gasoline example, suppose that, in response to a 50 percent decrease in the price of gasoline, you tripled your gasoline purchases to 300 gallons a week. What would be the effect on the service station's revenue? The second line in the table below provides the answer: a sharp increase in revenue.

Similarly, let's suppose that if the price of gasoline doubled, you would use only one fourth as much. This would generate revenue of $125, as shown in the third line of the table. (Incidentally, I am using numbers that illustrate the type of elasticity I am discussing. In reality, elasticity is all over the place, both for any given individual and for groups that use a product. Also, elasticity can be greater in response to a price increase than to a price reduction, or vice versa.)

	P	×	Q	=	R
Original situation	$2.50	×	100 gals.	=	$250
Price drops 50%	$1.25	×	300 gals.	=	$375
Price doubles	$5.00	×	25 gals.	=	$125

Here your demand for gasoline is characterized by elasticity of demand. In contrast to unitary elasticity, elastic demand occurs when a reduction in price increases the quantity demanded so that the seller's revenue increases. This is the way things *should* work for most businesses: the seller can sell more by cutting his price—and so it's worth it to the seller.

As the table also shows, however, this cuts both ways: the seller will lose revenue if he increases his price. With elastic demand, an increase in the price calls forth a decrease in the quantity demanded, which decreases the seller's revenue.

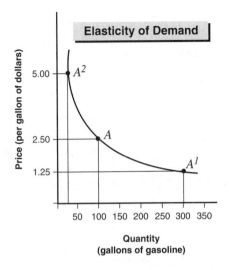

Figure 5.2

Figure 5.2 demonstrates that a decrease in price increases demand by more than unity. At the $1.25 price, demand increases to 300 gallons, bringing revenue up to $375 (which is equal to $1.25 × 300). With elasticity—as opposed to unitary elasticity or inelasticity—decreasing the price increases revenue. Also, the area of the rectangle formed by connecting the $1.25 price point with point A¹ and point A¹ with the 300-gallon mark is clearly larger than the area of the rectangle formed by connecting the $2.50 price point with point A and the 100-gallon mark. That, too, represents the higher revenue resulting from the price decrease.

The elasticity of demand chart also demonstrates that, with elasticity, a price increase will decrease demand to the point where revenue also decreases. At the $5.00 price, demand falls to just 25 gallons and revenue drops to $125.

ECONOTIP

A change in price may result in only a small increase in demand and revenue. The examples I'm choosing here use round numbers and simple relationships for the sake of clarity. But many producers face markets in which a price decrease of 10 percent may increase revenue by only 2 percent. This may or may not be a profitable decision for the producer. It depends on his costs. However, when a price reduction increases both the quantity demanded and revenue, it is, by definition, a case of elasticity of demand.

Are there situations in which a price change will cause the quantity demanded to drop to zero? Yes. Economists call this *infinite elasticity*. Cases of infinite elasticity are rare and usually confined to a single locale or a special situation.

For instance, the Internet has created an environment in which many users feel that everything on the web should be free. Now, it's not really free, because they've paid their Internet service provider for access to the web. But they feel they should not have to pay one penny more for information, music, or pictures pulled from websites. For some web users, this is a matter of principle, and they will not pay at all for something they believe should be free. Therefore, if a fee is requested as they are browsing a site, their demand for that site's offerings is zero. In such a situation, a price cut (let alone a price increase) is impossible because the price the buyer will pay is zero.

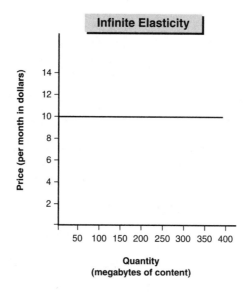

Figure 5.3

Figure 5.3 portrays infinite elasticity, the situation for our highly principled Internet user. He will pay $10 a month to his Internet service provider for access to the web, but he will not pay a penny more for any web-based content. Regardless of the price, if there is a price beyond the $10 access charge, his demand for web-based content is zero.

Inelastic Demand: No Price Cuts Here

Some sellers learn, to their dismay, that a price decrease does not increase revenue. For instance, say our service station reduces his price by 50 percent, but you increase your gasoline usage by only 20 percent.

Table 5.2   Inelastic Demand for Gasoline

	P	×	Q	=	R
Original situation	$2.50	×	100 gals.	=	$250
Price drops 50%	$1.25	×	120 gals.	=	$150
Price doubles	$5.00	×	80 gals.	=	$400

The result here is lower revenue and an instance of inelastic demand. In general, inelastic demand occurs when a price decrease calls forth an increase in quantity that results in a decrease in revenue. In other words, price goes down and quantity goes up, but revenue still goes down.

This means that the effect on quantity demanded is less than unity but greater than zero.

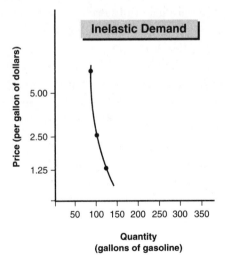

Figure 5.4

This chart depicts inelasticity of demand, meaning a decrease in price increases demand, but not by enough to raise revenue. Inelasticity basically means that people demand a certain quantity of the product and are not going to change that demand very much because of price decreases. They'll change it a bit, but not much.

THE REAL WORLD

Operators of tow trucks that cruise around during snowstorms understand inelasticity: if you need to be towed out of a snow bank, you'll pay the outrageous price. Your demand is inelastic.

However, this also cuts both ways. Inelasticity also means that demand will not decrease very much in the face of a price increase. Therefore, a seller of a product with inelastic demand can raise prices and people will generally pay the increase. Consumers can't really reduce their consumption all that much. As the chart shows, a doubling of the price calls forth a mere 20 percent decrease in demand. This boosts the gas station's revenue to $400, well above the $250 brought in before the price decrease.

Although consumers cannot reduce their consumption much in the short run, as we'll see later in this chapter, they can reduce their demand for almost any product in the long run.

Zero elasticity, or what economists call perfect inelasticity, occurs when a price change has no effect at all on the quantity demanded. Certain medicines and health-care services face perfectly inelastic demand (or close to it). For instance, people with AIDS require certain medicines and people with kidney disease require access to a dialysis machine regardless of the cost. Figure 5.4 (on the previous page) depicts inelastic demand, while Figure 5.5 (on the next page) depicts zero elasticity, also called *perfect inelasticity* (the quantity remains the same, regardless of price).

Perfect, or zero, elasticity means that no matter how the price changes, the quantity demanded remains the same. The consumer needs this amount of the product, regardless of how expensive or inexpensive it is.

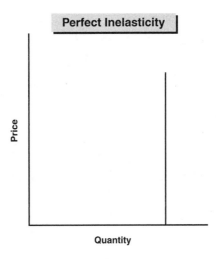

Figure 5.5

What Determines Elasticity?

If you produce or sell anything, or work for an outfit that does, you should have some idea of the elasticity of demand for your product or service. When the economy takes a downturn and people cut back their spending, can they cut back on your product or service? If you work for a hospital or sell basic consumer goods, like toothpaste, you have little to worry about. People who need essential medical services aren't worried about what it costs and people aren't about to stop brushing their teeth—their demand is relatively inelastic.

On the other hand, if you work in a high-end retail clothing store, travel agency, or fine restaurant, you may want to keep a Plan B handy. In general—as demonstrated in the 2008–2009 recession—inessentials or highly discretionary expenses have a higher elasticity of demand. If people can do without something when times get tough, they will. That recession hit luxury goods manufacturers, retailers, restaurants, and travel services very hard.

Either consciously or subconsciously, the issue of elasticity surfaces for consumers and producers in many everyday, real-world situations. Let's examine some of these situations and the main factors that determine the degree of elasticity of demand. These factors are:

- Availability of substitutes
- Short run versus long run
- Percentage of income spent on the product

Availability of Substitutes

Overall demand for gasoline in the United States is generally considered relatively inelastic, at least in the short term. Americans own cars and trucks, and the country is large and laced with highways. Americans need gasoline because there are few substitutes for it. In fact, the only real substitutes are public transportation, which is not always available, and the electric car, which is still a relatively new technology.

However, any individual consumer's demand for gasoline can be elastic or inelastic, depending on their access to a substitute. Suppose the price of gasoline were to double over the next two months. If you commute from a suburb into New York City or another city with good public transportation, you could start taking the bus or train to work and dramatically reduce your demand for gasoline. Your demand for gasoline is relatively elastic.

On the other hand, if you commute from your home in one suburb to an office campus in a distant suburb, your transportation options may be quite limited. You need gasoline, and therefore your demand for it is relatively inelastic.

If there are few substitutes for a product, the demand for it is relatively inelastic. That means that the price can change, but the quantity demanded doesn't change very much in response.

Short Run Versus Long Run

The long-run and short-run demand for many goods and services can differ substantially, and that affects elasticity. In our gasoline example, a driver whose demand for gas is inelastic in the short run may have elastic demand in the long run. She may find a job or start a business closer to home, or start a home-based business. She might buy a more fuel-efficient car, or—in an instance of substitution—buy a hybrid or an electric car when her vehicle needs replacement.

For most products and services, long-run demand is far more elastic than short-run demand. As a fossil fuel with a finite supply, gasoline itself will be unavailable in the long run. Over the long run, people can make any of a number of adjustments that will alter their demand for a good. In the short run, however, inelasticity tends to prevail relative to the long run.

THE REAL WORLD

The oil embargo of the early 1970s, which cut the supply of gasoline in the United States, showed the inelasticity of U.S. demand for gasoline. As you would reason from the law of supply and demand, the price increased dramatically. However, consumers' need for gasoline did not decrease very much. Indeed, they not only paid the higher prices but also waited in long lines to pay them.

Yet as the 1970s progressed, consumers reduced their demand for gas. They purchased smaller, more fuel-efficient cars. Japanese automakers, who were already making small cars for their island nation, were ready to meet that demand. Doing so helped manufacturers such as Toyota, Nissan, and Honda to establish themselves in the U.S. market. Soon U.S. auto manufacturers also began making smaller cars.

Then, in the 1980s and 1990s, oil and gasoline prices stopped rising and U.S. drivers moved into minivans and SUVs. Those were profitable vehicles for car manufacturers—until people stopped buying them. That happened when the war in Iraq, the 2008–2009 recession, and a falling dollar increased gas prices and uncertainty about future gas prices.

Percentage of Income

The higher the percentage of income that a product or service consumes, the higher the elasticity. The lower the percentage of income, the lower the elasticity. For example, if the price of Tic Tacs goes up by 10 percent, I doubt that many consumers would alter their demand for them. It's partly because the percentage increase would occur on a small base price relative to other common purchases, such as food, clothing, and gasoline. But it's also because the money spent on mints is a tiny percentage of most people's incomes.

Demand for items purchased with a small percentage of people's incomes is fairly inelastic. Price changes don't have a big effect on the quantity demanded. By that same token, cutting the price would probably do little to stimulate demand.

Things that people spend a higher percentage of their incomes on, such as cars, have much higher elasticity of demand. People will consistently seek out the best deal on a new car or buy a used car because the price represents a relatively high percentage of most people's incomes. Some people never buy a new car, only used ones. Meanwhile, few people are shopping for the best deal on Tic Tacs (or are willing to accept used ones).

Elasticity is worth knowing about because, first, it explains a lot of consumer behavior and, second, it lays the groundwork for understanding other aspects of consumer purchase decisions, as you will see in Chapter 6.

Tinkering with Markets

Up to now we have been examining the way markets operate when they are left to their own devices. However, markets are rarely left to their own devices. External measures are often introduced into a market—often by the government, sometimes by business. These *interventions* can affect the price of a product or service, the quantity demanded, and the behavior of producers and consumers. The rest of this chapter examines some of these measures—specifically, sales taxes, rent controls, and the minimum wage—and their effect on supply and demand.

ECONOTALK

Interventions in the market consist of steps by the government (price controls), businesses (monopolies), or even consumers (boycotts or trade unions) that affect the price, quantity, demand, supply, or some other aspect of the market. In general, however, the term market intervention refers to government actions. The parties doing the intervening generally believe that they are doing so for a good reason.

Please note that I intend only to show the effects of these measures on the market purely from the economic standpoint. I am neither addressing nor judging the social impact or political aspects of these measures.

A Sales Tax Is a Price Increase

Sales taxes are levied by all states (except Alaska, Delaware, Montana, New Hampshire, and Oregon) and many cities as a way of raising revenue. Each individual state or city decides the amount of sales tax to charge, usually ranging from about 4 to 7 percent of the purchase price.

The term *sales tax* refers to a general tax on purchases. In many jurisdictions, certain items such as food and medicine are exempt from sales tax. Also, the term *sales tax* does not usually apply to taxes on specific goods. For instance, taxes on gasoline and so-called *sin taxes* on cigarettes and alcoholic beverages are called gasoline taxes, cigarette taxes, and so on. Despite their titles, they are a form of sales tax and have the same general effect: to increase the price of the item being purchased. As you know by now, the law of supply and demand dictates that if the price increases, the quantity demanded decreases. As Figure 5.6 (on the next page) shows, that is exactly what happens when a sales tax is levied.

Here we return to our Chapter 4 example of the market for beef. Figure 5.6 shows that the equilibrium price without the sales tax is $6 a pound. At that price, consumers demand 60,000 pounds of beef. The chart assumes a sales tax of $2 per pound of beef (don't laugh, federal plus state cigarette taxes average over $2 a pack). The tax raises the price, but notice that overall demand for beef—the demand curve—*does not shift*. Instead, demand decreases along the existing demand curve to 40,000 pounds.

The price increase does, however, shift the supply curve. The shift reflects the new reality imposed by the higher price under the sales tax. Supply curve S^T in the chart shows that, given the decreased demand due to the higher price, suppliers are willing to supply less beef at all price levels. Therefore, the new equilibrium point (E^T) stands at a price of $8 (equal to $6 plus the $2 tax) and a quantity of 40,000 pounds.

As a result of the tax, the producers supply and consumers demand 20,000 fewer pounds of beef. In effect, the tax on beef takes 20,000 pounds of beef off the market. These dynamics hold true for most sales taxes on most products. There are arguments for and against sales taxes and sin taxes, but without question, they alter the prices and quantities that would prevail in the market if they were absent. However, they do raise tax revenues.

THE REAL WORLD

With anti-smoking zealot Michael Bloomberg as mayor, New York City raised its cigarette tax to $1.50 per pack, increasing the total price to over $9.00. The mayor made no bones about his goal of encouraging people to quit. Smokers felt they were being singled out as easy targets and bearing an unfair share of the city's tax burden.

Whatever your views on smoking, this highlights issues of both elasticity and sales taxes (which are generally related). Historically, those who levied cigarette taxes counted on fairly inelastic demand for cigarettes. The product is habit-forming, and those with the habit were generally not deterred by cost.

Until recent years, that is. The skyrocketing cost of cigarettes, due to manufacturers' price hikes as well as higher taxes, has encouraged many people to quit. High costs especially deter teenagers, who often can't pick up the habit due to the expense. And you know why: cigarettes consume a higher percentage of a teenager's income than an adult's income.

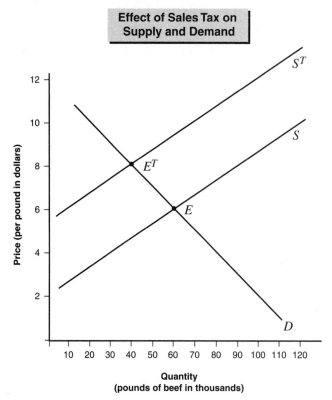

Figure 5.6

Rent Controls

Some communities employ rent controls to make affordable housing available to people without enough income to otherwise live in the community. In general, rent controls keep the price of rental units below the market price. Indeed, that is their goal, because at the market price there's not enough housing for people with lower incomes.

If you consider the relationship between price and quantity in a free market, you'll realize that, over time, the effect of rent control will be to limit the amount of housing available in the community. Why? Because if the *price ceiling* is below the market price (that is, the price at the equilibrium point), then the quantity of housing will be kept below the point that buyers would demand in a free market. Figure 5.7 illustrates this.

ECONOTALK

A **price ceiling** is a government-mandated maximum price that a seller can charge for a product or service. A price floor is a government-mandated minimum price that a seller can charge. Rent control is an example of a price ceiling, while a minimum wage is, in effect, a floor on the price of labor.

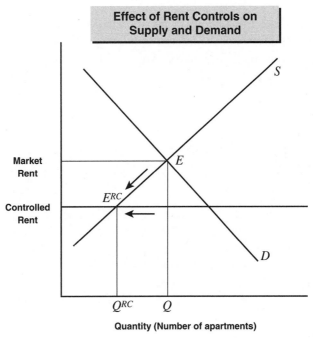

Figure 5.7

The price ceiling imposed by rent control creates a shortage of housing and leads to some renters being unable to find apartments. In Figure 5.7, the shortage is the difference between the imposed equilibrium quantity of Q^{RC} and the market equilibrium quantity of Q.

In practice, rent controls do limit construction of new rental units in the long run, as has been seen in New York City and other cities. New Yorkers lucky enough to live in rent-controlled apartments love the system. But, over time, landlords found that the costs of buying or constructing and maintaining a building outpaced the rent increases permitted under the controls. That made owning an apartment building a bad business proposition and led landlords to abandon buildings. A two-tiered system developed in which people with rent-controlled apartments paid rents well below market rates, and those in decontrolled apartments or new buildings not subject to rent control had to pay market-rate rents well above what they would have been in a free market.

Again, the social value of making affordable housing available to lower-income people is left out of this analysis. Yet the danger in rent controls (as opposed to other means of helping people afford housing, such as welfare payments to raise their incomes) is that a city can wind up with two levels of housing—very inexpensive and very expensive. This tends to squeeze middle-income families out of the city, which has also occurred in New York City, particularly in Manhattan.

The Minimum Wage

While rent control sets a ceiling on the cost of housing, the minimum wage sets a floor under the price of labor. Minimum wage legislation aims to provide every worker with a living wage, meaning an hourly rate that covers the cost of life's necessities.

The current minimum wage does not exactly do that. Working a 40-hour week at the current U.S. minimum wage of $7.25, a worker would earn $290 a week, or $15,080 for a 52-week year. According to the U.S. Department of Health and Human Services, the *poverty threshold* for one person in 2009 was an income of $10,830 a year. For a household of two people the threshold was $14,570 and for a family of three, $18,310. Therefore, the federal minimum wage keeps a household of two with one breadwinner just above the poverty line, and fails to do so for a household with one or more children and a full-time homemaker.

ECONOTALK

The **poverty threshold** (sometimes called the poverty line) is the level of annual household income, adjusted for household size, which officially defines poverty. A household that earns an income below the threshold is officially poor and eligible for certain types of public assistance. The U.S. Census Bureau updates these data every year to reflect changes in incomes and price levels.

All of this aside, an economist would analyze the effect of a minimum wage on the labor market as depicted in Figure 5.8. If the minimum wage is set above the wage that would otherwise prevail in the free market, then the wage floor will generate unemployment. Figure 5.8 shows why.

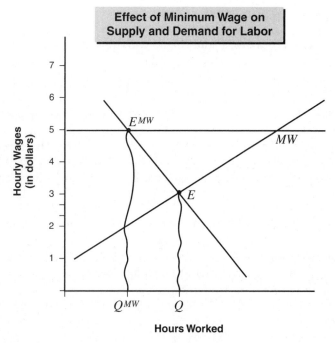

Figure 5.8

The line labeled MW at the $5.00 wage level represents the minimum wage, while the free-market wage stands at $3.00. The minimum wage creates an imposed equilibrium point (E^{MW}) at which the quantity of labor demanded (Q^{MW}) stands well below the quantity that employers would demand (Q) at the free-market wage of $3.00. This generates a surplus of labor (that is, idle workers) equal to Q minus Q^{MW}. Workers who are lucky (or skilled) enough to land a job at the minimum wage are happy. However, many of those who cannot command the minimum wage are unemployed.

THE REAL WORLD

The U.S. federal minimum wage, at $7.25 in 2009, is something of an unpleasant joke. It not only generates an income that would fail to support most people in most areas of the nation in any but subsistence conditions, but in real (inflation-adjusted) terms, it actually *decreased* in every year from 1978 to 1989 and in every year from 1997 to 2006, when it stood at $4.04, down considerably from its high in 1968 of $7.21 (both in 1996 dollars).

The Wages of Control

Thus in the case of rent control and the minimum wage, government intervention in free markets distorts the dynamics of supply and demand. In the case of rent control, a city winds up with too little housing or with a two-tier system. In the two-tier system, some lucky people enjoy apartments at below-market rates, while others are paying inflated rates for a scarcer number of free-market apartments.

In the case of the minimum wage, some workers are idle because the government is, in effect, requiring them to demand a wage that employers are not willing to pay. This may have the unintended consequence of actually putting less money into the workers' pockets.

There are good arguments for and against rent control and the minimum wage. Here, however, the goal is to examine their pure effect on supply and demand. To do this, we are leaving social aims and other factors, such as welfare payments and differences in the cost of living around the nation, out of the discussion for the moment.

This chapter extends the exploration of supply and demand that began in Chapter 4. As we've seen, several factors, including elasticity and government intervention in the market, can affect the demand and supply for a product or service.

In Part 2, we examine more of the workings of the market and the behavior of consumers and producers.

The Least You Need to Know

- Elasticity of demand refers to the change in demand that occurs in response to a change in price. Specifically, it is the degree to which an increase or decrease in price will change the quantity demanded.

- Unitary elasticity occurs when the quantity of a product demanded changes in response to price changes in a way that leaves total revenue unchanged. Elasticity occurs when a reduction in price increases the quantity demanded so that the seller's revenue increases. Inelasticity occurs when a reduction in price increases the quantity demanded by more than zero but less than unity.

- Elasticity can be affected by the availability of substitute goods or services, the percentage of income spent on the good or service, and whether the short term or long term is being considered.

- Interventions in the market consist of steps by the government (sales taxes), businesses (monopolies), or consumers (boycotts or trade unions) that affect the price, quantity, demand, supply, or some other aspect of the market. Those who intervene usually believe that they are doing so for a good reason.

Capitalism at Work

Buyers and sellers have different—even opposite—needs and motivations that must be resolved in markets. In this part, we unscrew the top of the consumer's head and find out how he or she makes buying decisions.

Most consumers are also sellers—of their labor. Everyone who works for a living (or plans to) should understand the dynamics of the labor market. This market has seen more than its share of turmoil, and we explore ways in which labor and management have tried to handle their differences. Speaking of management, we also examine businesses in this part. Production decisions are every bit as difficult as buying decisions, and there is usually a lot more riding on them. Therefore, we see what goes into making these decisions profitable.

Part 2 closes with an examination of the distribution of income and wealth, particularly in the United States. This chapter discusses poverty and income inequality and the causes of income inequality. It focuses on changes in the United States over the past few decades that have contributed to increasing income inequality during that period. The better you understand the determinants of higher incomes, the better you can position yourself to earn one.

Buyer Be Where?

In This Chapter

- How consumers make purchase decisions
- The true value of goods and services
- Why water is very valuable but very cheap
- What makes consumers better off

To understand the U.S. economy, you must understand consumers. Consumers drive the growth of the economy as well as its character. They drive its growth because consumption by households represents more than two thirds of gross domestic product (GDP). They drive the character of the economy—which is that of a consumer society—because of their wealth and buying behavior. The high levels of wealth, together with a low savings rate and high use of credit, have meant that Americans tend to buy what they want when they want it. This flows through to producers, who are always scrambling to produce more goods and services for this voracious market.

This is not to ignore the many U.S. households that cannot *afford* to buy what they want when they want it. Nor is it to say that every American is always on a buying binge. The recession of 2008–2009 left many economists (and businesses) wondering whether persistently high unemployment, curtailed use of credit, and newfound motivation to save money would lower U.S. consumer spending for several years. Still, relative to most other nations, the United States produces and consumes a broader array of goods and services in larger quantities. This is also why many foreign producers want to establish themselves in the U.S. market.

However, U.S. consumers are not unique. They respond to the same motivations and forces that drive consumers in other economies. This chapter examines those motivations and forces. It examines how consumers maximize their happiness and the constraints on spending that call upon consumers to make choices rather than simply buy whatever they want.

What's the Use? Demand and Utility

The entire demand curve for a product—let's stick with beef—is actually the sum of all consumers' demand for the product. If you could determine every single consumer's demand for beef—that is, the quantity that each would buy at various prices—and add up the quantities at each price, you would have the total demand for beef.

In other words, you would add them up horizontally. As Figure 6.1 shows, total demand is the sum of what individual consumers demand (say, per week) at various prices. Here, at $2 per pound, these two fictitious consumers, Jim and Diane, demand a total of 3 pounds of beef. Jim wants 2 pounds, and Diane wants 1 pound.

Obviously there are more than two people in the market for beef. But no one (not even an economist) is going to survey all consumers on their demand for beef at different prices. Thus the demand curve for a good or service theoretically represents total demand. That curve is—also theoretically—the sum of the demand of all the individuals in the market for that good or service.

I'm bringing this up because I want to focus on individual consumers for a while and show how they think and behave. Focusing on individual consumers (and thinking about your own buying behavior) is a good way to understand what drives buying behavior.

You Want *Another* One?

One key driver of buying behavior is *utility*. Utility is the reason you buy something. It is the value or benefit you get from buying a good or service. Utility varies from consumer to consumer. A pickup truck has no utility for people who would never buy one. But a pickup truck has a huge amount of utility for people who couldn't get along without one.

The utility of a pickup truck also varies among the people who do own one. Some people buy one because they need it to make a living. Others buy one to haul their firewood and dogs around. And others never haul anything. They buy a pickup truck because they think it makes them look cool. Whatever the benefit or enjoyment you get from buying a product, that is its utility.

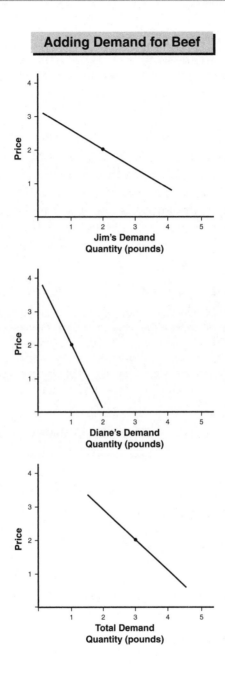

Figure 6.1

Marginal utility is the benefit you get from buying each additional unit of the good. For instance, most individuals who own a pickup truck own just one. If they bought a second one, do you think it would give them the same benefit as the first one? Would it have the same utility? How about beef? If you went to a restaurant and had a steak dinner tonight and then went out to a steakhouse again tomorrow night, would you enjoy tomorrow's steak as much as tonight's? What if you went to a steakhouse the night after that?

The answer to all these questions is generally no. You can only drive one vehicle at a time. You can only eat so many steaks before you want a plate of stir-fried vegetables. In fact, almost all products and services are characterized by *diminishing marginal utility*, depicted in Figure 6.2. The utility—that is, the benefit and enjoyment you derive from the last unit consumed—is less than that of the one previously consumed. Sooner (for pickup trucks) or later (for steaks), the benefit and enjoyment of the last unit consumed will be less than that of the unit before that.

ECONOTALK

Utility is the value, benefit, or enjoyment that a person receives in buying a product. **Marginal utility** is the value, benefit, or enjoyment a person receives from buying each additional unit of the product. **Diminishing marginal utility** means that the utility (the benefit or enjoyment) of consuming the last additional unit of a good is less than that of the previous unit consumed.

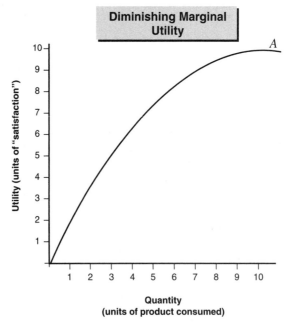

Figure 6.2

Note in Figure 6.2 that until point A, total utility is increasing—but it is increasing at a decreasing rate.

What does this have to do with buying behavior? Just this: each consumer is on a limited income or has a limited amount of wealth. (Remember scarcity? It applies to money, big time.) Each consumer spends his money with the aim of maximizing the overall benefit and enjoyment he can get for that expenditure. Therefore, each consumer will be best off if he spends his income so that the marginal utility of every product or service is in exact proportion to its price.

In other words, to maximize your well-being—the total utility you get from your purchases—the last dollar you spend on beef should bring you the same marginal utility as the last dollar you spend on anything else. Moreover, this has to be the case for everything else you buy.

Why? If you're not getting the same marginal utility on the last dollar you spend on each product you buy, then you would shift your spending around so that you did. Why would you spend money on something when something else would make you happier by providing greater marginal utility?

This is called the *law of equal marginal utilities per dollar.* It says that a consumer will buy each product she wants until the marginal utility per dollar spent on it equals that of any other product she buys.

ECONOTALK

The **law of equal marginal utilities per dollar** states that a consumer will buy each product she wants until the marginal utility per dollar spent on it is exactly the same as it is for any other product she buys.

It may be useful to picture a market basket of all the goods and services you buy in the average month with your average monthly income. This should include not just the products that would fit into a market basket, but also your housing, electricity, gasoline, entertainment—all the goods and services you buy.

Ask yourself these questions: Why do I buy these things? Why do I buy this particular mix of products and services? Am I allocating my expenditures in proportion to the marginal utility I derive from these products and services? Or could I be happier if I bought less of something and more of something else?

Every consumer out there is struggling to reach a point that economists call consumer equilibrium. That's the point where the consumer is maximizing the total utility he obtains from his total spending. With so many choices, it's no wonder we're all going crazy.

The Price of Utility

What could have more utility than water? You can drink it, bathe in it, swim in it, sprinkle your lawn with it, wash your car with it, and you would die without it. Yet water is one of the cheapest products you can buy—in the United States, that is, not on the planet Dune. Also, I'm discussing the water that comes out of your faucet and showerhead, not the water that comes in bottles labeled Evian.

Water has tremendous utility and value, yet its price is low. How can that be? This question stumped Adam Smith (of "invisible hand" fame), whom you learned about in Chapter 1. He wondered why water, one of life's essentials, was cheap, while diamonds, which you cannot drink or bathe in, are expensive. He never did figure it out.

However, later economists did. The answer is partly that water is plentiful, especially in comparison to diamonds. Water is also easy to produce and deliver, once reservoirs and pipelines are in place. Diamonds are tough to produce and deliver (requiring the services of diamond miners and diamond cutters). But the real economic issue is the total utility versus the marginal utility of water and diamonds.

The *total* utility of water is high, but its *marginal* utility is low. Water is so plentiful and we use so much of it that an extra glass of it or an extra minute in the shower has only a tiny bit of extra utility. Diamonds are scarce, and we use very few of them. Most of us buy one diamond, or at most a few, in our lifetimes; therefore, the marginal utility—the benefit and satisfaction—of, say, an engagement ring, is huge.

And that is the answer to Adam's Smith question about the price of water: the marginal utility—the utility obtained from the last unit consumed—and not the total utility determines the price of something. In general, the price of a good falls until it reflects the utility of the last unit sold. Why? Because if the price were any higher, then that last unit cannot be sold. Sellers want to sell as much as they can of whatever they sell, so they set their prices to clear out their inventory.

THE REAL WORLD

The theory of utility has been criticized. For one thing, utility really cannot be measured. In Figure 6.2, I labeled the vertical axis "units of satisfaction" and economists do that, too, but it's a theoretical concept. Of course, utility and marginal utility make sense: we buy things that benefit us, and that benefit does diminish as we consume more of the thing. But that benefit cannot be precisely measured.

Another criticism is that people don't walk around thinking about the benefit they will derive from spending another dollar on another pound of beef or another gallon of gas. So, say the critics, can marginal utility make a difference in buying behavior?

Economists acknowledge that these objections have some validity. However, regardless of whether utility can be measured or whether people think about it, people buy things they want, but they cannot buy *everything* they want. Therefore, they buy the things that give them the greatest satisfaction until they are satisfied with the amount they have. And they buy a mix of goods that somehow maximizes their overall satisfaction. This is, after all, rational behavior, and economics assumes that people behave rationally.

The Consumer's Surplus

Incidentally, because market prices are driven by marginal utility—the utility of the last unit sold—the earlier units we purchase are actually worth more to us than the last. This means that we get more utility than we are paying for from the earlier units we purchase. We're paying a price set by the utility of the last pound of beef for the first pound and second pound and third pound we buy. Economists refer to this extra utility as a surplus—more accurately, as the *consumer surplus*.

Consumers would actually be willing to pay more for the first and perhaps the second and third pound of beef than they are actually being charged. The difference between what a consumer would pay and what she does pay is the consumer surplus. For example, suppose that Diane would actually pay $7 for her first pound of beef, $6 for her second pound, $5 for her third pound, and $4 for her fourth pound—and that the price of beef is $4.

If Diane buys 4 pounds of beef, she pays the store $16 (for 4 pounds at $4 a pound). However, Diane is receiving $22 worth of beef. That's because she would have been willing to pay $7 for the first pound, $6 for the second, $5 for the third, and $4 for the fourth, and $7 + $6 + $5 + $4 = $22. In this situation, Diane's consumer surplus equals $6. That's the difference between the total utility she derives from the purchase and the actual purchase price. Again, that price is set by the market at the value of the marginal utility of beef.

This is depicted visually in Figure 6.3. Diane pays $16, which is represented by the square under the line labeled "Market Price," because 4 pounds (the quantity on the horizontal axis) times $4 (the market price on the vertical axis) equals $16. The $6 is represented by the shaded areas above the line labeled "Market Price." Although this whole situation still relies on the concept of utility and marginal utility, it has the advantage of expressing the concept in dollars instead of units of utility.

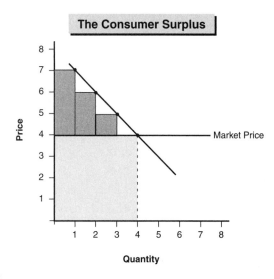

Figure 6.3

To grasp the impact of the consumer surplus on the larger economy, consider the fact that we are all Diane when we are shopping. We would *all* pay more for the things we really need and want. If you had a raging headache, what would you pay for your first aspirin and then your second? During a gasoline shortage, what would you pay for your first gallon, your second, and so on? Certainly, for both the aspirin and the gasoline, you would pay substantially more than the market price set by the value of the last unit sold. But you don't have to pay that, because the market prices goods and services based on their marginal utility, not total utility.

So consumers are out to maximize their total utility, given their budgets. And prices are set by marginal utility, rather than total utility. So far, so good. Now let's delve more deeply into the complex mind of the consumer.

Milk and/or Cookies

Let's consider the complex mind of a seven-year-old consumer. His name is Jimmy, and he only buys two things: milk and cookies. Jimmy loves milk and cookies. He loves milk and cookies so much that he will buy them in almost any combination. But he wants them both. He finds milk with no cookies to be insufferably dull. He finds cookies with no milk to be insufferably dry. But beyond that, Jimmy is indifferent to most combinations of milk and cookies. Over the course of his week in school, he'll find equal satisfaction among the following combinations of glasses of milk and cookies:

Indifference Combinations

	Milk	Cookies
A	2	12
B	4	6
C	6	4
D	8	3

These are called indifference combinations because Jimmy is indifferent regarding which combination he gets. He would derive equal enjoyment (that is, utility and benefit) from any of these combinations of milk and cookies.

Like so many things in economics, these indifference combinations can be plotted on a curve, as shown in Figure 6.4 (on the next page).

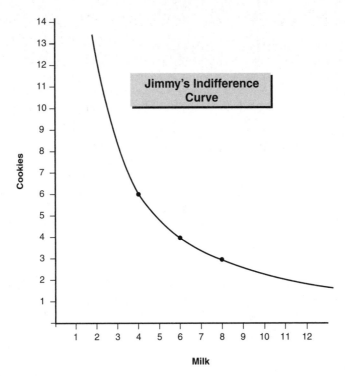

Figure 6.4

Jimmy will derive equal satisfaction anywhere along this curve, not just at the combinations in the small table of indifference combinations. Why? Because Jimmy is willing to trade off cookies for milk and milk for cookies in the proportions shown in his indifference combinations and anywhere along his *indifference curve*. All the combinations are equally satisfactory to Jimmy. He would be indifferent about which combination he actually received.

ECONOTALK

An **indifference curve** shows a series of combinations of purchases of two goods that are all equally acceptable to the consumer. The consumer is indifferent in the sense that he would be equally happy with any of the combinations plotted on the curve.

Consumers—all of us—are willing to trade off one good for another. We do it every day, don't we? We all buy some things instead of others. That's the case with Jimmy. However, at different points on the indifference curve, he will make trade-offs in different proportions of each good. For instance, when Jimmy has four glasses of milk and six cookies, he will give up two cookies to get another two glasses of milk. Say he makes that trade and winds up with four cookies and six glasses of milk. At that point, he will only give up one cookie for two glasses of milk. Why? Because at that point he has plenty of milk, but is starting to run low on cookies. In fact, from this point on, he will need more and more milk to separate him from each remaining cookie.

This illustrates an important concept: the *marginal rate of substitution*, also known as the substitution ratio, changes along the curve. (This, for the geometrically inclined—no pun intended—means that the slope of the curve is changing.) The various points on the indifference curve show the marginal rate of substitution between two goods for a consumer. This ratio changes along the indifference curve. It changes as the proportion of the two goods to one another changes. The less you have of a good, relative to another good, the less you want to trade it off. For many goods, you may reach a point where you simply won't trade it off.

ECONOTALK

The **marginal rate of substitution** is the rate at which a consumer will trade one good for another as one becomes scarcer to her and the other becomes more plentiful. In general, as a good becomes scarcer, a consumer will trade it only for increasingly greater amounts of the more plentiful good.

Jimmy will not trade every last drop of milk for a cookie or trade his last bite of cookie for more milk. He holds onto his cookies as they become scarce and milk becomes plentiful. Likewise, he holds onto his milk as it becomes scarce and cookies become plentiful. This is why the indifference curve flattens out at each end. The curve eventually becomes vertical for cookies and horizontal for milk, because Jimmy does not want all milk and no cookies (too dull), nor does he want all cookies and no milk (too dry).

In econospeak, this means that, to Jimmy, the marginal utility of milk increases as milk becomes scarce and cookies become plentiful (and his mouth becomes dry). And it means that the marginal utility of cookies increases as they become scarce and milk becomes plentiful (and Jimmy longs for variety in his life). In general, the more you have of something, the lower the marginal utility of each additional unit you receive. After our study of marginal utility earlier in this chapter, that should make complete sense.

An indifference curve is also called an equal utility contour. (It's a contour as well as a curve, you see.) It's an equal utility contour because the curve (or contour, if you must) depicts a series of points where the relative marginal utilities of the two goods—in this case, milk and cookies—are equal for the consumer—in this case, Jimmy.

More (Or Less) Cookies and Milk

Believe it or not, the indifference curve in Figure 6.4 is just one of many that I could have drawn for Jimmy. That's because there are many other combinations of milk and cookies that will satisfy the boy, as shown in Figure 6.5.

For instance, along curve I^2, Jimmy would be as happy to have four cookies and four glasses of milk as he would be to have two cookies and seven glasses of milk. However—and this is important—no combination along curve I^2 would make Jimmy as happy as any combination on the original curve I^1 (which is the original curve in Figure 6.4). That's because, at any point on curve I^1, Jimmy has more cookies *and* more milk, in various combinations.

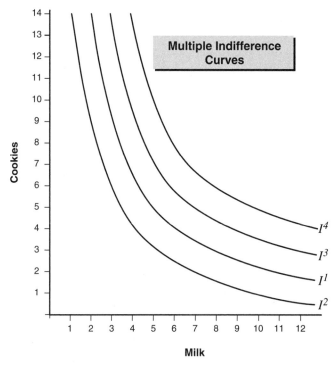

Figure 6.5

Similarly, Jimmy would be happier with any combination on curve I^3 than on curve I^1, and even happier with any combination on curve I^4.

Please file these thoughts where you can get at them easily, because we'll be coming back to them soon. First, though, we need to examine Jimmy's financial situation.

That Awful Thing Called a Budget

There's no such thing as free milk and cookies (or a free lunch). At Jimmy's school, cookies cost 50¢ each, and milk costs 75¢ a glass. Jimmy's on a meal plan, so his lunch is paid for in advance. But he foots his own cookie-and-milk bill out of a cookie-and-milk allowance of $6 a week. Jimmy can spend that $6 allowance on cookies and milk, in any combination he chooses.

Figure 6.6 illustrates the possible ways in which Jimmy could spend that money. If he wanted to (which he doesn't), Jimmy could allocate his whole cookie-and-milk budget to cookies—and buy 12 of them at 50¢ each—or to milk—and buy 8 glasses at 75¢ each. Those two points, and all the points between them—that entire line on Figure 6.6—is called the *budget line*. It's also known as the *consumption-possibility line*. That's the perfect name, because that line shows all the possible combinations of cookies and milk that Jimmy could consume with his $6.

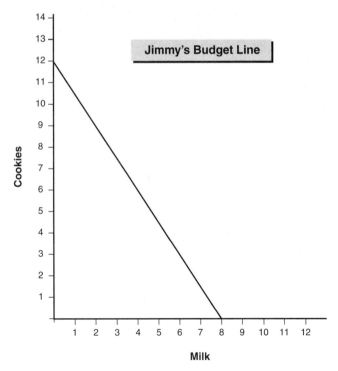

Figure 6.6

At the end of the week, however, Jimmy will have purchased only one combination of cookies and milk. He'll buy the combination of cookies and milk that will give him the greatest total utility. To find that combination, we could wrack our brains running a bunch of numbers—but, because we have charted Jimmy's indifference curves and his budget line, there's a much easier way.

In Figure 6.7, we lay Jimmy's consumption-possibility line on top of his multiple indifference curves. This clearly reveals the cookie-and-milk combination that will give Jimmy the greatest utility given his budget—or, as economists say, the biggest bang for the buck: six cookies and four glasses of milk. This point rests on the highest indifference curve that Jimmy's budget will carry him to, and it is called the *optimal equilibrium point*. At this point, the marginal utility of the last dollar spent on each product is equal.

ECONOTALK

The **budget line** or **consumption-possibility line** shows the range of combinations of two goods that a consumer can afford, given his budget. The consumer's **optimal equilibrium point** is the point on the highest indifference curve that the budget line just touches. That is the combination of purchases in which the marginal utility of each dollar spent on the two goods is equal.

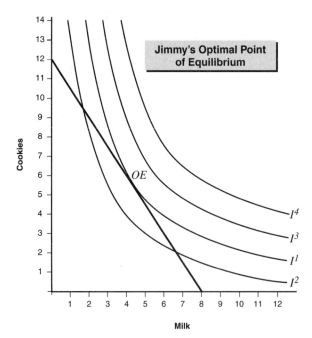

Figure 6.7

What About Changes?

Changes in the price of products and services (such as cookies and milk) and in the consumer's income (or allowance) will change these pictures and the underlying situations.

An increase in the price of either cookies or milk will change the budget line. If the price of cookies increases, Jimmy will be able to afford fewer than 12 of them on his $6 allowance. That will cause the budget line to pivot downward and place the optimal equilibrium point in Figure 6.7 out of reach. An increase in the price of milk will have a similar effect. Moreover, an increase in the price of both cookies and milk will shift the entire budget line lower. In all of these cases, Jimmy winds up on a lower indifference curve and at a lower optimal equilibrium point.

A decrease in the price of either cookies or milk, or both, will have the opposite effect, and will move Jimmy to a higher indifference curve and a higher equilibrium point.

Changes in income have similar effects. An increase in income moves the entire budget line—that is, the consumption-possibility line—higher. A decrease in income moves the entire budget line lower. When the line moves higher, the consumer winds up on a higher indifference curve and at a higher equilibrium point. When the line moves lower, the consumer is on a lower indifference curve and at a lower equilibrium point.

ECONOTIP

The cookies and milk example simplifies an extremely complex situation in which a consumer, facing a vast number of choices, attempts to optimize the marginal utility of her expenditures. The theory of marginal utility and consumer equilibrium is, admittedly, theory. However, something very much like this process goes on in consumer behavior.

A shopper doesn't go to the store and buy 40 pounds of beef and no potatoes, even if she and her family really enjoy beef. At a certain point, the marginal utility of beef will diminish, particularly if the shopper has no potatoes in the house. Think of the entire market basket of goods and services you buy. Isn't there a subconscious analysis of marginal utility going on in your buying behavior?

There are, of course, other drivers of consumer behavior. We will examine some of them in Chapter 7. Yet the mechanism of choice plays out along the lines of utility, marginal utility, and consumer equilibrium—whether the consumer knows it or not.

The Least You Need to Know

- Utility is the value, benefit, or enjoyment that a person receives in buying a product. Marginal utility is the value, benefit, or enjoyment a person receives from consuming each additional unit of the product. After a point, marginal utility diminishes with each additional unit consumed.

- In general, the price of a good falls until it reflects the utility of the last unit sold. If the price were any higher, then that last unit could not be sold. In this way, the consumer derives more benefit from the first units of a product she bought, because the product is actually priced at its marginal utility.

- Indifference curves show a series of combinations of purchases (of two goods) that are all equally acceptable to the consumer. The consumer is indifferent in the sense that he would be equally happy with any combination of goods plotted on the curve.

- The budget line, or consumption-possibility line, shows the range of combinations of two goods that a consumer can afford, given his budget. The point on the highest indifference curve that the budget line just touches is the consumer's optimal equilibrium point. That is the combination of purchases that he can afford that will make him happiest. That is also where the marginal utility of each dollar spent on the goods is equalized.

- Changes in prices and income affect a consumer's well-being. Lower prices or higher income will leave the consumer better off, while higher prices or lower income will leave her worse off. Here, better and worse off are defined as points on higher or lower indifference curves. On higher curves, the consumer has more goods; on lower curves, she has fewer goods.

Income, Outgo, and Investment

In This Chapter

- Sources of income
- Propensity to spend and to save
- The consumption function
- The multiplier effect

In Chapter 6, we examined consumers' buying behavior based upon their individual wants and needs. In this chapter, we look at consumers on a larger scale as a driving force in the economy.

It's well worth doing. Consumers' choices about how much of their income to spend and to save strongly affect the growth of the economy and, over time, its size. That's because, as you recall, the spending of households on goods and services accounts for at least two thirds of U.S. gross domestic product (GDP). Consumer spending boosts production of goods and services. Meanwhile, the savings of households are channeled into businesses' investment in productive capital, which determines the long-term ability of the economy to produce goods and services.

Where Income Comes From

Households receive income mainly in exchange for providing businesses with labor and other factors of production—the essential things needed to produce goods and services. Economists define the *factors of production* as land, labor, and capital. Land is self-explanatory and includes not only farmland but all land devoted to factories, offices, terminals, and other commercial purposes. Labor refers to all human effort aimed at producing something or performing a service for payment.

ECONOTALK

The **factors of production** are land, labor, and capital. Capital refers to productive plant and equipment—any tangible thing that is created in order to create another product. Plant and equipment are also called capital goods, meaning goods that produce other goods.

The term capital requires more explanation. Economists define capital as any product created to make more products. Capital includes factories and equipment, computers and tools, vehicles and roads—the entire productive infrastructure and its individual components. Interestingly, economists do not include financial capital—that is, money—in their definition of capital, only productive capital.

There is one other factor. In a capitalist system, an entrepreneur organizes the factors of production into a business to produce a product or service, sell and deliver it to customers, and, in the process, earn a profit for herself and her investors. This entrepreneurial function is essential to a developed economy because the factors of production do not organize themselves. (They couldn't, even if they tried.)

The process of capital formation generates capital goods. Capital formation—building productive capacity—is an essential step in developing an economy that can produce goods and services beyond farm and handmade products. Capital formation is also called investment and is the *I* in C + I + G you learned about in Chapter 2. As you will see in Part 5, capital formation is a crucial issue for the developing economies of the world, which face the challenge of attracting financial capital and then channeling it into productive capital.

Each factor of production receives a specific kind of payment, although it's all money. Landlords, who provide the land, receive *rent*. Workers receive *wages* (or salaries). Capitalists, who provide the productive capital (or more accurately, the money that finances that capital), receive *interest*. And entrepreneurs, who organize the factors of production, receive *profit*.

I've italicized these terms because each one has a specific meaning: each relates to the factor being provided and paid for in the production process. Economists use these four types of income—rent, wages, interest, and profit—to calculate a figure for national income.

It All Adds Up

National income is the total employee compensation, rent, interest, dividends, and profits paid to all of the factors of production in the economy in a year, including corporations.

Personal income is the amount paid to households for their contribution to production during a period, such as a quarter or a year. The following are the personal income figures for the years 1990, 2000, and 2009.

Table 7.1   Personal Income (in billions)

	1990	2000	2009
Wages & salaries	$3,326	$5,789	$7,787
Proprietors' income	365	818	1,041
Rent	50	215	268
Interest	752	984	1,239
Dividends	169	377	554
Government transfer receipts	595	1,083	2,105
Less gov't transfer contributions	−410	−706	−967
Personal income	$4,847	$8,560	$12,027

Source: Bureau of Economic Analysis, National Income and Product Accounts

Figure 7.1 (on the next page) shows how national income and the factors of production relate to one another and flow through the economy.

ECONOTALK

National income is the total amount paid to all the factors of production in a quarter or a year. **Personal income** is the amount paid to households in a period, mainly in the form of employee compensation, interest, and dividends. National income equals GDP and personal income equals about 85 percent of national income.

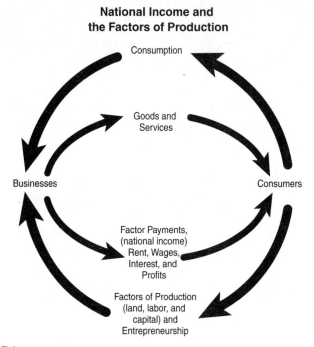

**National Income and
the Factors of Production**

Consumption

Goods and
Services

Businesses

Consumers

Factor Payments,
(national income)
Rent, Wages,
Interest, and
Profits

Factors of Production
(land, labor, and
capital) and
Entrepreneurship

Figure 7.1

In the lower half of the diagram, consumers (households) provide the factors of production to businesses, which make factor payments to consumers in return. In the top half, consumers pay businesses and receive goods and services in return. The diagram shows a circular relationship between consumers and businesses because that's what it is. Businesses pay consumers to produce goods and services, and consumers pay businesses for those goods and services.

Propensity to Save and to Consume

Disposable income is what's left of personal income after taxes, and there are only two things a consumer can do with that income: spend it or save it. Either way, that income is being recycled into the economy as part of consumption—the C in C + I + G—or as part of investment—the I in C + I + G.

Up to now in this book, I have spent a good deal of time discussing demand. We will discuss it again, even in this chapter—but first, let's focus on the investment aspect of GDP. Investment in capital goods does not simply represent a boost to GDP in the year it is made. It represents a boost to the economy in the years ahead. Remember, investment in capital goods expands our economy's productive capacity.

When people save part of their income, they forgo current consumption for later consumption. The saver engages in this act of delayed gratification for his own good, not to provide money for businesses to invest. He wants to make an expensive purchase in several months or years, or wants to have money for retirement. The problems of businesses searching for money to finance capital goods are the furthest things from his mind.

Businesses are equally unconcerned about the saver's situation. They also don't give a thought to the larger economy and the issue of raising I in the GDP formula. They are interested in growing. They are concerned about latching onto (or developing) a new technology, building a new factory or office, or getting a new product out to market.

You'll recall that the impersonal dynamics of supply and demand work themselves out in the market through the price mechanism to bring consumers and producers to an equilibrium point. Similarly, the dynamics of saving and investment are resolved in the market by interest rates (the price of money) and by unemployment and income levels. Too little savings will boost interest rates. A surplus of savings will cause interest rates to fall. Too little investment will generate unemployment. Too much investment can cause inflation, thus eroding the purchasing power of income.

Let's look more deeply into those dynamics.

Spend or Save?

As you may imagine, people with high incomes save more money than people with low incomes. The poor don't save at all, while families in the higher income brackets do most of the saving. Many economists, financial planners, and public officials have expressed concern that the U.S. personal savings rate—the amount of disposable income that an individual saves instead of spends—has plummeted over the past 40 years. Indeed the overall personal savings rate (personal savings as a percentage of disposable income) fell from 9.6 percent in the 1970s to 8.6 percent in the 1980s to 5.5 percent in the 1990s to 2.9 percent in the 2000s.

Those concerned about the savings rate usually worry more about the long-term well-being of the savers (actually, the nonsavers) than the pool of investable funds. Although the U.S. personal savings rate is undoubtedly low, both historically and compared with other nations (notably Japan and Germany), you should keep two things in mind.

First, the savings rate does not consider the appreciation of financial securities or home values. Many nonsavers have a good deal of wealth in those forms. Although unrealized appreciation is not the same as money in the bank, it is a form of wealth. Second, as a large, stable, prosperous economy, the United States attracts more foreign investment capital than any other nation in the world.

However, the home-price collapse and recession of the late 2000s encouraged many U.S. consumers to resume saving. In 2009, the savings rate reached 4.7 percent, well above the low of 1.4 percent in 2005.

So, overall, we can infer that Americans today have a lower propensity to save and, therefore, a higher propensity to consume than they did in the 1970s. The *average propensity to save* is equal to the savings rate. It is the amount saved in a period divided by disposable income in a period. Similarly, the *average propensity to consume* is consumption expenditure in a period divided by disposable income in the period.

The average propensity to save rises as income rises. This is true for a single household and for the population as a whole. By that same token, the average propensity to spend decreases as income rises. At the lowest levels of income, savings are negative, meaning that people borrow to make ends meet. As income rises, people generally save an increasingly larger fraction of their income.

However, as is so often the case in economics, the *marginal* propensity to consume and to save is often more important than the averages. The marginal propensity to consume is the percentage of another dollar of disposable income that a person, household, or population will spend. The marginal propensity to save is the percentage of that dollar that will be saved. As we will see when we look at government fiscal policy in Part 3, the marginal propensity to consume and to spend—and the values of these propensities at various income levels—have serious implications for economic policy.

Picking Apart Propensities

To understand the propensity to consume or save, let's focus on one household, that of the Hobstweedles. On the next page is the Hobstweedles's average propensity to consume and to save and their marginal propensity to consume and to save.

Table 7.2   Average and Marginal Propensity to Consume and to Save (for one hypothetical family)

(1) Disposable Income	(2) Amount Spent	(3) Average Amount Saved	(4) Average Propensity to Consume	(5) Average Propensity to Save	(6) Marginal Prop. to Consume	(7) Marginal Prop. to Save
$10,000	$11,000	$- 1,000	1.10	-.10	—	—
20,000	20,000	0	1.00	0	.90	—
30,000	28,500	1,500	.95	.05	.85	.15
40,000	36,000	4,000	.90	.10	.75	.25
50,000	42,500	7,500	.85	.15	.65	.35
60,000	48,500	11,500	.81	.19	.60	.40
70,000	54,000	16,000	.77	.23	.55	.45
80,000	59,000	21,000	.74	.26	.50	.50

As I walk you through this table, I'll refer to the columns by number. The first three columns are straightforward. Column 1 is disposable income, that is, the Hobstweedles's household income after taxes over the years as their careers progressed and their salaries rose. Column 2 is the dollar amount of disposable income that they spent each year. Column 3 is the amount of disposable income that they saved each year.

Notice that in the first year, their disposable income was $10,000 and they borrowed another $1,000 to spend. In that year, they realized what economists call a dissavings of $1,000. The following year, they earned $20,000 after taxes and spent the whole amount. That, incidentally, means that $20,000 is their break-even point—the level of disposable income at which they neither save nor borrow. After that break-even point, they start saving a portion of their disposable income every year.

So much for the dollar amounts. Column 4 is the percentage (expressed as a decimal value) of total disposable income spent that year. It is calculated by dividing the value in Column 2 by the value in Column 1. Column 5 is the percentage of disposable income (again, expressed as a decimal) that the Hobstweedles saved that year. This value is calculated by dividing the value in Column 3 by the one in Column 1.

In the first year, the 110 percent average propensity to spend indicates that the Hobstweedles spent 10 percent more than they earned. That amount is offset by the negative 10 percent propensity to save.

As income rises, the average propensity to consume decreases and the average propensity to save increases. This is the case for most people. Households with rising incomes save more money than lower income households, and not just because they make more money. They also save a higher percentage of their income than lower income households.

Once again we come to the issue of what happens at the margin of an economic phenomenon. In economics, the term *marginal* usually means *one additional* or *an added amount.* The marginal propensity to consume—which is listed for various income levels in Column 6—refers to the percentage of *additional* income that is spent. Marginal propensity to consume is calculated by dividing the increase in consumption over the previous level of consumption (in Column 2) by the increase in income over the previous level (in Column 1).

In our table, the increase in consumption varies from one level to the next. For instance, at the $40,000 income level, the increase in consumption is $7,500 over the previous year. This $7,500 equals the $36,000 in consumption at the $40,000 level minus the $28,500 spent the previous year. The increase in income is always $10,000 in Column 1. So we divide $7,500 by $10,000 and get the .75 propensity to consume shown in Column 6.

The marginal propensity to consume is the answer to the question, "If a person receives one more dollar of income, how much of it does he spend?" In Table 7.2, I have used the income increments of $10,000 to make the example clear and a bit more realistic. (No one really thinks in terms of an extra dollar of income—except economists.)

As the table shows, the marginal propensity to consume decreases as income increases. Moreover—and this point is key—as income reaches higher levels, the marginal propensity to consume is usually lower than the average propensity to consume. The reason for that is simple. As income rises, more of that additional income is saved, and less is spent. In other words, people spend more of the $10,000 they earn between $20,000 and $30,000 than they do of the $10,000 they earn between $50,000 and $60,000.

The flip side of the marginal propensity to consume is the marginal propensity to save. The marginal propensity to save—in Column 7—is the percentage of *additional* income that is saved. It is calculated by dividing the *increase* in savings over the previous year's savings (in Column 3) by the increase in income over the previous year's income (in Column 1). As income rises, people save a larger percentage of the added income than they saved when they were making less. Therefore, as income rises, the marginal propensity to save rises.

For the Hobstweedles, the marginal propensity to save rises all the way to 50 percent at the $80,000 level of household income.

The Consumption Function

Plotting some of the values in Table 7.2 will give us a clearer picture of how consumption and savings relate to disposable income. Figure 7.2 (on the next page) plots the values for consumption (on the vertical axis) as a function of disposable income (on the horizontal axis). The curved line on the chart represents the amount spent from Column 2 at the various levels of disposable income in Column 1.

What about the line on the chart at a 45-degree angle? That line shows what would happen if consumption and disposable income were always equal: if all disposable income were spent. Thus the line shows that consumption is $10,000 at disposable income of $10,000; $20,000 at income of $20,000; $30,000 at income of $30,000; and so on. If that's what the 45-degree line shows, then a line showing any deviation from the 45-degree line will represent consumption that is either above or below disposable income.

That is exactly the case here. For the Hobstweedles, consumption is $20,000 at disposable income of $20,000. That is called the break-even point for them, and I have therefore labeled it BE. The break-even point is the point where consumption and disposable income are equal—all disposable income is spent.

At any point on the consumption function to the left of the break-even point, the situation of dissavings exists. If the household is spending in excess of its disposable income, then they must be borrowing. Likewise, at any point to the right of the break-even point, there are savings. If the household is spending less than it brings home in income, then they are saving the difference.

In addition, a vertical line drawn upward from any point on the disposable income axis (as I have drawn at $80,000) will show the area under the consumption function to represent consumption expenditures and the area between the consumption function and the 45-degree line to represent the amount saved.

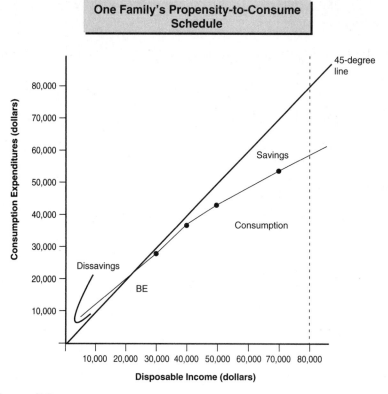

Figure 7.2

THE REAL WORLD

The consumption function, and this discussion of propensities to consume and save, implies that income is the main driver of spending and saving behavior. Income is one of the most important factors, if not the most important. However, other factors affect a family or nation's spending and saving behavior. Cultural norms, for example, play an important role at both the household and national levels.

Having lived in both New York City and New England, I believe that cultural norms in New York City predispose people to spend more freely than they do in New England. Many New Yorkers strive to present themselves to others in a fashionable, even impressive, manner. That costs money—money that could be saved instead.

New Englanders tend to place more value in the old Yankee habit of thrift and generally devote less attention (and less money) to fashion.

The Savings Function

If there is a consumption function, there must be a savings function. There is, and we will examine it briefly, because it is basically the mirror image of the consumption function.

The savings function for the Hobstweedle household is shown in Figure 7.3. The curve is plotted from the values for disposable income and savings in Table 7.2.

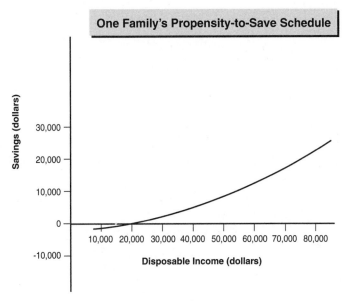

Figure 7.3

Figure 7.3 shows the dollar amounts that our sample family saves as their disposable income rises. As income rises, savings increase at an increasing rate. That is why the line curves gently upward.

Notice, too, that savings is less than zero at the $10,000 income level due to the dissaving I discussed earlier. At $20,000, savings is zero, and thereafter, savings increase as income increases.

Meanwhile, At the National Level

The real issue for economic policy is not what the Hobstweedles will do with added income, but rather what large segments of the population or the entire population will do with it. In other words, we need a consumption function for the whole United States. Table 7.3 shows the values we need in order to plot the function.

Table 7.3   Disposable Income, Consumption, and Personal Saving (in billions of current dollars)

	2000	2001	2002	2003	2004
Disposable income	7,327	7,649	8,010	8,378	8,889
Less: personal outlays*	–7,114	–7,444	–7,728	–8,088	–8,586
Equals: savings	213	205	282	290	303
Savings rate	2.9%	2.7%	3.5%	3.5%	3.4%

	2005	2006	2007	2008	2009
Disposable income	9,277	9,916	10,403	10,806	10,924
Less: personal outlays*	–9,150	–9,681	–10,224	–10,520	–10,459
Equals: savings	127	235	179	286	465
Savings rate	1.4%	2.4%	1.7%	2.6%	4.3%

Personal Outlays include consumption, interest payments, and transfer payments

Source: Bureau of Economic Analysis, National Income and Product Accounts Tables (Values may be off by one due to rounding error.)

Note that the savings rate rose from 2.9 percent of disposable income in 2000 to 3.5 percent in 2002 and 2003 but remained well below the historic highs of 10 percent achieved in the 1970s. For Americans, the 2000s were not exactly the Age of Thrift.

Figure 7.4 shows the relationship between actual U.S. disposable income and consumption for the 10 years from 2000 through 2009. It is called a consumption function because it shows consumption as a function of disposable income. I have drawn a line of best fit (which you learned about in Chapter 3) through the 10 data points for the 10 years to serve as the consumption function.

The area between the consumption function and the horizontal axis for disposable income represents total consumption. The area between the consumption function and the 45-degree line represents savings. With the consumption function so close to the 45-degree line, the chart clearly shows that savings were low over the entire period.

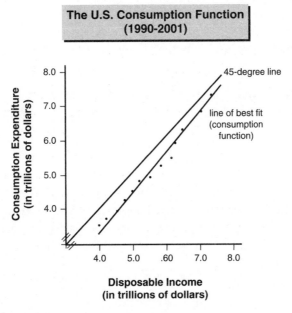

Figure 7.4

The Importance of Investment

Up to now, I have discussed consumers and households, consumer demand, savings by households, and so on. I've focused heavily on the *C*—consumption—in C + I + G. Now, however, we must shift the focus to investment—the *I* in our GDP formula—in order to understand more fully how the economy really works.

You'll recall that consumption represents about two thirds of GDP—that's a signifi-cant portion of the economy. However, in a very real sense, investment determines economic growth, particularly long-term economic growth. Keep in mind that economists define investment as investment in productive capacity by businesses. This includes building and expanding factories and offices and purchases of equip-ment and vehicles. It also includes one other item: increases in inventories of goods to be sold. Inventories are obviously not productive capacity, but they are the product of that capacity. Therefore they represent a store of wealth that will be delivered to consumers.

Productive capacity is a store of wealth, too. A machine is not simply a machine. It is a device that converts raw material into saleable, usable products. It also requires an operator—and a repairman, a manager, a laborer to pack the products into boxes, a salesperson to sell them, a driver to deliver them to customers, a customer service person to explain how to use them, and … you get the idea.

Most of the income that households get to dispose of comes from businesses. When businesses invest in plant and equipment, they create employment and incomes. When they stop investing in plant and equipment, they diminish employment and incomes.

In a sense, consumer demand is more or less a given, but income is not. Who doesn't want a new car, new kitchen, new clothes, vacations, restaurant meals, and plasma screen TVs? The problem is, all of these things cost money—disposable income— and income comes from employment, and employment, by and large, comes from businesses. If they're not investing in productive capacity, businesses aren't going to need more employees in which case consumers won't have enough disposable income to generate increasing demand.

ECONOTIP

When an investor purchases shares of stock that have already been issued, the money does not go to the company that issued the stocks. Instead, the money goes to the party that was holding the stock. Only new shares of stock sold by a company raise money for the company to use for expansion.

However, if consumers have income, they will generally spend most of it and fuel demand. Investment is another story. It's a much longer-term decision, made with much more deliberation than the decision to eat out tonight or buy a new sofa. It depends on profits, which are often reinvested in productive capacity, and it depends on interest rates. But most of all, it depends on expectations and estimates of the future, and often the distant future at that: it can take as long as three to five years to build a factory and get it up and running.

In addition, business investment decisions are made independent of the spending-versus-saving decisions made by households. That means that the amount of investment that businesses want to do may not match the amount of saving that households want to do. That, too, has implications for the economy.

Mismatches Between Savings and Investment

When businesses want to invest more or less than households want to save, or house-holds want to save more or less than businesses want to invest, we have disequilibrium. As you saw in the case of supply and demand for goods and services, when disequilibrium occurs, economic forces push buyers and sellers toward a point of equilibrium.

A similar situation prevails when it comes to savings and investment. Figure 7.5 depicts the situation.

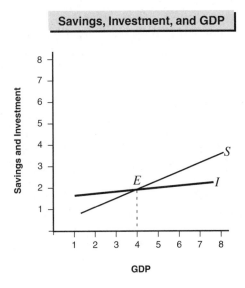

Figure 7.5

Notice in Figure 7.5 that both lines—S, representing savings, and I, representing investment—slope upward (as you go to the right). This indicates the positive relationship between savings and GDP growth and investment and GDP growth. Both savings and investment increase as GDP increases. Similarly, GDP increases as savings and investment increase. So we do not have a downward sloping demand curve for investment in this situation.

But we do have a mismatch between savings and investment. At levels of GDP to the right of the equilibrium point (E), savings are greater than investment. Households are saving more than businesses want to invest. What forces will move the economy toward equilibrium GDP?

If households are saving more than businesses want to invest, then they are not spending their money. Consumers are sitting on their wallets, or banking their money instead of spending it. This means that inventories of goods will pile up, and businesses will reduce production. Workers will be laid off, and machines will stand idle. Investment—expansion of productive capacity—will stop when people aren't buying the goods already being produced. When the layoffs occur, income will start to fall, and so will savings. As a result, GDP will contract—it will move to the left, toward the equilibrium point.

Conversely, at levels of GDP to the left of the equilibrium point (E), households are saving less than businesses want to invest. That means they are also spending freely. They are buying more goods and services than businesses can produce with their current productive capacity. No wonder businesses want to invest in more factories and equipment!

If people are buying more than businesses can produce, businesses will sell off their inventories and step up production. They will hire new workers, put current workers on overtime, and leave no machine idle. This will increase incomes and, as we have seen, when incomes increase, savings increase thanks to the increasing marginal propensity to save. This stepped-up production also increases GDP, which will move to the right, toward the equilibrium point.

Equilibrium GDP tends to remain elusive. In a way, that's good; in a capitalist, growth-oriented society, we always want GDP moving to the right—the direction in which it gets larger. We want businesses to always be adding workers and capacity so that the economy keeps growing. Does this mean that we can make this happen by spending instead of saving? To an extent, it does, and that is part of the secret of continual U.S. economic growth. But saving must also occur if businesses are to have funds to invest. There must also be profitable opportunities if businesses are to decide to invest.

As important as consumer spending is to the U.S. economy, investment is equally important. In the next and final section of this chapter, I want to show you one more reason that this is so.

How Investment Flows Through the Economy

In the previous section, you learned that an increase in investment causes an increase in employment and income, and that a decrease in investment causes a decrease in employment and income.

What I didn't tell you is that the effect of a dollar increase or decrease in investment is actually greater than one dollar. The effect on GDP is multiplied. In other words, a $10,000 investment by a business does not simply increase the *I* in C + I + G, and thus GDP, by $10,000. It increases GDP by a multiple of that amount. That's why this effect is called the *multiplier effect*.

For such a technical concept, the multiplier effect is quite easy to grasp. When a company invests $10,000 to expand its building, it hires workers, buys materials, pays for building permits, and so on. And I do mean "and so on." When the building is complete, the business will equip it, furnish it, and hire workers to staff it, clean it, and repair it as needed.

ECONOTALK

The **multiplier effect** refers to the fact that an increase in investment eventually raises or lowers national income by an amount greater than itself. The **multiplier** is the number that expresses the magnitude of that effect. For example, if a $100 investment eventually increases national income by $300, then the multiplier is three.

Unfortunately, the multiplier works both ways. When a business decides to slash its inventories and reduce its production, it will buy fewer materials and less fuel and lay off workers. Say the business saves $10,000 through these measures. The sellers of the materials and the fuel, and the laid-off workers, receive less money to pump back into the economy. As a result, the economy contracts by more than the $10,000 that the business chose not to spend.

The multiplier stands as another case of everything relating to everything else in economics. The economy is one system in which, one way or another, sooner or later, all players are linked.

The Least You Need to Know

- Households must either spend or save their disposable income—that is, their after-tax income. The average propensity to consume is the percentage of disposable income that a household spends. The marginal propensity to consume is the percentage of additional income that goes to consumption.

- The average propensity to save is the percentage of total disposable income that a household, population segment, or nation puts into savings. The marginal propensity to save is the percentage of additional income that goes into savings.

- As income increases, the marginal propensity to save increases and the marginal propensity to consume decreases.

- Saving and investing are done by two very different sets of players in the economy and for unrelated reasons. Consequently, the levels of savings and investment in the economy often do not match one another. Therefore, forces relating to production, employment, and income are usually pushing the economy toward an equilibrium point, which tends to remain elusive.

- The multiplier amplifies the effect of business investment on the economy.

The Business of Business

In This Chapter

- Production decisions and how they are made
- How to analyze a business's cost structure
- All about economies of scale
- How monopolies and cartels operate

Having examined the consumer in some depth, let's take a look at his counterpart, the producer. Everything that makes its way into the market, every good or service that's up for sale, must somehow be produced. In Adam Smith's world, the butcher, the baker, and the candlestick maker are guided in their production decisions by the famous "invisible hand." Modern economists, however, have worked hard to make that hand at least partly visible.

In this chapter, we learn how production decisions are made, how fixed and variable costs add up, and how some businesses become so large. We'll also examine some of the ways that businesses intervene in the market with the aim of increasing their profits.

Business Realities

A business takes inputs, which it pays for, and transforms them into outputs, which it gets paid for, and must make a profit in the process. As anyone who has ever run a lemonade stand knows, to make a profit you must sell the output for more than you paid for the inputs. Profit is what remains after the cost of the inputs—land, labor, plant, equipment, raw materials, transportation, and so on—is subtracted from the revenue received for the output. (Actually, taxes must also be subtracted.)

How does a business manage its costs? How does a business find the right mix among the factors of production? Let's find out.

THE REAL WORLD

Politics in the United States, like politics elsewhere, has often been characterized by hostility toward profits. As you learned in Chapter 1, Karl Marx blazed a trail in this area, believing that businesses made profits only by exploiting labor.

Although some political viewpoints are hostile to profits, from the economic standpoint, profits are necessary. First, entrepreneurs provide a valuable service in organizing the factors of production. If they weren't compensated for providing that service, why would they do it? Second, profits reward the entrepreneur for taking the risks associated with failure. Rents, wages, and interest are guaranteed by contracts, but profits are not guaranteed. Entrepreneurs must be rewarded for risking their time and talent to produce goods and services that may or may not sell. Third, profits encourage investment and are often used to buy more productive capital for the business.

Many people are misinformed not only about the purpose of profits, but about the level of profits most companies earn. A number of years ago, a survey revealed that many Americans believe that 20 to 25 percent or more of a company's revenue goes to profits. The actual figure averages about 5 percent.

Decisions, Decisions

Every business owner or management team must combine the factors of production, particularly labor and capital, in a way that generates profits. Let's take a very simple business—landscaping. Landscaping is fairly *labor-intensive* as opposed to *capital-intensive*. It requires a good amount of human labor, but the productivity of that labor can be boosted with machinery. Giving the workers power mowers rather than hand mowers and leaf blowers rather than rakes will increase their productivity.

ECONOTALK

A **labor-intensive** business relies more heavily on labor than capital as a primary input. Restaurants and most personal service businesses are labor-intensive. A **capital-intensive** business relies more heavily on equipment than labor. Mining is a highly capital-intensive industry.

However, power mowers and leaf blowers are more expensive to purchase, operate, and maintain than hand tools. They increase insurance expense by increasing the risk of injury. Transporting equipment to the work site requires larger trucks, which require fuel, drivers, and insurance. The purchase price of the equipment and trucks and the insurance premiums are all fixed costs. Labor and the fuel to operate the equipment are the major variable costs.

Suppose that, over the first few years in operation, the owner of the landscaping outfit developed the figures shown in Table 8.1.

Table 8.1   Fixed, Variable, Total, Marginal, and Average Costs

(1) Quantity (Acres)	(2) Fixed Costs	(3) Variable Costs	(4) Total Cost	(5) Marginal Cost Per Acre	(6) Average Fixed Cost	(7) Average Variable Cost	(8) Average Total Cost
0	5,000	0	5,000	—	—	—	—
50	5,000	300	5,300	6.00	100.00	6.00	106.00
100	5,000	550	5,550	5.00	50.00	5.50	55.50
150	5,000	750	5,750	4.00	33.33	5.00	38.33
200	5,000	1,050	6,050	6.00	25.00	5.25	30.25
250	5,000	1,550	6,550	10.00	20.00	6.20	26.20
300	5,000	2,250	7,250	14.00	16.67	7.50	24.17
350	5,000	3,150	8,150	18.00	14.29	9.00	23.29
400	5,000	4,250	9,250	22.00	12.50	10.63	23.13
450	5,000	5,550	10,550	26.00	11.11	12.33	23.44
500	5,000	7,050	12,050	30.00	10.00	14.10	24.10

Please follow along as I walk you through this important table. Column 1 shows the number of acres the company can landscape in, say, a week. Column 2 shows fixed costs of $5,000—fixed because they remain the same regardless of the number of acres. Column 3 shows the variable costs—labor, fuel, repairs, and so on—which increase as the number of acres landscaped increases. Column 4, total cost, is simply the sum of the fixed costs (Column 2) and the variable costs (Column 3) for a given number of acres.

Now here's where it gets interesting, because a business person is always interested in costs per unit. In this case, the unit of production is an acre. Marginal cost per acre, shown in Column 5, is the *increase* in total cost divided by the *increase* in acreage. So at 150 acres, total costs are $5,750. That's an increase of $200 over the previous level of cost, which is $5,550. If it costs another $200 to landscape 150 acres rather than 100 acres, then the marginal cost per acre is $4.00, which equals the additional $200 divided by the additional 50 acres.

As volume increases, marginal cost per unit decreases *up to a point*. Notice that, in this example, marginal cost per unit is lowest at that 150-acre volume. After that point, marginal cost rises. At 200 acres, it is back up to $6.00. We'll examine the reason for this in a moment.

Average fixed cost, shown in Column 6, is just the fixed cost in Column 2 divided by the number of acres in Column 1. Average fixed cost decreases as volume increases. The reason for this is simple: average fixed costs are the fixed cost *per unit*. As the number of units increases and fixed costs remain constant, the fixed cost per unit must decrease. The more units that a piece of equipment produces, the more cheaply it is producing each unit.

Average variable cost, shown in Column 7, is the variable costs in Column 3 divided by the total acres in Column 1. Average variable cost, which is variable cost per unit, also decreases *up to a point* and then increases. Again, we will see why in a moment.

Finally, average total cost, shown in Column 8, is the total cost in Column 4, divided by the number of acres. Average total cost, which is total cost per unit, also decreases and then increases.

Diminishing Returns

Figure 8.1 shows the behavior of various per-unit costs at various levels of output. Let's start with average fixed costs, represented by the curve AFC. Average fixed costs decrease as volume increases, so the curve slopes downward as the number of acres landscaped increases.

Average variable costs, represented by the curve AVC, first decrease and then increase as volume rises. This is due to the *law of diminishing returns*, which states that, if fixed inputs are held constant, additional units of a variable input will yield higher returns up to a point. After that point, each additional input will produce less output. In other words, at some point the extra worker will produce less than the worker who was added before him.

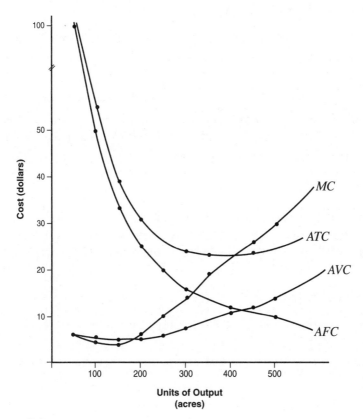

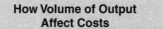

Figure 8.1

ECONOTALK

The **law of diminishing returns** states that, after a certain point, each additional unit of a variable input will yield less output than the previous unit of input. This concept also underlies diminishing marginal utility, which consumers experience.

In our example, adding more laborers will at first enable the business to landscape more acreage. More workers can get more work done *until* they start running into limiting factors. For example, if they don't have enough equipment, their contribution to output will be less than that of workers with equipment. (They will only be able to pick up leaves by hand, for instance.) If the business kept adding workers, they would ultimately undermine the productive process by trampling the grass and bushes. There simply wouldn't be enough land for them to work on.

The diminishing returns to labor are reflected in the variable cost curve AVC. Variable costs first decrease, but then increase as the productivity of each added worker decreases.

Average total costs are the sum of average fixed costs and average variable costs. That is, Column 8 in Table 8.1 is the sum of Columns 6 and 7. Similarly, the distance of the average total cost curve ATC from the horizontal axis equals the distance between curve AFC and the horizontal axis plus the distance between curve AVC and the horizontal axis.

One final point: the marginal cost curve MC intersects the average total cost curve ATC where the cost of the marginal unit equals the cost of the average unit. After that point, marginal cost—the cost of producing each added unit (each additional landscaped acre)—increases, which in turn *raises* the average total cost.

Voodoo Accounting

Managers of small businesses usually combine fixed and variable inputs intuitively and figure their costs using accounting rather than economics. But managers in heavy manufacturing operations analyze their costs more scientifically.

For instance, microchip manufacturers such as Intel and AMD work very hard to drive their costs down. Fixed costs in the business run into the billions for factories and equipment before chips can be produced. A chip manufacturer must produce as many chips as possible to spread these fixed costs over as many units as possible. To control variable costs, each company produces as many chips as it can from each silicon wafer it processes.

Intel claims that its costs are the lowest because it has more advanced factories that can process larger silicon wafers. This enables Intel to produce more chips per wafer. AMD claims that its costs are lowest because its chips are smaller. This enables AMD to produce more chips per wafer, even from the smaller wafer.

External analysts believe that the companies' costs per chip are about equal. Whichever company is the lower-cost producer, each of them uses very sophisticated economic analyses to determine the type of factories to build and the size of the wafers to be processed and chips to be produced.

What's a Business Person to Do?

What does all this mean for the business owner? First, a business owner must understand the cost structure of her business—the costs of the fixed and variable inputs needed to produce various levels of output.

Second, she must find the right mix of fixed and variable inputs. Sometimes the decision to replace people with capital is a no-brainer. For example, one worker with a leaf blower will be more productive than two workers with rakes.

Third, the owner must minimize total costs by using the right mix of inputs to produce the right quantity. The mix of inputs that will minimize costs will be the combination where the *marginal product per dollar* of the variable inputs is equal to the marginal product per dollar of the fixed inputs.

ECONOTALK

Marginal product per dollar is the amount of additional output produced by the last dollar spent on input. This can be calculated for variable inputs, for fixed inputs, or for total inputs.

Here, marginal analysis does for the producer something like what it does for the consumer. You'll recall that the consumer maximizes his total satisfaction when the marginal utility produced by the last dollar he spends on an item equals the marginal utility of the last dollar spent on any other item he buys. Otherwise, he could get more satisfaction by changing the mix of items he buys—and, presumably, he would change to that mix.

The same is true, in its way, for the producer. The marginal product of the last dollar spent on variable inputs should equal the marginal product of the last dollar spent on fixed inputs. Otherwise, he would get more output for the money spent by changing the mix of variable and fixed inputs, just as the consumer could get more satisfaction by changing the mix of items he buys.

Output is the utility that the producer wants to maximize for the money he spends on variable and fixed inputs. This happens at the volume of output where the marginal cost curve MC intersects the total average cost curve ATC. In Figure 8.1, this output level is about 400 acres. Finally, the owner will maximize profits by producing the right level of output at the right price. In a competitive market, a business trying to maximize its total profit should produce the quantity of output where the marginal cost per unit equals the price.

Think about it. If the marginal cost—the total fixed and variable cost—of the last unit produced is greater than its price, then the company loses money on the last unit. If the marginal cost is below the price, the company is not maximizing its profits because it is producing fewer units than it could profitability produce. The company makes additional profit as long as the marginal revenue (from selling one more unit) is higher than the marginal cost (of producing one more unit).

So total profit is maximized when the company produces the level of output where marginal cost per unit equals the price of the unit. But in reality, prices—even prices of the same brand of product in the same size—fluctuate with changes in demand, competitive conditions, and so on. Therefore, a business must use pricing strategies that take the external market—as well as internal costs—into consideration.

Let's take a look at these pricing strategies.

Three Pricing Strategies

There are three basic pricing strategies: cost-plus pricing, competitive pricing, and value pricing.

In *cost-plus pricing*, you look at the cost of what you sell—that is, the total marginal cost—then add on the profit you need to make. That's your price. Cost-plus means cost plus profit. So if it costs the landscaper $25 to landscape an acre, and he has targeted a pre-tax profit of $5 per acre, he should charge $30 per acre. (There are other ways to set the price using cost-plus pricing, but all are based on clearing a certain profit above the costs.)

This method of pricing is straightforward and ensures that you will make money on what you sell. Unfortunately, it does not ensure that you will sell it. The success of this pricing strategy depends on targeting a reasonable profit and controlling your costs. It also depends on not being under-sold by a competitor.

A *competitive pricing* strategy aims to price the product at the lowest price among all recognized competitors. Low prices are one way to compete effectively, and sometimes competitive pricing is essential. For instance, in an industry selling a *commodity*, the outfit with the lowest price will usually succeed. That's because when the products themselves are not differentiated, price becomes the differentiating factor.

Competitive pricing is not just for commodities. In retail, for example, portable CD players are not a commodity, but once a customer has decided she wants to buy one, price will play a big role in which type she buys. So competitive pricing is common in retailing. In fact, some retailers offer to beat any other advertised price.

In general, the success of a competitive pricing strategy depends on achieving high volume and low costs—preferably the lowest in the industry—so you can maintain the lowest price and still make a profit. Success also depends on avoiding a destructive *price war.*

ECONOTALK

A **commodity** is a product that is the same in characteristics and performance regardless of who is selling it. There are, however, grades of quality associated with commodities. Copper, coal, and other metals and minerals; lumber; and most grains and other agricultural products are commodities.

In a **price war,** two or more competitors repeatedly undercut each other's prices. This usually occurs in a commodity business: two gas stations on opposite corners is the classic example. In a price war, each competitor can wind up selling the product at a loss. When that occurs, they are trying to drive one another out of business. The winner will be the one that can afford to lose money the longest and still stay in business.

A *value pricing* strategy is the alternative to basing your prices on your costs or your competitors' prices. Instead, you base your prices on the value you deliver to customers. In this strategy, you deliver as much value as possible to your customers—and charge them for it. With this strategy, you charge a high price and justify it by delivering high value. Value pricing is common in high technology and luxury items, such as clothing, restaurants, and automobiles.

In practice, a business considers all three pricing strategies. You have to consider your costs, or your profits will suffer. You have to consider your competitor's prices, even if you're not competing on price. You must consider the value you deliver because, no matter what you sell, customers want value for their money.

Why the Big Get Bigger

Why are so many industries in the United States dominated by a handful of very large companies? For decades, the Big Three automakers—General Motors, Ford, and Chrysler—dominated the U.S. market. Now they share it with several other foreign car companies that are the large automakers in their nations: Toyota and Honda of Japan, Mercedes Benz and Volkswagen of Germany, Volvo of Sweden, and several others.

Three major companies—General Mills, Kellogg's, and Post—dominate the cereal business. Proctor & Gamble and Colgate Palmolive dominate personal care products, such as soap and toothpaste. Independent booksellers have been supplanted by chains such as Barnes & Noble and Borders. Other chain operations, such as CVS, Kinko's, and McDonald's have superseded the local drugstore, copy shop, and hamburger joint.

These companies all became large partly due to *economies of scale*. In many businesses, there are very real advantages to large size, but not in every business. It all depends on how much the level of output increases when the scale of the business increases. Scale here means the size of the business. As the business becomes larger (or scales up), it can experience constant, decreasing, or increasing economies of scale.

Constant economies of scale mean that a certain percentage increase in scale brings about an equal increase in output. If you double the size of the operation, you double the amount of output. There are no true economies of scale in such a business. Many personal service outfits face this situation. If a hair salon doubles the number of chairs and hair stylists, it will roughly double its output. This doesn't mean that a chain of hair salons couldn't compete more effectively by establishing a first-rate training program and a strong brand. Nor does it mean that a chain of salons couldn't cut costs by buying supplies in volume. It means that the output of 10 stylists is about double that of 5 equally skilled stylists.

Decreasing economies of scale mean that a certain percentage increase in the size of the business brings about a less than equal increase in output. If you double the size of the operation, output will increase by less than 100 percent. This amounts to dis-economies of scale in which too many cooks make less broth. Many companies find that inefficiencies arise with large size and people become less productive (probably because they spend so much time in meetings!).

Increasing economies of scale mean that a certain percentage increase in scale brings about a greater increase in output. If you double the size of the operation, output more than doubles. Business people typically refer to increasing economies of scale simply as economies of scale.

ECONOTALK

Increasing economies of scale means that when the size of an operation increases by a certain percentage, output increases by a greater percentage. **Decreasing economies of scale** means that as the size of an operation increases, output increases by a smaller percentage—or decreases. **Constant economies of scale** means that increases in the size of an operation yield the same percentage increase in output.

Increasing economies of scale are why the large companies get larger. They are also why a few large companies dominate many industries. And they are why Karl Marx predicted that most industries would become dominated by a few large companies, or one large company.

The returns to scale can be enormous. Here are several factors that both contribute to, and result from, increasing economies of scale:

- **Capital intensiveness:** In a highly capital-intensive business, large size is essential for survival, let alone success. The extractive industries (oil, gas, coal, and metals) are so capital-intensive that a small outfit is not economically feasible. The fixed costs of drilling rigs, refineries, and pipelines demand a high volume of production. High volume drives down the average fixed costs, which increases cost-effectiveness.

- **Volume buying:** Average variable costs also decrease for many large operations thanks to volume buying. A high-volume producer usually passes some of the cost savings on to high-volume buyers in the form of lower prices. A high-volume buyer of raw materials can, in turn, lower its prices and compete more effectively against lower-volume producers. In this way, high-volume operations often push low-volume ones out of business—and then sometimes raise their prices when the competition is gone.

- **Administrative efficiencies:** Administrative costs include the finance and personnel departments, the cost of employee benefit plans, and so on. There are both fixed and variable costs involved. For instance, every company needs a computerized billing system and someone to run it. That's a fixed cost. The variable costs occur when the number of customers grows and accountants must be hired. These costs, however, typically do not grow as fast as the output. Therefore, large size brings increasing economies of scale in administration.

- **Distribution:** Some transportation costs, such as the cost of a truck, are fixed. Others, such as the cost of gasoline, are variable. But in general, the more product that can be delivered for the fixed costs, the more efficient the operation will be. For example, a company that delivers office supplies to small businesses will typically prospect aggressively for new customers along its established delivery routes, because new customers on the route will drive down delivery costs.

- **Market and marketing power:** A large operation can allocate its marketing costs over a larger number of customers. Plus, large advertisers get volume discounts from the media. Perhaps even more important, global brands benefit from brand power because of their size. It is easier for most people to trust (and notice) a globally known brand.

Economies of scale have driven much of business history over the past century. Many U.S. industries—oil, automobiles, food processing, financial services, consumer packaged goods, advertising, and software—started out with many competitors and are now dominated by a few large companies.

Large companies and the economics of mass production have provided a tremendous range of goods and services to consumers at reasonable prices. But the concentration of power and profits among the largest players in an industry can be quite significant.

THE REAL WORLD

The merciless economics of economies of scale are most evident in farming. In 1935, there were over 6.5 million family farms in the United States; today there are fewer than 2 million. The major reason for this is consolidation in the farming industry, driven mainly by economies of scale. By some measures, which omit social costs, large farms are more efficient than small ones. Large agribusiness companies, such as ConAgra, Cargill, Tyson, and Dole, drive down the costs of food production, and thus prices, and force smaller farms out of business.

Political storms surround farming. First, all developed nations have government programs to temper the financial difficulties of farming that arise from weather, crop damage, and market forces. These programs cost taxpayers money, which some taxpayers resent. Second, many—but not all—Americans, Europeans, and Asians believe that family farms should be preserved as a way of life and as strong threads in the social fabric.

Finally, the definition of efficiency can change once items beyond the cost of inputs are considered. The costs and impact of pesticides, hormones, ecological damage, lower food quality, food-borne illnesses, and inhumane treatment of animals are often thought to be higher in large-scale farming. Thus, while large scale may yield efficiencies in farming, it may also yield serious inefficiencies.

Let's examine ways in which concentrated power can be, and has been, used and abused in business.

Monopoly and Oligopoly

As you learned in Chapter 4, in a free market, the dynamics of supply and demand are resolved through the price mechanism. Yet this occurs only when numerous suppliers must compete for customers, and customers bid up or bid down the price.

If there is one supplier, the result is a monopoly. If there are several suppliers, the result is oligopoly. First, we'll examine monopoly and oligopoly, and then we'll look at how a cartel works.

Monopoly: The Power of One

A monopoly occurs when a single producer controls the supply of a good or service that has no real substitute and where the *barriers to entry* are high.

ECONOTALK

Barriers to entry are conditions that make it hard for new suppliers to enter a business. Any business presents some barriers to entry, but in many industries they are quite low—for example, web-based businesses. Essentially, all you need is a computer, Internet service, and a great idea. The Internet has in fact lowered the barriers to entry in businesses such as publishing, retailing, and travel services. However, even on the Internet, barriers can include historical position, brand recognition, patent protection, and the like.

Many people think of a monopoly as a company that set out to dominate its industry illegally. In fact, many monopolies develop for more benign reasons. A natural monopoly occurs because a single supplier owns the entire supply (or most of it), or a single provider can supply the market at a lower cost than several competitors could.

Single suppliers often own the supply for historical reasons. De Beers diamond company has dominated the diamond market since 1889 by controlling most of the world's diamond mines and the supply of rough diamonds. For many decades, Dun & Bradstreet had about 90 percent of the commercial credit-reporting business to itself because they started the industry in the mid-1800s and kept building it.

The economies of scale in some industries result in a lower cost to the consumer if a single, and often regulated, supplier serves the market. Until the late 1980s, power generation was thought to be such an industry. Competition among electric utilities was deemed inherently inefficient compared with having a single utility serve a designated area, subject to regulation of its prices. Power generation was deregulated and opened to competitive market forces in certain areas in the 1990s, with decidedly mixed results. California consumers were overcharged billions of dollars by producers who created artificial shortages to drive up electricity prices.

Another type of natural monopoly centers on a single standard of technology for an industry. A single standard ensures compatibility and helps users get the most from the technology. Microsoft is the best example of this. Microsoft developed DOS (Disk Operating System), which enabled personal computers to run applications software. DOS served as a single platform that enabled software developers to write software for a large market. The common platform provided by DOS created a large installed base that would allow a successful software developer to spread its costs over a huge number of users. This introduced real efficiency into the personal computer market. The Windows operating system had the same effect.

Many people believe that the worst aspect of a monopoly is the excess profit it receives by charging a price above the free-market price. That's bad. But worse yet, consumers may also receive a lower quantity of the product than they would in a competitive market. A monopoly usually limits the supply and moves the supply curve to the left. This raises the forced equilibrium price upward on the demand curve, so consumers pay an above-market price for below-market quantity.

THE REAL WORLD

In the late 1800s, John D. Rockefeller founded Standard Oil (now ExxonMobil) to standardize the oil business, which had been composed of small drilling and refining operations battered by wild price fluctuations. With sometimes ruthless but legal tactics, Rockefeller bought up refineries and consolidated them into larger operations.

As Standard Oil became larger, increasing economies of scale kicked in, making it impossible for smaller outfits to compete. In the process, Rockefeller created the template for the modern corporation and executive team. Although he was vilified as a "robber baron," Rockefeller also established a model of corporate and personal philanthropy that endures to this day.

In the 1980s and 1990s, the United States broke up several monopolies and introduced market forces into some formerly regulated industries, such as telephone service, power generation, and air travel. Results have been mixed. In the telephone business, greater innovation and lower prices for services have resulted. Lower prices have also resulted in air travel, but extremely high costs may render the industry ill-equipped to function in a truly competitive environment. The jury is still out on power generation, but the signs from California have not been promising.

Oligopoly: The Chosen Few

Oligopoly occurs when a few producers share a market, but no single one among them controls the supply or the price of the product. Oligopoly tends to occur in industries with high barriers to entry, high fixed costs, and the need for large size (relative to total demand) to reach the optimal size for efficient production.

Oligopoly occurs in situations where marginal costs persistently decrease as larger quantities are produced. The key feature of an oligopoly is tacit agreement (as opposed to actual *price-fixing*) to not undercut one another's prices. The oligopolists maximize their long-run profits by maintaining a level of prices designed to do exactly that.

ECONOTALK

Price-fixing refers to agreements between producers to maintain a certain level of prices for certain goods or services. This enables the producers to maintain their profits above the level they would earn if they did compete on price. This and other forms of collusion are generally illegal.

Oligopolists try to avoid competing on price. In oligopoly-like industries such as breakfast cereal and consumer packaged goods—prices are pretty much in line with one another. However, the players pour huge sums into advertising to differentiate products that are actually quite similar, such as raisin bran and shampoo. Competing on price would be potentially destructive and almost certainly result in lower total profits for all the major companies.

Cartels Mean Control

Members of a cartel agree to limit the supply of a good in order to raise its price and their profit. Cartels arise in industries with few producers, because too many producers would present too much temptation to compete by raising production or cutting price. Competition is exactly what the members of a cartel don't want—especially among themselves.

The Organization of Petroleum Exporting Countries (OPEC), which, depending on the year, pumps about 30 to 40 percent of the world's crude oil, is the best current example of a major cartel. Representatives from the 14 member nations meet periodically and agree to a target price per barrel of crude oil and agree to limit the amount of oil they produce to a level that will achieve that target price.

The share of the total output that each nation gets to produce is decided through quotas, which have a mixed history of success. In any cartel, there is an incentive for a member to produce more than its quota in order to sell more and profit at the expense of the members who stick to their quotas. One thing that has made OPEC successful is the willingness of Saudi Arabia to cut its production when another nation does exceed its quota and to absorb the revenue loss. With the world's largest proven oil reserves, Saudi Arabia may well be able to afford this gesture.

OPEC must play its game carefully. If it targets too low a price, it may not maximize its profits (while encouraging usage of the finite resource it depends on). On the other hand, if OPEC targets too high a price, it encourages oil production among non-OPEC nations. A higher price increases the amount supplied by other producers, gives OPEC more competition, and puts downward pressure on prices.

OPEC clearly benefits its member nations and does bring some price stability to the oil market. On its website (www.opec.org), the cartel admits to acquiring a major say in the pricing of crude oil on world markets in the 1970s, but states that, since then, larger forces have more effect on price. In fact, for a public relations piece, the "Brief History" section on the OPEC website provides an interesting, generally accurate accounting of the organization's role in oil markets over its more than 50 years in existence.

Meanwhile, Out in the Marketplace

Regardless of how a business structures its costs, it must make a trade-off between fixed and variable inputs. Also, every business must decide how large or small it wants to be. Of course, market realities and management skills have as much to do with the growth of a business as its underlying economics. However, managers and investors ignore the microeconomic fundamentals of their business at their peril.

The Least You Need to Know

- The costs of every business can be broken down into variable costs and fixed costs. Variable costs are expenses that change with the volume of production. Fixed costs do not change with the level of production.
- Total costs are minimized at the point where the marginal product of an additional dollar spent on variable inputs equals the marginal product of an additional dollar spent on fixed inputs.

- Total profits are maximized at the level of output where, for the last unit produced, marginal cost equals marginal revenue.

- Increasing economies of scale occur when a percentage increase in the size of an operation brings about a higher percentage increase in production.

- A monopoly is a single supplier that can control the price of a product. A monopoly raises the price and lowers the supply of a good beyond the market levels.

- An oligopoly is a group of a few suppliers who price their products in a way that limits price competition among them and maximizes their long-term profit.

Wages, Workers, and the Workplace

In This Chapter

- Labor and management relations
- The effect of unions on supply, demand, and wages
- Wages for skilled versus unskilled workers
- The economic effect of discrimination

Steve Martin once said, "All I've ever wanted was an honest week's pay for an honest day's work." It is an aspiration that has taken him pretty far. Those of us less fortunate, meaning most of us in the workforce, face the harsher economics of the labor market. This market is unique among all markets because the commodity being bought and sold is a human being's time, talent, and energy. That may indeed be the case when any product is sold. After all, everything we buy in stores and showrooms is the product of human labor. However, in the labor market, the exchange is extremely direct and personal.

Employees rent *themselves*, not their land or machinery, out to the employer. Employees are then largely under the control of the employer. While it's true that workers are usually free to leave their jobs, the loss of any single employee does not threaten the income of most employers. But if the employer abandons the employees, for example, by laying them off or moving the business out of the region, the employees lose their livelihoods. Without the protection of union contracts or other legal agreements, most employers in the United States are free to lay off employees or move the business at will.

Although the exchange is direct and personal, impersonal economic forces prevail in the workplace. In this chapter, we examine some of those forces and the behavior of people in the workplace. We'll start with an overview of the economic relationship between employers and employees.

Fighting Over the Pie?

Many business people—particularly entrepreneurs, capitalists, and business owners—picture wages coming out of the pockets of landlords, capitalists, and entrepreneurs. It's especially easy for entrepreneurs, managers, or business owners to conjure this image. They often feel that every dollar paid in wages is a dollar less going to profits. Similarly, workers often feel that the profits of the business are coming out of their wages. In every picket line, you will see a striking worker or protester holding a sign that says, "People before profits."

The traditional battle—wages versus profits, employees versus employers—still goes on. But the terms of engagement, and even the scene of the battle, have shifted a bit. The old terms of engagement called for collective bargaining, in which union officials confronted tightfisted employers with demands for higher wages and better working conditions. The battlefield was the sidewalk, the shop floor, the union hall, and the smoke-filled rooms where union chiefs and factory bosses argued far into the night.

All of that still exists (although the rooms may be less smoky). Yet for most workers, the terms of engagement have shifted because they are no longer represented by unions. Many traditionally unionized jobs have been moved to foreign production facilities by companies eager to avoid the relatively high costs of U.S. workers. As manufacturing jobs have been moved out of the country, they have been replaced by nonunion service jobs. Most service industries, such as retail, restaurants, and personal services (for example, beauticians and masseurs) have been slow to unionize.

Moreover, expanded access to education over the past 50 years has created a huge class of knowledge workers, such as financial analysts, computer programmers, and engineers, and swelled the ranks of the professions, which traditionally have included law, medicine, accounting, and architecture. Knowledge workers and professionals—and, of course, managers—are rarely, if ever, unionized in the United States.

Much of the battle has shifted from the plant floor and the union hall to the Senate floor and the halls of Congress. Today, regulations, mandated employee benefits and work rules (for instance, the Employees with Disabilities Act), and international trade policies can affect both employers and employees as much as any union contract.

THE REAL WORLD

In reality, the conflict between management and workers goes beyond the issue of profits versus wages. It also centers on salaries (of management) verses wages (of hourly employees). Given the finite sum available to pay managers and workers, managers may feel that they are taking money out of their own pockets when they give workers a raise. They often act that way.

The clearest case of managers pocketing salaries at the expense of workers (and profits) has been the skyrocketing compensation of CEOs at major corporations. According to *The State of Working America 2008–2009,* published by the Economic Policy Institute, from 1980 to 1990 the ratio of CEO total compensation to the average worker's pay rose from about 35 to 71. By 1993, the ratio had climbed to 126, and by 2000 it had reached 299. The ratio fell to 150 during the recession, but by the end of 2009 it was around 300 again. In virtually all other industrial nations, the ratio of CEO to average worker pay is far lower.

Many books on economics, particularly textbooks, delve deeply into the history and effect of unions. We will examine their effect, but unions are on their way to becoming history, at least in the United States. According to the Bureau of Labor Statistics (BLS), from 1984 to 2009, union membership declined from 20.1 percent to 12.3 percent of the workforce. In 2009 about 15.3 million workers were union members. In 1983, the first year for which there are comparable data, there were 17.7 million union workers. Before the 1980s, union membership was even higher, although union membership peaked at about 36 percent in the early 1950s.

For many workers, the demise of unions has probably not been a good thing.

The State of the Unions

Unions exist to address the imbalance of power between employer and employee. In a union, workers band together to bargain collectively with management regarding their pay, hours, and working conditions. Under collective bargaining, the union leaders negotiate a contract that governs these and other aspects of work at the company or in the industry. A union shop is a plant or other location, such as a construction site, where the workers are covered by the union contract. In many instances, workers are obligated to join the union in order to work at the location.

During contract negotiations or protests of management decisions, a union may hold a strike or slowdown. A strike usually shuts down an operation, costing the business large amounts of money, hurting its customers and the public, and putting pressure on management to meet the union's demands. Striking workers form a picket line to protest management's reluctance to meet their demands. Anyone attempting to cross a picket line to work in the place of a striking worker is subject to at least some intimidation (sometimes even physical violence). When they can, managers will often take the place of striking workers to keep the business functioning on some level. Nonunion workers who work in the place of striking workers are known as scabs.

For their part, managers work fairly hard to avoid unionization of their businesses in the first place. The history of the labor movement in America offers as many tales of violent union-busting and strike-breaking as there are of union intimidation and violence. In some cases, where the economic well-being of the nation, region, or industry is at stake, the president of the United States will order the workers back to work.

THE REAL WORLD

When the air traffic controllers' union went on strike in 1981, President Ronald Reagan declared the strike illegal (which it was, according to established regulations) and ordered them back to work. When they refused to return to work, he authorized the Federal Aviation Administration to hire and train new workers, which it did.

In 2002, President George W. Bush ordered the dock workers on the West Coast back to work after deciding that their strike against the shipping industry was causing too much damage to the economy and the shipping and farming industries. In this case, the workers complied.

In 2009, President Barack Obama partly accommodated the United Auto Workers to save jobs and General Motors and Chrysler. Critics said this was politically motivated, and it may have been. However, it also saved thousands of jobs, a sound goal given the worst recession and unemployment since the early 1980s.

Government workers and protective service workers, such as police officers and fire fighters, make up the greatest portion of union membership. Less than one in ten private-sector workers belong to a union. Unionization rates for government workers have held steady at about 37 percent since 1983, while those of private-sector employees have fallen to 9 percent. The highest unionization rate occurs in the protective services at 38 percent. (Note, however, that this means that, even in this line of work, over 60 percent of the employees are *not* in unions.)

According to the Bureau of Labor Statistics, the private-sector industries with the highest rates of union workers include transportation and utilities (22.2 percent), telecommunications (16 percent), and construction (14.5 percent). The industries with the lowest unionization rates are agriculture (1.1 percent) and financial activities (1.8 percent).

Despite the decline of their influence in the private sector, unions remain a powerful force in America. They make the news in stories ranging from baseball and basketball players' strikes to controversies over how to improve public schools in which unions make it hard to fire teachers. The major point of contention in the legislative battle over the Department of Homeland Security (DHS) in 2002 was whether the government workers being moved into the department would still be covered by union rules. Democrats favored continued coverage, while Republicans did not. The legislation creating the DHS was passed without protection of the employees' union rights. Since then, however, some government workers' unions have been pressing to establish union rights for DHS workers.

 THE REAL WORLD

Traditionally, the Democratic Party has been viewed as the labor party in America while Republicans are viewed as the party of big business. In reality, elected officials at all levels cheerfully accept campaign contributions from all sources. Major labor unions, corporations, and industrial groups contribute to both parties. Yet in general, unions still tend to favor the Democrats and vice versa, and big business still tends to favor the Republicans and vice versa.

Speaking of politics, union membership and political influence tends to be much stronger in Europe than in the United States.

What Good Are Unions?

Labor unions, like most aspects of labor, are mostly about money. They generally perform the function of getting more money for their members fairly effectively. Table 9.1 (on the next page) shows the median full-time wages, and the wage differentials, between union and nonunion workers for the U.S. workforce and by gender and race. (More recent data has not yet been reported in comparable form as I write this, but these figures have generally remained stable. One exception has been that union membership has grown faster among black workers than among white workers in recent years.)

Table 9.1 Union versus Nonunion Wages Median Full-Time Weekly Wage for 2000 (current dollars and percentage differential)

	Union Members	Nonunion Members	Differential*
All workers 16 years and older	$696	$542	28.4%
Men	739	620	19.1
Women	616	472	30.5
White workers	716	565	26.7
White men	757	641	18.1
White women	631	482	30.9
Black workers	596	436	36.7
Black men	619	479	29.2
Black women	564	408	38.2
Hispanic workers	584	377	54.9
Hispanic men	631	394	60.2
Hispanic women	489	346	41.3

* Calculated by subtracting nonunion wage from union wage and dividing the difference by the nonunion wage.

Source: Bureau of Labor Statistics

The difference between union and nonunion wages is significant in all cases. White men who are members of unions earn about 19 percent more than their nonunion counterparts. Hispanic men who are union members earn about 60 percent more than Hispanic men who are not union members. The differential between the median union and nonunion wage is greater for women than for men in all categories of workers excluding Hispanic women.

ECONOTIP

When is a difference significant in economics? The rule of thumb that I use is 10 percent or more. If an indicator moves at a rate that's at least 10 percent more than the previous period's rate or if the difference between two values is at least 10 percent, it *could* be significant. In many cases, however, a smaller difference could also be significant.

Please view these wage statistics with caution. While the differences between union and nonunion wages are significant for all groups, union membership is only one factor in that difference. First, to some extent, unions choose their members. Perhaps they choose better-educated workers, leaving those less educated in the nonunion workforce. Second, unions typically try to unionize established, profitable industries that are able to pay a decent wage. Third, the Hispanic population in particular includes many recent immigrants, who may have a harder time getting into a union. Fourth, the same gender and racial differences in pay occur for both union and nonunion workers. White men are paid more than white women in both union and nonunion settings. White workers are paid more than black and Hispanic workers in both settings. However, the differential between the median wage for men and women is smaller in the union wage than in the nonunion wage for all categories of worker except Hispanic.

Finally, the jobs of unionized government workers, police officers, firefighters, and teachers tend to be very secure. As workers gain seniority in these jobs, their wages steadily increase. In the private sector, workers deemed too expensive can be laid off, and they often find it difficult to find new jobs at their previous pay.

Yet, these qualifiers notwithstanding, workers in unions are, on average, doing significantly better than their nonunion counterparts.

How Unions Skew Labor Economics

We saw the effect of a minimum wage on the supply and demand of labor in Chapter 4. Now let's turn to the effect of unions on the labor market, which is like that of a minimum wage. A union aims to enforce a minimum wage either by demanding one or by restricting the supply of workers by limiting the number of workers in the union.

Figure 9.1 shows the general effect of unions on the supply of labor. Note that this effect does not apply to the overall labor market, but to the specific supply of and demand for the type of workers covered by the union.

The goal of the union is to raise the wage from W^1 to W^2 by making wage demands in the union contract or to reduce the supply of workers from S^1 to S^2 by limiting union membership. In practice, a union often does both. In any case, the effect is essentially the same. If the wage is increased to W^2, the supply curve shifts from S^1 to S^2. If the supply curve shifts to S^2, then the wage increases to W^2.

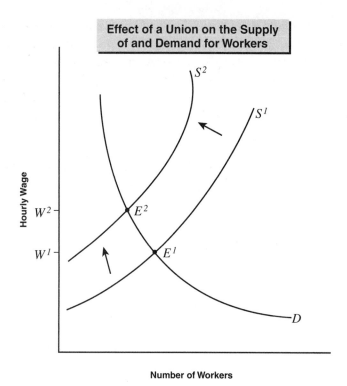

Figure 9.1

In both cases, the supply of workers is artificially limited. (By artificially, I mean by means other than free-market dynamics.) If the union demands a high—that is, above-market—wage, then the business hires fewer workers, just as it would if the minimum wage were well above the market wage. If the union limits the number of workers, then the labor supply falls and management must pay the higher wage that prevails at that lower level of supply.

Unions also try to shift the demand curve upward. Union work rules are a common way of doing this. For example, a railroad union contract might stipulate that there must be a conductor for every two cars on a passenger train when one for every three or four cars would be enough. A bricklayers' contract might state that a mason may lay only so many bricks per seven-hour shift, leaving the contractor no choice but to hire more masons or pay overtime to get more done.

Although a union affects the supply and demand only for its members, the effects extend to the general labor market and to the overall economy. These effects are both positive and negative.

Among the negatives, unions raise the cost of doing business and of products because they move the cost of labor above its market equilibrium level. This *can* make U.S. products less competitive in the global market. (I stress *can* because if skilled union workers produce higher-quality products, the higher prices may indeed be fair and competitive.) Also, businesses try to avoid or escape unions by moving to *right-to-work* states or moving jobs out of the country. This takes jobs away from an area that was used to having them. To avoid unions, companies have moved jobs in the textile industry from the North to the South, jobs in the garment industry from the United States to Asia, and jobs in the auto industry from the United States to Mexico. Unions protest these management decisions but are also at least partly responsible for them.

ECONOTALK

In a **right-to-work** state, a worker cannot be required to join a union or pay union dues or fees in order to get or keep a job. However, there are some exceptions. For example, in certain states, airline or railroad employees may have to pay union fees but are not required to join a union. Twenty-two states have right-to-work laws.

Among the unions' positives, they have helped neutralize the power of employers over individual employees. In doing so, they have probably required managers to manage more professionally and to maximize the productivity of capital equipment. Unions have also raised the standard of living of millions of workers and have boosted their purchasing power and thus the nation's economic growth.

By and large, unions are both a negative and positive force, just like the management teams that they often oppose. Unions are a blunt instrument for accomplishing economic goals, but one that has often worked.

Peace over the Pie?

Whatever your personal and political views on unions, management, and the positions of each side—both of which have validity—another fact has altered the dynamics between labor and management. Unions in America enjoyed their most rapid growth between 1930 and 1960. During those years, Marx's view of the worker as an exploited pawn of capitalism became familiar to much of the public even in fervently nonsocialist nations, such as the United States, as well as in those more open to socialism, such as Russia.

But since the middle of the last century, capitalism has proven itself to be quite effective at bringing prosperity to workers as well as to landlords, capitalists, and entrepreneurs. By some measures, it has brought more prosperity to workers than to the other players in production. Since 1950, the entire pie—measured by wages and salaries, rent, interest, profits—has grown larger, and workers (including salaried managers) have shared in that growth. Table 9.2 shows this to be the case.

Table 9.2   Shares of Employee Compensation, Rent, Interest, and Profits as Percentages of Total

	1950	1960	1970	1980	1990	2000	2009
Wages & Salaries	64	69	73	74	72	72	70
Rent	20	16	12	9	9	9	12
Interest	1	3	5	8	10	10	9
Profits	15	12	10	9	9	9	9
Total	100	100	100	100	100	100	100

Source: Bureau of Economic Analysis, National Income and Product Accounts

Since 1970, the share of national income going to wages and salaries has been 70 to 74 percent, and the share going to profits has been about 9 percent. Money is not being steered away from wages and toward profits. Instead, both workers and entrepreneurs—and, since 1980, landlords and capitalists—are maintaining fairly steady shares in the growth of the U.S. economy. (Rent here includes proprietors' income—income of business owners—as well as rental income of persons.)

THE REAL WORLD

When corporate profits skyrocket, be aware that profits can sometimes be manipulated through accounting gimmicks. For instance, in the 1990s, before certain accounting scandals came to light in the early 2000s, some economists examining the National Income and Product Account (NIPA) data—where the profits reported have to be real—were puzzled by the companies' continual claims of record profits (and by lofty stock prices).

The NIPA income data have to be real because they are based on tax-accounting rules, which deal in actual receipts and expenses. In contrast, the income figures reported on financial statements released to the investing public are based on financial accounting rules, which are more, ah, liberal in their treatment of revenue and expenses.

In other words, Karl Marx's vision of workers exploited by employers hogging profits has not come to pass. As we will see in Chapter 10, the *distribution* of income among wage earners has become uneven. That has to do with higher wages for skilled workers and lower wages for unskilled, as well as with the shift to a service economy in the United States. But the shares of national income going to wages and to profits clearly indicate that workers and shareholders *overall* are sharing equitably in the growth of the economy.

But, if workers' slice of the national income pie has remained the same, why did I say that the demise of unions may be a bad thing for many workers? Because a much larger slice of the wage and salary pie is going to people in upper-income brackets. If you are an educated, skilled, flexible knowledge worker, manager, or professional, you don't (necessarily) need a union to represent you. As it happens, there are more such people in the workforce than ever. Yet less-educated wage earners are having a tougher time making a good living. Lack of union jobs is one—but only one—of the reasons.

Yet unions are having a hard time maintaining, let alone increasing, their membership. They have failed to unionize even poorly paid white-collar workers, such as clerks and other office workers, and many workers in the retail and restaurant industries. So unions are not going to save most American workers from the realities of the domestic and international labor markets. Two things that can help American workers would be increasing their skills and ending racial and gender discrimination on the job.

Got Skills?

Skilled workers earn more than unskilled workers for several reasons. First, if the law of supply and demand is operating (and it usually is), the supply of workers with a specific skill is far smaller than the supply of people without that skill. If the demand is high relative to the supply, people with that skill can command a wage well above the wage of unskilled workers.

Second, it takes time to acquire a skill. Time is money, so people who learn a skill forgo some or all of their earnings during the education or training period. Few people will forgo earnings unless they can make more money later by doing so. Therefore, people must be compensated for their training. This is one reason that doctors are paid more than nurses, and why nurses are paid more than orderlies.

Third, relative to unskilled workers, skilled workers add more value to the goods and services they produce. That means that they also generate more revenue. This is also true of people with a higher level of skills than other people with the same skill set. For instance, a senior partner in a law firm who litigates cases adds more value for her firm's clients than an associate two years out of law school. She therefore bills out at a much higher rate—and is paid a lot more—than the associate.

As we saw in Chapter 8, economists analyze the factors of production at the margin— they examine the effect of adding one more unit of the factor being analyzed, including labor. Recall that the marginal product of a factor is the extra output added by one extra unit of that factor, holding all other factors constant. Remember also that the worker will be paid an amount equal to his or her marginal revenue product. That fact clearly works to the advantage of skilled workers.

In general—and this will be quite apparent when we look at the U.S. distribution of income in Chapter 10—education, training, and skills are the key determinants of higher wages.

Discrimination Doesn't Pay

To an economist, the issue of job discrimination is one of optimizing the value of *human capital* and, on a more political note, economic justice. From the truly dismal economics of slavery to recent efforts to exclude immigrants, the United States has a long history of discrimination in the workplace.

ECONOTALK

Broadly, **human capital** is the total of all that people bring to an economy. It is also the base of knowledge and skills that the population, or a subset of a population, has acquired through training, education, experience, and similar endeavors (including reading!). People invest in human capital through education, research, job training, scholarships, coaching, and mentoring.

What, exactly, is the economic effect of job discrimination? Let's take racial discrimination against African Americans as a case in point, although the effects also apply to gender and to other racial and ethnic discrimination.

You can probably guess that the overall effect of discrimination would be to artificially increase the wages of white workers and decrease those of black workers. White wages increase because whites are given greater access to higher-paying jobs while blacks are relegated to lower-paying jobs. This reduces the supply of labor for higher-paying jobs and, as a result, the white wage rises.

However, society pays a price in lost productivity from African American workers. If a black person who qualifies for a position as a loan officer is kept in the position of bank teller, or a black customer service representative is refused a promotion to salesperson, their productivity—their contribution to GDP in that higher, better-paying position—is forgone.

Therefore, when discrimination ends, the wages that white workers lose is small relative to the gain that black workers—and the economy—achieve. White workers do lose a portion of their wages, because the total supply of workers, black and white, for higher-paying jobs increases. When the supply of labor increases, the wage decreases. Yet most of the gains that black workers achieve come from their increased productivity in their new jobs. Those new jobs enable them to contribute higher marginal revenue product. In addition, the (often white) business owners obtain that increased productivity at a slightly lower total wage.

Although white workers do lose a bit, the overall gain to those discriminated against, and to society as a whole, warrants the end to discrimination on economic grounds. Of course, there are no moral grounds for discrimination, either.

What Works?

On an economic level, human labor is just one more factor of production. However, unlike land, materials, and machinery, people think and talk back. They form unions, engage in collective bargaining, move jobs to other nations, differentiate themselves by their skills, practice discrimination, and generally behave in ways that skew the forces of the free market.

Labor economics is among the most fascinating areas of economics. In no other part of the economy have buyers and sellers come to such deep, lasting, and violent conflict. There are few areas where the stakes are as high. The best path forward for workers and employers lies in understanding the role of human capital and how to enhance it and put it to the best use for the greatest number of people. When all factors of production—including human labor—reach their highest degree of functionality, an economy will realize the greatest good for the greatest number of people.

The Least You Need to Know

- In a union, workers band together to engage in collective bargaining with management regarding their pay, hours, and working conditions. Union membership and influence has waned in the United States, yet about 15 million workers still belong to a union.

- Union membership is heaviest among government workers, police officers, firefighters, and teachers. About 37 percent of government workers are union members compared with about 9 percent of private-sector workers.

- Since 1970, the share of national income going to wages and salaries has been about 72 percent, and the share going to profits has been 9 percent. Money is *not* being steered away from wages and toward profits.

- Skilled workers are paid more because of supply and demand, the need to compensate them for the time and money spent in school and training, and their higher marginal revenue product compared with less-skilled workers.

- Discrimination relegates the minority to lower-paying jobs, leaving more highly paid jobs to the majority. However, society loses a portion of the productivity of the minority. When discrimination ends, the majority loses some pay, but less than the wage gain to the minority and the productivity gain to the business owner.

To Have and Have Not

In This Chapter

- How economists define wealth and poverty
- Income patterns in the United States
- Public policy and income redistribution

People tend to be quite judgmental when it comes to wealth and poverty. On the one hand, the so-called Protestant work ethic—the idea that wealth comes to those who work—leads many people to blame the poor for their poverty. On the other hand, compassion for the poor (and perhaps envy of the wealthy) leads others to blame the wealthy for poverty, judging them too selfish and unfeeling to assist the poor.

Here is where the science of economics comes in handy. As a social scientist, an economist examines wealth and poverty from a more objective viewpoint than the noneconomist. In this chapter, we examine poverty and wealth from the economist's viewpoint. The goal is, first, to develop a clear picture of the extent of wealth and poverty and, second, to examine trends in the distribution of income in America. Finally, we will examine the government's current role in addressing poverty.

What Is Poverty?

Economists measure wealth and poverty in several ways. The three most common measures are income, assets (meaning accumulated wealth in the form of money, securities, and real estate), and socioeconomic metrics. Measures in the last category go beyond financial data to account for health, nutrition, infant mortality, sanitation, and other aspects of human well-being.

In this chapter, I will usually examine wealth and poverty in terms of income. Data on income is readily available, reliable, and relevant, especially in discussing poverty in the United States, where inherited wealth is a minor factor and most people live on wages and salaries.

It's useful to think of wealth and poverty in relation to one another. That's because *income inequality* is really the underlying issue in poverty, especially in developed nations.

ECONOTALK

Income inequality refers to the differences in income between and among various groups of individuals and households in an economy.

Human social systems being what they are, it is often the differences in wealth that make people feel rich or poor. In a third-world nation, a family with indoor plumbing, running water, decent food and clothing, and access to health care and education is quite well off. In the United States, however, millions of people who have those things are considered poor because they have little else, and those things constitute the bare essentials in America. In this most developed of economies, dwellings without plumbing are not legally fit for habitation; public assistance programs, such as the Supplemental Nutrition Assistance Program (food stamps), Medicare, and Medicaid, assure at least adequate levels of nutrition and health care; and public education is compulsory for children.

Perhaps Webster's Dictionary provides the most accurate definition of poverty, at least in America: the state of one who lacks a *usual or socially acceptable amount* of money or material possessions (italics mine). This is not to minimize the plight of the poor in America. It's easily arguable that poverty of any kind is unacceptable in a society with the riches and opportunities of the United States. Also, many poor Americans do live without adequate nutrition, shelter, and health care. This is especially true of the rural poor (for instance, in Appalachia) and for the physically, emotionally, and mentally disabled poor. I am only pointing out that poverty can be a relative condition.

For instance, the World Bank identifies areas of the world where significant portions of the population live on less than $1 a day. These are the poorest people in the world's poorest regions, where food, shelter, health care, and other necessities are in dangerously short supply. Table 10.1 reveals the sad statistics.

Table 10.1   People Living on Less Than $1 a Day in 2000

Region	Total Population (millions)	People Living on Less Than $1 a Day (millions)	Percent of Region's Population
Latin America and Caribbean	432	49	12
West Asia and North Africa	204	5	3
Sub-Saharan Africa	388	169	44
South Asia	1,266	515	41
East and Southeast Asia	1,726	320	19

Source: World Bank

Poverty is most widespread in Sub-Saharan Africa and South Asia, where over 40 percent of the population lives on less than $365 a year. All told, over 1 billion people in the world are in this situation, which is considered absolute, rather than relative, poverty. This represents an improvement. The World Bank reports that in 1981, 1.5 billion people were living on $1 a day or less, but that the figure dropped to 1.2 billion in 1990 and to 1.1 billion in 2000, the most recent official figure. The World Bank has targeted and forecasted a drop to 0.6 billion people in this extreme poverty in 2015.

We will look at the economic issues of the developing world in Part 5. But one of the worst of its problems is the human suffering caused by persistent poverty.

Who's Got How Much?

To measure income inequality—a measure of wealth and poverty that can be applied to any geographical area—economists use quintile rankings. These rankings divide households into five groups according to income. Each group accounts for one-fifth of the number of households. Table 10.2 shows the income breakpoints for each quintile of U.S. households for 2007, 2000, 1990, 1980, and 1970, according to the U.S. Census Bureau.

Table 10.2   U.S. Household Income Limits by Quintile (upper limit of each quintile—with the exception of the fifth quintile—in current dollars, rounded to nearest 100)

Lower Limit of Year	Lowest	Second	Third	Fourth	Top 5%
2007	20,300	39,100	62,000	100,000	177,000
2000	18,000	33,000	52,300	82,000	145,500
1990	12,500	23,700	36,200	55,200	94,700
1980	7,600	14,100	21,600	31,700	51,500
1970	3,700	7,100	10,300	14,700	23,200

Source: U.S. Census Bureau

Just to clarify, this table is saying that in the year 2007:

- 20 percent of U.S. households had incomes of $20,300 and under
- 20 percent had incomes between $20,301 and $39,100
- 20 percent had incomes between $39,101 and $62,000
- 20 percent had incomes between $62,001 and $100,000
- 20 percent had incomes above $100,000

It is also saying that in 2007, 5 percent of households had incomes of $177,000 and higher. (This 5 percent is also counted in the top 20 percent.)

To analyze the data in this table accurately, however, we should use real, rather than nominal, dollars to correct for the effects of inflation. Table 10.3 shows the same data in real dollars (adjusted for inflation by the Census Bureau using the Consumer Price Index).

Table 10.3   U.S. Household Income Limits by Quintile (upper limit of each quintile, in real dollars, rounded to the nearest 100)

Lower Limit of Year	Lowest	Second	Third	Fourth	Top 5%
2007	20,900	40,200	63,700	102,700	182,000
2000	18,500	33,900	53,700	84,200	149,600
1990	16,400	31,100	47,500	72,500	124,400
1980	15,400	28,700	44,000	64,500	104,800
1970	14,600	27,900	40,600	57,900	91,500
Increase in breakpoint, 1970–2000	26.7%	21.5%	33.3%	45.4%	63.5%
Increase in breakpoint, 1970–2007	43.2%	44.1%	56.9%	77.4%	99.0%

Observers who point out that the wealthiest Americans have been doing better than the rest of the population are clearly correct. In real dollars, from 1970 to 2000, the upper limit of the fourth quintile (that is, the lower limit of the fifth quintile) rose by 45.4 percent while the upper limit of the lowest quintile rose by only 26.7 percent. Meanwhile, the lower limit that defines the top 5 percent—the very wealthiest households—rose by 63.5 percent. Income gains in the seven-year expansion from 2001 to 2007 continued this trend. In fact, according to the Center on Budget and Policy Priorities, the top 1 percent of households reaped two thirds of the income gains realized by households in that expansion.

Changes in the *share* of total income going to the various quintiles tell an even more interesting story. Table 10.4 shows the percentage share of total income going to each quintile and to the top 5 percent of households.

Table 10.4   Share of Income Received by Each Quintile and the Top 5 Percent

Year	Lowest	Second	Third	Fourth	Fifth	Top 5%
2007	3.4	8.7	14.8	23.4	49.7	21.2
2000	3.6	8.9	14.8	23.0	49.8	21.9
1990	3.8	9.6	15.9	24.2	46.5	18.6
1980	4.2	10.2	16.8	24.7	44.1	15.8
1970	4.1	10.8	17.4	24.5	43.3	16.6

Source: U.S. Census Bureau

It doesn't take a raving socialist to see that the shares of total income going to U.S. households in the top 20 percent—and in the top 5 percent—increased from 1970 to 2000, while the shares going to those in the lower four quintiles—the lower 80 percent—decreased. This trend tempered slightly in the 2000s expansion, but the recessionary years of 2008 and 2009, for which official U.S. Census data on income distribution is not yet available as I write this, were not good to the poor. In fact, many families fell out of the middle class (and onto the rolls of the Supplemental Nutrition Assistance Program and unemployment insurance recipients) during those years.

What you think should be done about this well-established overall income distribution trend, if anything, is another matter. Yet clearly, over the past 30 years, a larger share of income has gone to those who were already earning the highest incomes.

That is a major point of contention in the political, social, and economic argument over income distribution in the United States. Very few Americans seriously argue that income *equality* is a reasonable, or even desirable, goal. Americans recognize that the incentive to earn a higher income drives people to get an education and work hard, fuels economic growth, and informs our national character. If incomes were equalized through taxation or other means, the labor market would fall into disarray and people would lack economic incentives to better themselves.

ECONOTIP

Don't confuse income distribution with income redistribution. Income distribution refers to the amounts and shares of income that go to various segments of a population. Income redistribution refers to government programs to even out income disparities to some degree. This involves taking money from relatively wealthy segments of society and transferring it to relatively poor segments, through public assistance and other government programs.

However, despite very real disparities in income, Americans pride themselves on being a classless society, or at least on being a nation with such a large middle class that it may as well be composed of one class. This may be wishful thinking given the actual distribution of income.

Through work, education, innovation, and financial savvy, people in America can move to a higher socioeconomic class more easily than in most other societies. This is another source of national pride and economic incentive in the United States. Might that change if people with the largest slice of the economic pie keep getting an even larger slice? If we became a nation in which the economic deck is stacked against average people—those with average education and skills—both social mobility and incentives to work could diminish. Moreover, with much of the fruits of economic growth going to a relatively small segment of the population, the once-tight social fabric of the country could fray.

There is some evidence that that fabric has frayed since the glory days of World War II and the 1950s. The urban riots of the 1960s arose in part from economic issues. The character of many U.S. cities changed during and after that period, in many instances leaving a much smaller middle class to fill jobs, attend schools, spend money, and pay taxes. Suburban sprawl, "white flight," and the need for more housing transformed large portions of cities like Detroit, Baltimore, Los Angeles, and New York into urban societies with two classes: wealthy and poor.

Some people point out that even if the lower four quintiles each have a lower share of the economic pie than they did 30 years ago, their incomes are still higher than they were back then. That may be true, but relative to the top quintile, they are poorer, and the distribution of the shares of national wealth is the key measure of wealth and poverty in a nation as rich as the United States.

Why Incomes Are Becoming More Unequal

Incomes have become more unequal in the United States for three primary reasons:

- Changes in employment patterns
- Increased returns to education
- Changes in households

Let's take a look at each of these reasons.

Changes in Employment Patterns

As we discussed in Chapter 9, the percentage of workers who belong to a labor union decreased dramatically in the past 40 years. That in itself results in a lower wage for millions of workers, because unions exist to push wages upward, and they usually succeed.

As a result, however, management often moves jobs to lower-wage locations. Many high-paying U.S. manufacturing jobs have been replaced by lower-paying jobs in service industries, such as retail and restaurants. This trend is expected to continue.

The Bureau of Labor Statistics states that, of the 10 occupations with the largest projected job growth from 2008 to 2018, 6 pay average wages of $25,000 a year or less (office clerks, nursing aides, home health aides, retail salespersons, personal and home care aides, and food preparers).

Growth in service-sector employment is also being driven by changes in consumers' spending patterns. Spending on services has been growing faster than spending on nondurables, such as food, beverages, and clothing, and that trend is also expected to continue. Spending on durables, such as motor vehicles, furniture, appliances, and consumer electronics was growing, paused during the 2008–2009 recession, and resumed growth after it. But much of the manufacturing in those industries has been moved to lower-wage nations, such as Mexico, Malaysia, and China.

Increased Returns to Education

More educated and highly skilled workers have always earned higher incomes than less-educated and less-skilled workers. That tendency has become more pronounced in the United States due to increased demand for knowledge workers and managers in an economy where industries such as high technology, financial services, media, communications, and academia have been growing.

Table 10.5 relates education with income levels for men and women.

Table 10.5   Higher Education Means Higher Income (average annual income in dollars, rounded to nearest 100)

	Men	Women
No high school diploma	22,600	14,200
High school graduate	32,400	21,200
Some college or Associate's degree	41,300	27,000
Bachelor's degree	57,400	38,600
Advanced degree	77,200	50,900

Source: U.S. Census Bureau, 2007

For both men and women—admittedly with a significant gender gap—income increases with education. However, that gender gap narrows (but only a bit) with education. A man with a bachelor's degree earns 77 percent more than one with a high school diploma. A woman with a bachelor's degree earns 82 percent more than one with a high school diploma. This translates to a gender gap in which a man with a high school diploma earns 53 percent more than a comparably educated woman, but a man with a bachelor's degree earns 48 percent more than a comparably educated woman.

Higher education also means lower unemployment. In 2000—a low-unemployment year—unemployment was 3.5 percent for high school graduates and, at 1.7 percent, about half that for college graduates. However, in the recession of 2008–2009, people with less education were hit much harder than those with more education. For example, in 2008 the average unemployment rate for non–high school graduates was 9.0 percent; for high school grads, 5.7 percent; for workers with some college, 5.1 percent; and for workers with bachelor's degrees, 2.8 percent. I am *not* saying that if everyone had a college degree, unemployment would have been 2.8 percent in 2008. I am saying that overall, for individuals, higher education increased the chances of being employed even during the recession.

A bright, motivated individual worker stands a good chance of earning a higher income by obtaining more education. But increased education and skills training will not be enough to shift the current trend in income distribution significantly. Even if it were possible to give all U.S. workers a college education, millions of the jobs being created in the future—in retail, restaurants, home health services, and so on—simply don't require high levels of education. Getting a college degree only to wind up selling hardware or frying potatoes makes no economic sense. Nor does paying a hardware salesperson or a fry cook $25 an hour.

These structural changes in the labor force represent a high obstacle to improving the incomes of the bottom 40 percent of households.

Changes in Households

Households themselves have changed, and these changes have affected household income. The tendency toward more single-adult households (due to people marrying later and divorcing more frequently) has, over the past 30 years, created more households for a given level of population. When people marry later and couples divorce, the number of households increases in proportion to the population. Indeed, this is exactly what has occurred in the United States since 1970.

Table 10.6 summarizes key population statistics for 1970 and 2008.

Table 10.6   Population, Households, and Married Couples (1970 and 2008, nearest million)

	1970	2008	Change
Total Population	203,000,000	299,000,000	47%
Households	63,000,000	117,000,000	86%
Average Household Size	3.2 people	2.6 people	–19%
Married Couples	45,000,000	58,000,000	29%
Married Couples as Percent of Pop.	22.2%	19.4%	—

From 1970 to 2008, the U.S. population increased 47 percent while the number of married couples increased by only 29 percent, due to later marriage, increased divorce, and, perhaps, increased acceptance of gay lifestyles. The rise in the number of households relative to the population (86 percent versus 47 percent) increases the number of households that total income is divided by, resulting in lower income per household.

Consider this: if a married couple heading a household—even a two-earner household—divorces, their income is divided between two households rather than one. That halves the household income figure generated by that couple. (And that's assuming that their incomes remain the same, which is not always the case: women's incomes often decrease after divorce.)

On the surface, this may seem to be a mathematical issue rather than a true problem of income inequality. After all, if people want to remain or become single, why shouldn't they? They probably should. But being divorced or an unmarried head of a household (or both) falls harder on the poor. As difficult as divorce and single parenthood can be, it's tougher for people in the lower-income quintiles, because they lack the income and other resources that help a person cope with child-rearing and other challenges of daily living. Society also bears the social cost of a continuing cycle of poverty and the ills that poverty generates.

What's the Government's Role?

The U.S. government is already working to address income inequality and poverty. Some people believe that the government should be doing more, some believe it should be doing less, and some feel that the current role is about right.

Here are some of the policies that the government has in place to address income inequality and assist poor households.

Progressive Income Tax

A *progressive income tax* taxes people with higher incomes at higher rates. In the United States, federal tax rates start at about 10 percent and reach a high of 35 percent, with four intermediate brackets. Except for transfer payments and public assistance programs, all U.S. citizens receive the same basic federal services in terms of defense, law enforcement, food and drug regulation, and so on. Yet wealthier citizens pay more for these services. This smacks of the Marxist principle, "From each according to his means …," yet most Americans (but not all) feel that progressive taxation is ultimately fair. So while the wealthiest Americans have a larger share of the income pie, they also pay more in taxes. In fact, given high federal deficits and decreased tax rates on the wealthy over the past few decades (relative to the 1950s through the 1970s), it is likely that taxes on the wealthy will rise.

ECONOTALK

A **progressive income tax** levies higher taxes on higher incomes. Typically, marginal income is taxed at marginally higher rates. For example, income up to $20,000 may be taxed at 15 percent, income between $20,000 and $35,000 at 20 percent, and so on. (If only the tax code were that simple.) In other words, the higher rate does not apply to all income, but rather to the marginal income.

Public Assistance Programs

Federal unemployment insurance, Medicare, and programs such as the Supplemental Nutrition Assistance Program all help poor and temporarily hard-pressed households make ends meet. While Social Security and Medicare are not welfare programs (because workers pay specific taxes to fund these benefits), they do provide assistance to millions of retirees and people unable to work.

Economic Development Programs

Federal programs that help finance minority- and women-owned businesses, such as those of the Small Business Administration, help redress the imbalances created by job discrimination in the past, and so do efforts that encourage these businesses to apply for government contracts. Federal money also finds its way into state and municipal programs to train unskilled workers and encourage business formation—for instance, in enterprise zones designed to foster redevelopment in the inner city.

Managing the Economy

The federal government implements economic policies aimed at generating full employment and low inflation. While this benefits wealthy Americans as well as the less well off, the emphasis on controlling unemployment arguably helps wage earners more than it does the moneyed class. Of course, as proven in the recession of 2008–2009, business cycles will continue, and government policies can do only so much to address unemployment.

All of that said, the United States generally provides its citizens with a lower level of government support for health and human services than developed European nations. This is true for services that benefit the middle class as well as those for the poor. Most European nations provide, insure, or mandate higher levels of health care, childcare, employee benefits, and job security. They also generally levy higher taxes on their citizens, particularly on the wealthiest, to finance these programs.

In Parts 3 and 4, we will examine the role of the federal government in managing the economy. The government's role in addressing income inequality falls into the political realm, and this is not a book about political economics. Very few people, regardless of their political persuasion, want to see their fellow human beings in poverty. However, there is no political consensus on further addressing the effects of poverty in the United States.

Other Aspects of Wealth and Poverty

Before completing our examination of wealth and poverty, there are a few related topics to cover: general spending patterns, consumer debt, and inflation.

Where It Goes

As I mentioned earlier, there are three broad classes of personal consumption expenditure: durables, nondurables, and services. Table 10.7 shows the dollar amounts of spending and the growth rates in these categories for 1977 and 1993, and for 1995 and 2009.

Table 10.7   Personal Spending Patterns Are Changing (billions of 2005 dollars)

	Personal Spending 1977	Personal Spending 1993	Average Annual Percent Growth 1977–1993
Durables	280	490	4.7
Nondurables	820	1,079	2.0
Services	1,197	1,890	3.6
Total	2,297	3,459	3.2

	Personal Spending 1995	Personal Spending 2009	Average Annual Percent Growth 1995–2009
Durables	512	1,101	8.2
Nondurables	1,438	2,037	3.0
Services	4,208	6,088	3.2
Total	6,158	9,226	3.6

Source: Bureau of Economic Analysis

As the table shows, consumers spend most of their money on services. In fact, the share of goods and services spending (leaving aside energy) devoted to services increased from 52 percent in 1977 (= 1197 ÷ 2296) to 66 percent in 2009 (= 6,088 ÷ 9,226). The five largest service expenditures are housing, health care, financial services, utilities, and transportation. Spending on nondurables—food, beverages, clothing, toys, and so on—is the next largest category. Although spending on durables—motor vehicles, furniture, appliances, home computers, and so on—is the smallest, it was the fastest growing category of spending from both 1977 to 1993 and particularly from 1995 to 2009.

As household income falls, the percentage of income spent on necessities such as food, housing, utilities, and transportation becomes larger. This leaves less to save and to spend on durables such as new cars, furniture, and appliances. Therefore, much of the growth in spending on durables has been fueled by educated, higher-income baby boomers purchasing vehicles, as well as homes and condominiums that require furniture and appliances, as they have moved through adulthood. During the economic expansions of the 1990s and 2000s, spending on durables increased over that of the late 1970s, 1980s, and early 1990s. The housing boom of the 2000s helped boost this growth, as did an expansion in consumer debt.

New Highs in Deep Debt

American consumers use large amounts of credit. Consumer credit takes two basic forms: mortgages, which are used to buy real estate and are *secured* by the homes, condominiums, or other property being purchased; and consumer loans. Home-equity loans, which are personal loans secured by the equity in houses and condominiums, may be lumped in with mortgages. Consumer loans include both secured loans, such as auto loans, and *unsecured* loans, such as purchases made with credit cards.

ECONOTALK

A **secured** loan is one in which the borrower provides a tangible or financial asset—such as a home, car, boat, stocks, or bonds—to the lender as collateral. In the event the borrower cannot repay the loan, the lender takes possession of the collateral and sells it to recoup the borrowed money. An **unsecured** loan is one on which the borrower provides no collateral.

In the first decade of the new millennium, consumer debt in all forms has reached record levels, both in absolute terms and as a percentage of income. Mortgages to finance America's widespread homeownership are one reason, but so is the proliferation of credit cards and other installment debt. It's a fact that a good part of the economic growth from 2001 to 2007 was fueled by consumer debt. From 2003 to the end of 2007, outstanding personal loans, auto loans, and credit card balances increased almost 25 percent, from $2.1 trillion to $2.6 trillion. That's not counting mortgage and home-equity lines—and it's a record high. This is why offering consumers credit wouldn't get the economy moving in the recession of 2008–2009, and why banks were reluctant to lend. Consumers were loaned up, and very concerned about their prospects for continued employment.

The consequences of high consumer debt are twofold. First, it usually indicates a low rate of savings, and, as we saw in Chapter 7, that is indeed the case in the United States. Second, when a recession results in fewer working hours and lower incomes, consumers can find repaying their debt difficult or even impossible. Indeed, according to the October 9, 2002, *Wall Street Journal*, auto repossessions, personal bankruptcies, and mortgage foreclosures were all at or near their highest levels in decades at the time—and they reached higher levels still, as did home foreclosures, during the 2008–2009 recession.

During the 2008–2009 recession, consumers found it difficult to maintain, let alone increase, spending while under their debt burden. That prolonged the lackluster economic growth and made further borrowing impossible for many households. Also, if interest rates rise, many consumers who had difficulty making debt payments at lower rates may find themselves unable to do so at higher rates. That occurred from 2005 to 2008, when the rates on many adjustable rate mortgages (ARMs) increased and sent hundreds of thousands of homeowners into default.

Inflation Hurts—and Helps

Inflation is generally considered bad, especially by government finance officials, who are charged with keeping the value of the currencies of their nations sound. Except in times of stagflation (a combination of stagnant economic growth and inflation), incomes generally rise during periods of inflation. But if incomes are not rising as fast as prices, then inflation is eroding the currency's purchasing power. This hurts everyone—wealthy, middle class, and poor—but can make life especially hard for the poor.

That's because of a second effect of inflation. During inflation, the value of assets—particularly real estate, but also financial assets such as stocks—generally rises. This rise in asset values helps the wealthy and the middle class because they own real estate and stocks. The poor do not. The rise in stock values in the 1990s and of home prices in the early 2000s produced what is known as a wealth effect, which occurs when even people who don't sell their homes or portfolios feel wealthier because they are wealthier on paper. As a result of the wealth effect in those periods, consumers probably spent (and borrowed) more freely than they otherwise would have.

Price stability and high employment are the goals of government economic policy. A stable currency enables everyone, wealthy or poor, consumer or business person, debtor or creditor, to make better, more confident financial plans and decisions. That said, moderate inflation—say, in the neighborhood of 2 percent or so—is generally viewed as tolerable by governments and as an assist to economic growth and low unemployment.

The Ultimate Issue: Quality of Life

Ultimately, wealth and poverty are quality-of-life issues. Wealth obviously improves it, but poverty undermines the quality of life for everyone in an economy, not just the poor. Poverty generates crime, broken families, drug addiction, illness, illiteracy—and more poverty. Many people decry the cost of government programs to deal with poverty and its side effects. However, the hidden costs of poverty, which go beyond the suffering of the poor, are staggering. These costs include property loss, deteriorating real estate values, bodily injury, and increased public and private expenditures for insurance, law enforcement, court cases, prisons, and health care, plus the lost productivity of people who could be employed or more gainfully employed.

These costs are borne by everyone. The wealthy arguably bear the largest share of the cost because they pay the largest share of income taxes. They also insulate themselves from the effects of poverty by inhabiting exclusive enclaves, using private schools, and so on, yet the social repercussions of poverty are difficult to escape.

Ensuring minimum levels of nutrition, shelter, safety, health care, and education for everyone may well be within the capabilities of the most productive economy in human history. Again, however, that is a political issue. Moreover, as we will see in the next two parts, the federal government has its hands full simply managing its budget and keeping the economy stable and growing.

The Least You Need to Know

- Often, it is income inequality rather than actual destitution that creates poverty in an economy.
- Income inequality is a fact of life in the United States, and it became more pronounced from the 1970s through the 2000s.
- The reasons for growing income inequality include changing employment patterns, increased returns to education, and changes in the composition of households.
- The U.S. government helps the poor through progressive income taxes, public assistance programs, economic development programs, and management of the economy for low inflation and unemployment. Yet the United States provides a lower level of government support for health and human services than most developed European nations.
- Many Americans who are not poor use debt freely in order maintain what they see as middle-class lifestyles. The levels of debt incurred by households in the early 2000s contributed to the recession late in that decade and to its severity.

The Government and the Economy

Part

3

Although the government plays a smaller role in the U.S. economy than the governments of most other nations play in theirs, that role is important and multifaceted.

First, it is through the government that society produces goods and services that everyone needs but that markets can't really deliver—defense is a good example. Second, total government spending accounts for about 28 percent of GDP, and that spending has a huge effect on the economy. Third, the government has the power to levy taxes, and the way in which it uses that power generates strong responses in people as well as in the economy. Finally, the government issues currency and controls the supply of money in the economy.

In this part, we examine all of these government roles except for the last one, having to do with the money supply, which we cover in Part 4. We begin by examining a key reason for the government to be involved with the economy to begin with—the business cycle and its effects.

The Ups and Downs of the Business Cycle

In This Chapter

- The nature of the business cycle
- Causes of expansions and recessions
- Unemployment, inflation, and the economy

The forces of supply and demand play themselves out in the economy in ways that tend toward equilibrium but never quite get there. Over the very short term or in very specific areas of the economy, supply, demand, employment, unemployment, wages, and prices may remain somewhat steady. That can create the impression that a kind of equilibrium has been reached. But the short term, by definition, never lasts long, and here we are focusing on the economy as a whole.

The economy as a whole is always either growing or contracting at a rate that usually changes from one quarter—or even one month—to the next. In this chapter, we examine the dynamics of growth and contraction. As I mentioned earlier, every business wants to grow, every household wants higher income, and every government wants a growing economy. Over the long term, the U.S. economy does grow at the average of about 3 percent that I mentioned earlier, but that's the average. In this chapter, we look at the swings around that average.

What Is the Business Cycle?

The economy, as measured by gross domestic product (GDP), goes through alternating phases of growth and contraction. Phases of growth are called *expansions*, upswings, or recoveries. Phases of contraction are called *recessions*, downturns, or periods of negative growth (yes, it's an oxymoron, but one that economists insist on using).

The exact beginning or end of a recession or expansion can be difficult to determine, particularly as it is happening. It can be a challenge even after the fact. The National Bureau of Economic Research (NBER) in Cambridge, Massachusetts, does the official dating of recessions and expansions, but not always in the timeliest manner. They took about 20 months to declare the official date of the end of the 11-month recession of 2001. In fairness, however, the NBER considers a number of factors other than GDP growth or contraction, including unemployment, job growth, incomes, and industrial production.

ECONOTALK

Informally, a **recession** is defined as two consecutive quarters of contraction in GDP (or negative growth). An **expansion** is growth in GDP, but unless it lasts, the result can be a double-dip recession—a recession in which the economy recovers for one, two, or three quarters and then contracts again. A flat economy is one registering zero growth—neither growth nor contraction.

During an expansion, consumer, business, and government demand all usually rise, but not at the same pace or at the same time. Expansions are often led by the consumer. In a consumer-led expansion, households demand more goods and services. In response, businesses increase production, put existing employees on overtime, and eventually hire new workers. This sets off a virtuous cycle of rising consumer demand, rising sales for business, and rising employment. Rising employment generates rising incomes for consumers, which fuels rising consumer demand, rising sales for business, and so on. Businesses increase their purchases of raw materials and expand their productive capacity by investing in new plant and equipment and offices. This kicks the sales of other businesses—contractors, builders, and producers of materials and capital equipment—into high gear.

Meanwhile, the federal government enjoys rising tax receipts. Elected officials can spread the wealth among their constituents by funding programs and increasing pay for government workers and the military (and themselves). They also usually increase government purchases and employment in health and human services, defense, public works, space exploration, and scientific research. If the federal budget runs a surplus, in which tax receipts exceed the federal budget, officials may even pay down some of the nation's debt—but don't count on it. We'll discuss the national debt in Chapters 12 and 13.

Even poor people fare relatively well in an expansion—that is, relative to their situation during a recession. As unemployment approaches the full-employment level of 4 percent, almost every worker can find employment. Unfortunately, those without skills are destined to remain relatively poor and vulnerable to job loss when the next downturn arrives.

In a recession, demand falls—we'll examine why in a minute—and when demand falls, production contracts. In a typical recession, a decrease in consumer demand sets off a vicious cycle. When consumer demand decreases, businesses cut back production. They buy fewer raw materials, stop hiring workers, and even lay off some workers. They put expansion plans on hold, and may even shut down plants and offices.

These moves by businesses decrease consumers' incomes, which prompts consumers to reduce their consumption. When consumption falls further, businesses cut back production even more, laying off workers, further reducing income, and so on.

So in a typical recession, consumption—the C in C + I + G—and investment—the I in the GDP formula—both fall.

What happens to government spending? You would expect it to fall, particularly when tax receipts decrease as incomes decrease. However, the federal government usually continues to spend during a recession. That provides a cushion—a baseline level of demand—so demand doesn't fall too far too fast. How much to spend is a fiscal policy decision for the government. We will deal with fiscal policy in Chapter 13.

When does a recession end? When demand is rekindled and starts rising, setting off a new virtuous cycle. Demand usually increases again because consumers reach a point where they simply have to increase their spending. Cars have to be replaced. Clothing wears out. Appliances break down for the fifth time. Even during a recession, most consumers continue to spend, although not at normal levels and not at levels that make the economy grow. It is the rekindling of demand from the consumers who cut back because they lost their jobs, overtime pay, or sense of security that kicks off the next expansion.

Often, however, the consumer needs help. In the Great Recession of 2008–2009, for example, the government applied significant fiscal and monetary stimulus to the economy. We discuss monetary policy in Part 4, but fiscal policy, explained in Chapter 13 enables the government to support demand—for example, through unemployment insurance and job-creation programs—so that the economy does not contract to the point where a serious, long-term recession, or a *depression*, occurs.

 ECONOTALK

A **depression** is a prolonged period of extremely low consumer demand and investment, reduced business activity, high unemployment, and pessimism about the future of the economy.

The Inflation-Unemployment Trade-Off

For much of the past century, economists and business people believed that there was a trade-off between inflation and unemployment. Many still do. Here's the theory, which has often (but not always) been borne out in the real world.

An economy enjoying high demand and high employment experiences inflationary pressure—that is, upward pressure on prices. That's because when demand for goods and services is high, consumers bid up the prices of goods and services. Sellers, of course, are happy to accommodate them. This is called *demand-pull inflation*, because buyers' increasing demand pulls up prices.

There's another type of inflation, too. When the unemployment rate is low (say, around the full-employment rate of 4 percent), we have a tight labor market. In a tight market, employers increase wages in order to keep good workers and hire new ones. This upward pressure on wages raises the cost of doing business. To maintain their profits, businesses have to raise their prices. This is called *cost-push inflation*, because the increased costs push prices upward. (It is also, more properly but less commonly, called *wage-push inflation*.)

> **ECONOTALK**
>
> **Demand-pull inflation** occurs when consumers bid up prices, usually because employment is strong and incomes are increasing. **Wage-push inflation** occurs when businesses must raise wages to keep and attract workers in an environment of low unemployment, and therefore must also raise their prices. **Cost-push inflation** can include wage-push inflation, but also refers to price increases by business due to increased costs of one or more inputs other than labor.

Regardless of which comes first—the chicken of increased prices or the egg of increased wages (or is it the other way around?)—the result can be a price-wage inflation spiral. Demand for goods pushes up prices and keeps production high and unemployment low. Low unemployment pushes wages up. With higher incomes, consumers can afford the higher prices. Production is stepped up even further, and that pushes unemployment even lower and wages even higher, and so on.

Where does the spiral end? It ends when the government reins in the money supply or when the level of demand and the level of real wages reach the equilibrium, full-employment level and stays there. We will see how the government reduces the money supply in Part 4. The demand and supply for goods and services, which determine prices, and the demand and supply of labor, which dictate wages, reach equilibrium levels when demand cools down but does not fall too sharply.

If demand falls too sharply, the economy is pushed into a recession. A recession wrings inflation out of an economy by reducing income. When businesses cut back, people lose their jobs and overtime pay. That stops the wage inflation and dampens consumer spending. When consumers cut back their spending, businesses lower their prices—or at least stop increasing them—to get people to buy. That stops the price inflation.

The inflation/unemployment trade-off is the classic view of the two phenomena and of the business cycle. However, two relatively recent developments have complicated things: the stagflation of the 1970s and changes in the business cycle, as evidenced in the low-inflation booms of the 1990s and 2000s.

Stagflation

Stagflation, a combination of stagnation and inflation, means rising prices in the face of fairly high unemployment. Why would such a thing occur? If unemployment is relatively high, how can people have the income to bid up prices of goods and services?

They don't. Stagflation results from an increase in the price of inputs other than labor. It's not wage-push inflation. In fact, the price of even one input can generate inflation, even in a slack economy, if that input is important and widely used—like oil, for instance.

Indeed, the term *stagflation* arose to describe the economy of the 1970s after the Organization of Petroleum Exporting Countries (OPEC) sharply increased the price of oil in 1973. Oil, gasoline, and other petroleum products are key inputs in virtually every aspect of the U.S. economy, as either raw material or fuel. There are few short-term substitutes for oil and gasoline, so the economy had to absorb the oil price shock. Businesses raised their prices, but incomes didn't rise and consumer demand stayed sluggish.

Stagflation can be quite persistent. In the short term, there is little to be done about it. Over the longer term, people can use less of the input or develop substitutes. They also absorb the shock and ride it out until overall wage and price levels adjust and stabilize. This eventually occurred after the oil shock of the early 1970s and after the milder, but also jarring, oil shock of the early 1980s.

In the 2000s, oil prices increased sharply after the 9/11 attacks and with the war in Iraq and rising demand from China. Although these increases hit consumers in the form of higher heating oil and gasoline prices and higher airfares, the U.S. economy saw scant increases in inflation, even during the 2000s boom. Reasons for this are not entirely clear, but the most likely ones include increasing use of foreign labor to produce manufactured goods coupled with a strong dollar (which keeps prices of imports low); increased productivity of U.S. workers due to better technology and static incomes; and changes to the method of calculating inflation (for instance, using equivalent rents rather than actual housing prices).

Indeed, in the late 1990s, some economists concluded that increased productivity in the U.S. economy had done away with the traditional trade-off between inflation and unemployment. During the 1990s expansion, inflation remained quite low—about 2 percent or less per year—even as unemployment approached the rock-bottom rate of 4 percent. Other economists argue that the inflation/unemployment trade-off may still exist because the 1990s and 2000s were unusual periods of unsustainable productivity growth and that lackluster income growth and a strong dollar also helped keep inflation low.

Changes in the Cycle

The business cycle and the relationship between inflation and unemployment that I've described are those that prevailed in theory and reality until the 1970s. There have been some changes since then. Most important among these are the following:

- Lower inflation

- Higher productivity

- Faster response by businesses

- Fed-fueled booms and bubbles

Inflation erodes the value of the currency, and therefore the government, by means of monetary policy administered by the Federal Reserve, tries to prevent or at least control it. We will examine monetary policy in Part 4. In recent years, the Fed has been quite successful in keeping inflation low—although, as noted earlier in the previous section, other factors have also played a role.

Some economists believe that increased productivity in the U.S. economy has moderated the trade-off between inflation and unemployment. If productivity rises, businesses can produce more with roughly the same resources. That means that prices don't get pushed up. During the 1990s and 2000s expansions, productivity generally increased due to improved technology and management methods. Also, real incomes have not grown substantially, which increases workers' productivity but not the workers' living standards.

Businesses now respond more quickly to changes in the business cycle than they did before the 1980s, thanks to better information systems and inventory management. Businesses reduce production more quickly, lay people off faster, and do not rehire workers as quickly as they did in past business cycles. When businesses respond faster to changing demand, they shift a bit more of the burden of recession to consumers, who are laid off faster. Many employees have learned to cope with this by working as independent contractors and supplementing their incomes, but many have not and were particularly hard hit by the Great Recession.

During the expansions of the 1990s and 2000s, the Federal Reserve failed to raise interest rates aggressively enough to ward off asset price bubbles. (Part 4 explains how and why the Fed does this.) The Fed's easy money policies allowed increases in liquidity that contributed to rising tech-stock prices in the 1990s and rising home prices (fueled by cheap mortgage money) in the 2000s. Although it may be a bit harsh to lay all the blame at the Fed's doorstep, the Fed clearly contributed to these increased asset prices and the overall easy credit conditions. The Fed may point out that inflation had remained low, but low inflation is hardly the only measure of a healthy economy.

Businesses improved their responses to recessions even if the Fed did not improve its responses to unrestrained growth. We will see as future business cycles unfold how each party—and the consumer—continues to adjust. Even so, the fundamental dynamics of the business cycle remain largely unchanged except for the lack of significant inflation over the past 20 years. The mechanism of increased demand leading to increased production and rising incomes (or debt) followed by a decrease in demand, decreased production, and falling incomes still operates in the economy.

But we've yet to answer one question: what causes demand to decrease in the first place?

Seasons of Wither

Demand falls because consumers reduce consumption, businesses reduce investment, or the government reduces spending. But *why* do they reduce these activities?

Let's start with the government. The government may curtail its spending because it sees less need to spend in certain areas. This has not been a determining factor in a recession since the early 1960s. But up to then, periodic (postwar) cutbacks in military spending without increases in other spending or reductions in taxes occasionally caused a contraction in demand that flowed through to the broader economy.

Since the late 1960s, government has occasionally tried to produce *mild* recessions to reduce inflationary pressure in the economy. This is done through monetary policy. To solve the problem of too many dollars chasing too few goods, the Federal Reserve increases interest rates, which makes borrowing more difficult, and curtails the growth of the money supply, which takes some of those excess dollars out of the economy. (Don't worry, Part 4 will cover this in detail.) If the Fed miscalculates and raises interest rates too fast or too high, the result is a not-so-mild recession.

So, believe it or not, the government sometimes initiates a recession. This was the case in the 1981–1982 recession under Fed Chairman Paul Volker, which was designed to wring the inflation of the 1970s out of the economy. It worked—but one of the costs was an unemployment rate of more than 9.5 percent in 1982 and 1983. This did, however, set the stage for the boom of the 1980s.

Businesses generally want to invest, but they need to see opportunities. If they go on an investment binge, as they did in the 1990s when they expanded operations and bought large amounts of information technology, they need time to integrate the plant and equipment into their operations.

They also need money to invest. As we saw in Chapter 7, a mismatch between the amount households want to save and the amount businesses want to invest can cause trouble. If consumers want to save more than businesses want to invest—if consumers sit on their wallets—production may decrease. If it decreases enough to raise unemployment and lower incomes, recession may follow. (Oversaving by consumers has not been a problem in the U.S. economy lately.)

Consumers (bless 'em) are predisposed to demand goods and services. They want to buy, but they need two things: income, which we've discussed, and *confidence* in the economy.

ECONOTALK

Consumer confidence, also known as consumer sentiment, is a measure of the mood of consumers regarding the current economy and their optimism or pessimism about their economic prospects. There are two widely followed measures of the consumer's mood: the Conference Board's Consumer Confidence Index and University of Michigan Consumer Confidence Index. Both are explained in Chapter 22.

The Great Recession

The recession of 2008–2009 was not a normal downturn in the business cycle. Rather it was a cyclical downturn exacerbated by several extraordinary factors.

The housing bubble and subprime mortgages buried within globally distributed mortgage-backed securities touched off a crisis in the financial markets and banking system that made it far more difficult to pull out of the recession. Banks were very reluctant to lend, and bank lending helps businesses and consumers to spend and thus boost demand.

Consumer debt was already at record levels going into the recession, which also meant that households were unable and unwilling to borrow more. In times of financial stress, consumers reduce spending and focus on paying for necessities and on reducing their debt.

Expansionary fiscal policy in the form of tax cuts and deficit spending, and expansionary monetary policy in the form of low interest rates during the expansion of 2002 to 2007, left both the Bush and Obama administrations with very few policy options. Yes, during the recession both administrations engaged in deficit spending and interest rates were kept low, but those policies could do little to reignite vigorous growth, although they did keep the recession from getting worse and prevented the economy from falling into a depression.

However, government debt also stood at record levels, which prompted opposition concerns about deficit spending when Obama took office. Unfortunately, those voices had been silent through the tax cuts, war costs, and huge increases in government debt that occurred during the expansion under the preceding administration.

The turmoil in the financial and housing markets caused a very real loss of wealth for consumers, as well as a feeling that they were losing ground economically. Add to that long-stagnant real-wage growth and a nationwide unemployment rate that topped 10 percent, and you have a very wary consumer and a relatively slow recovery.

Businesses also remained very wary. As I pointed out, businesses have become more aggressive in their response to downturns; they are faster to lay workers off and slower to rehire. That makes for sharply increasing unemployment when recession hits and slow job growth when recovery begins.

In addition to these factors, the U.S. industrial base and relations between employers and employees changed dramatically from the 1980s to the 2000s. Millions of manufacturing jobs had been exported to lower-wage nations. That means that the traditional pattern of layoffs followed by rehiring changed. Now the rehiring may or may not happen because the employers don't have factories that need to be staffed. They more often hire part-time or temporary workers and independent contractors. Relatively few private-sector workers (about 9 percent) belong to unions, and unions have far less power. In fact, much of the risk of downturns was shifted from employers to employees from the 1980s to the 2000s.

All of these factors made what could have been a normal recession much worse. That recession also left a number of problems in its wake. These include lingering high unemployment, a housing market that may take years to recover, a smaller U.S. auto industry, and many baby boomers facing retirement with low savings and financially stressed Social Security and Medicare programs. That said, at least the economy managed to avoid an economic depression, although a double-dip recession remained possible.

Serious Depression

Economists call a deep, prolonged contraction a depression. A depression is not as clearly defined as a recession, but is characterized by rising unemployment, falling incomes, falling prices, excess inventories and productive capacity, lack of confidence, and a generally low level of business activity. Fortunately, depressions are very rare. The Great Depression of the 1930s was the only true depression to occur in the United States and Europe in the past century.

The Great Depression lasted from 1929, when the stock market crashed on October 25 (Black Thursday), to about 1940. During the Depression, unemployment reached 25 percent, families lost their savings and homes and survived on charity and odd jobs, farms and banks failed by the thousands, and two generations formed lifelong memories of tough economic times. Real GDP contracted by 8.6 percent in 1930, 6.4 percent in 1931, 13.0 percent in 1932, and 1.4 percent in 1933.

Economists disagree about the exact causes of the Great Depression, but a stock-market bubble driven by the wild buying of the Roaring Twenties is one suspect. Much of that buying was on margin, meaning with borrowed money, so when stock prices peaked and a sell-off began, it quickly snowballed into a crash. Although the Crash of 1929 did not actually *cause* the Great Depression, it certainly reduced people's wealth and, perhaps more importantly, induced pessimism and fear regarding their economic prospects. That lack of confidence prevailed for much of the 1930s.

In the view of many economists, the Federal Reserve's decision to reduce the money supply in the very early 1930s reduced demand too sharply. Some economists blame the Fed for pushing the nation into depression, but a lot of money was actually taken out of the economy by bank failures. When people put a run on a bank—that is, when all or most depositors want to withdraw their money at once—the bank typically fails. The bank will close its doors, because the depositors' money is not in the bank—most of it has been loaned out as mortgages, auto loans, and personal loans. Bank failures reduced the money supply and that, apart from the Fed's actions, reduced demand.

Moreover, business investment collapsed. Why? The market crash hobbled companies' efforts to raise capital by selling stock. Consumer pessimism and falling demand left businesses with fewer reasons to invest. A reduced money supply and high interest rates made money harder to come by and expensive to borrow.

Actually, economists agree that all of these factors—the stock market crash, collapse in confidence, reduction of the money supply, bank failures, high interest rates, and reduced business investment—played a role in initiating, prolonging, or worsening the Great Depression. The disagreement concerns their exact roles and relative importance in the debacle.

Fortunately, economists agree that the United States now has safeguards in place that make a repeat of the Great Depression unlikely. These safeguards include a social safety net in the form of unemployment insurance, welfare, Medicaid, and Medicare. They also include a more active government role in economic policy, better regulation of the securities markets, and insurance of bank deposits up to $100,000 (increased to $250,000 until the end of 2013) thanks to the Federal Deposit Insurance Corporation (FDIC), which was created in 1933 to insure bank deposits and put an end to runs on banks. Overall, the U.S. government and governments elsewhere in the developed world are far more willing to intervene in the economic cycle than they were before the Great Depression.

THE REAL WORLD

In March 1933, Franklin D. Roosevelt succeeded Herbert Hoover as president of the United States. Roosevelt immediately began efforts to reform the banking and securities industries, provide relief for farmers and the unemployed, and stimulate the economy. By June 30, the Emergency Banking Relief Act (providing for federal bank inspections), Agricultural Adjustment Act and Farm Credit Act (subsidizing farmers), Reforestation Relief Act (putting people to work on conservation projects), and the Federal Securities Act and the since-repealed Glass-Steagall Act (reforming the securities industry) were all passed. The FDIC and the Tennessee Valley Authority were both created in that period as well.

These measures initiated the New Deal, which expanded the role of the government in the economy as both regulator and participant. This made Roosevelt a hero to many and a demon to others, depending on their politics and economic situation.

Booms and Busts

When consumers and businesses increase or decrease demand gradually, the cycle of recession and recovery will be relatively smooth, although hardly painless. But exaggerated responses by consumers or businesses can create a boom or a bust. (A bust is a colloquial term for a sharp, severe downturn.)

A boom occurs when demand increases sharply over a sustained period. The increase in demand can be broad-based and affect the entire economy, or it can be more specific. For example, a nationwide housing boom may be driven by a dramatic increase of adults in the population who are ready to become homeowners. More specifically still, a housing boom can occur in a rapidly growing city, as occurred in Las Vegas from the late 1980s through most of the 1990s.

In general, an economic boom means good times for most people. However, if a boom continues long enough and strong enough, it can generate overexpansion by businesses or inflation. If businesses overexpand, they wind up with too much productive capacity and too many employees for the existing level of demand. When that happens, they must cut their costs by cutting back on purchases of materials and equipment and decreasing the number of employees through layoffs. When employees are laid off, they cut back their spending, too. If businesses and employees cut back their spending sharply enough for long enough, a recession begins. If economic conditions become bad enough, the result can be a bust.

Look Out Below: Falling Prices

Until recently, very few economists worried about *deflation*, but since the early 2000s many have started re-examining the phenomenon. Deflation is defined as a sustained period of falling prices for most goods and services. It is a situation of too few dollars chasing too many goods and is therefore the opposite of inflation.

ECONOTALK

Deflation is a period of falling prices across a broad range of products and services. It is the opposite of inflation, in that too few dollars are chasing too many goods. In such a situation producers have no choice but to reduce their prices.

For this reason, deflation might strike you as a wonderful development. Indeed, it helps households, at least initially. Consumers can buy more for their money because, if prices are falling *and* wages remain stable, the purchasing power of the currency is rising. But that is about the only benefit to consumers, and it can be short lived.

During deflation, a business that's able to increase its sales volume enough to offset the effect of lower prices may continue to do business more or less as usual. But many businesses find that lower prices mean lower sales or lower profits, or both. (Recall our discussion of elasticity of demand in Chapter 5?) Businesses facing declining profits will have to reduce their payrolls and other costs. This reduces employment and income, which can set off the vicious cycle of lower demand, lower production, and recession.

In addition, deflation hurts debtors because they must pay back their debts with more expensive dollars. This is in contrast to the benefits debtors derive from inflation, when they repay their debts with cheaper dollars. Also, returns on savings and investments may decrease during deflation because interest rates tend to fall along with profits and, by extension, stock prices and dividends. Remember, the goal of sound economic policy is a stable currency, one that is neither gaining nor losing purchasing power. For this reason, economists take a dim view of deflation.

The cause of deflation is too much capacity—the ability to produce too many goods and services given the level of demand. In the United States, the huge investment in technology made during the 1990s expanded capacity while reducing production costs.

One cure for deflation is to reduce capacity, which is painful for the businesses that must close factories or stores—and for their employees. The other is to increase demand, which isn't always easy to do. Lower interest rates can help spur borrowing and spending, but sometimes the only cure is time. Sooner or later the car, clothes, and appliances need replacing, demand rises, and the virtuous cycle begins again.

The Least You Need to Know

- The business cycle is the alternating pattern of expansion and recession caused by fluctuating demand by consumers, businesses, and (to a lesser extent) government, and by mismatches between supply and demand and between savings and investment.

- Demand-pull inflation occurs when consumers bid up the prices of goods and services. Wage-push inflation occurs when businesses must raise wages to keep and attract workers in an environment of low unemployment. Cost-push inflation refers to price increases by businesses due to increased costs of inputs other than labor.

- A recession is informally defined as at least two consecutive quarters of contraction in GDP. The formal definition is a period of high unemployment, and low or contracting income growth, business investment, and economic activity. A depression is a prolonged period of rising unemployment, falling incomes, falling prices, excess inventories and productive capacity, and lack of confidence.

- The long-accepted relationship between inflation and unemployment is that low unemployment eventually generates inflation, and a mild recession is the cure for that inflation. However, the phenomenon of stagflation shows that inflation can occur even in the presence of relatively high unemployment.

- The business cycle and the traditional relationship between inflation and unemployment may have changed in the past 30 years due to faster responses by businesses, the Federal Reserve's success at controlling inflation, and higher productivity.

Hey, Big Spender! The Federal Budget

In This Chapter

- What the government does in the economy
- The federal budget and where it goes
- Government agencies that affect the economy

The main title of this chapter—Hey, Big Spender!—is meant to be somewhat ironic. Many Americans tend to distrust government in general and big government in particular. But, as I've noted, the U.S. government plays a smaller role in the U.S. economy than the governments of most developed nations play in theirs. U.S. taxes are lower, and public programs are smaller.

Still the government's role in the economy is one area where politics can be expected to intrude on economics, and it does. In this chapter, I will try to keep politics at bay and *describe* the role of the government, the money involved, where it comes from, where it goes, and the government agencies that most affect the economy. In other words, in this chapter our goal is to understand the government as the *G* in the C + I + G formula for gross domestic product (GDP).

The Role of Government in a Capitalist Economy

In a way, the political arguments that rage on in America are relatively trivial. There are serious situations to address—poverty, crime, drugs, and terrorism—but the vast majority of Americans largely agree on the basic economic principles.

Most Americans agree on the individual's right to private property; the government's right to issue currency, levy taxes, and borrow money; and the rights of businesses and consumers to enter agreements and to resolve their differences through legal channels. (Immigrants marvel at how easy it is to start a business in America.) Few people believe that laws regarding child labor, toxic waste, food and drug purity, and the financial markets should be repealed.

For some 90 percent of the population, the political and economic arguments really amount to whether the federal government should account for 20, 22, or 18 percent of the economy. Legislators of both parties in both houses of Congress grab as much federal money as they can carry back to their constituents, and the constituents don't send it back to Washington in protest.

Among voters, despite an occasionally intense partisanship and lack of knowledge about economic policy, there is general agreement on the role of government in the U.S. economy, which is to:

- Provide the public goods and services that society requires

- Issue currency, levy taxes, and borrow money

- Maintain economic order, stability, and growth

Let's examine each of these roles.

The Government Provides Public Goods

Public goods are those that society requires and that benefit everyone but that the private sector has little or no economic incentive to provide. Public goods benefit everyone, whether they pay for them or want them or not. The most basic public good is defense of the populace from attack and invasion. This begins at our borders and extends inward to the formation of police forces at the federal (the Federal Bureau of Investigation), state, and local levels. Other public goods include the highway system and traffic lights, clean air and water, and public education.

ECONOTALK

A **public good** is one that society requires and that benefits everyone but that the private sector has no economic incentive to provide. Public goods such as national defense, local policing, and clean air and water are made available to everyone, and everyone benefits from them.

There is a trade-off—as always in economics—between public goods and private goods. Societies allocate their resources to both in a mix that works for them. Some societies employ a mix weighted toward private goods, while others prefer a mix weighted toward public goods. In general, the more developed an economy becomes, the more resources it devotes to public goods.

The government provides public goods by administering the budget and overseeing the delivery of the goods. However, in most cases the goods are actually provided by the private sector. The personnel for the armed services are an exception, but even for defense, most of the equipment and weapons are manufactured by the private sector. Also, in the 2000s war in Iraq, the government used private security and support forces.

Currency, Taxes, and Borrowing

The federal government issues the nation's currency, levies taxes, and, when taxes don't cover federal spending, borrows money by issuing government securities. These three functions are subject to debate, especially taxes and deficit spending, which we cover in Chapter 13. Currency arouses little debate, although some people object to the Federal Reserve's attempts to control the money supply, a subject covered in Part 4. Debate over taxes and spending intensified when the recession of 2008–2009 led to higher deficits on top of those piled up during the preceding expansion.

ECONOTIP

In economics, the term *government* often means government at all levels: federal, state, and local. For instance, the *G* in C + I + G includes all three levels of government. In this book, I have generally indicated which levels of government are under discussion.

Order in the Economy!

The federal government tries to maintain order and growth in the economy. Disorder in the economy leads to social unrest and political upheaval. Lack of economic growth leads to unemployment, which also generates unrest. If poor economic growth persists, a nation may even wind up unable to defend itself from attack or invasion. For instance, the economy of the USSR under socialism could not sustain itself during the Cold War, which led to the breakup of the Soviet Union.

Most modern governments manage their economies through policies that aim to maintain a stable currency and economic growth at a rate that balances inflation and unemployment. In communist economies, such as China and North Korea, the government uses central planning to gauge demand and make production decisions. This stands in sharp contrast to the role of government in a market economy. In a market economy, the government usually acts as a referee, ensuring that the market works properly and achieves the goal of delivering the greatest good to the greatest number of people.

Toward that end, the U.S. government regulates certain activities in the market. For example, the Department of Justice occasionally launches *anti-trust suits* to limit monopolistic business practices, as it did against Microsoft in the late 1990s. The federal government will occasionally levy tariffs and erect other barriers to trade to protect a domestic market from foreign competition, as it did with certain steel imports in 2002. The Securities and Exchange Commission initiates suits against companies that violate securities law, as it did in 2001 and 2002 and again in 2009 and 2010.

ECONOTALK

Anti-trust suits are legal actions initiated by the Department of Justice to stop companies from engaging in anti-competitive practices or from becoming so large that they constitute a monopoly. Anti-competitive practices include any agreements or actions designed to limit competition, such as agreements among competitors to fix prices at a certain level.

In other words, society uses the government to limit behaviors that could distort the workings of the market for the benefit of a few unscrupulous or powerful competitors at the expense of everyone else.

The Government Share of the Economy

The most comparable measure of tax rates among nations is their percent of GDP. By that measure, U.S. taxes are well below those of most other countries in the Organization for Economic Cooperation and Development (OECD). According to the OECD, total U.S. taxes—including state taxes—average about 28 percent of GDP, compared with about 34 percent in the rest of the OECD. Opponents of taxes compare metrics such as tax rates, but what matters is what those rates are applied to, and definitions of income vary among nations.

With 28 percent of the U.S. economy accounted for by government at all levels, private spending makes up the other 72 percent. That 28 percent figure breaks down as shown in Figure 12.1.

As the figure shows, of the 28 percent of GDP that government spending represents, direct federal programs (programs administered by the federal government) represent 16 percent, while state and local spending represents the other 12 percent. Of that 12 percent, about 9 percent is raised by the states and local jurisdictions, and about 2 percent comes from federal government grants. The two numbers (9 and 2) don't add up to 12 because of rounding differences in the government data.

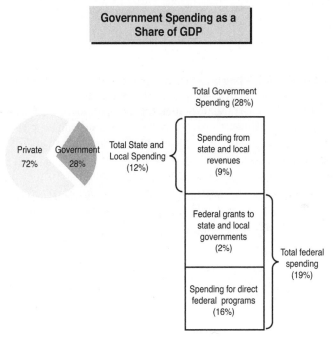

Figure 12.1

The government share of GDP is substantially larger in most European economies. In the 2000s in Italy, France, and the United Kingdom, government expenditures accounted for 45 to 55 percent of GDP, and in Germany, Spain, and Ireland, 40 to 45 percent.

Budgeting Billions

As is the case in most financial situations, understanding the budget is the key to understanding the government's finances. Each year the federal government undergoes a budgeting process in which the White House Office of Management and Budget (OMB) develops a budget that the president proposes to Congress.

Congress reviews this proposed budget and goes through its own budget process. In that process, Congress passes a budget resolution with targets, expressed in dollars, for total spending and revenues and for the surplus or deficit. Congress also allocates total spending between *discretionary spending* and *mandatory spending*. Finally, Congress approves its spending and revenue bills, which then are turned over to the president to be signed.

 ECONOTALK

Discretionary spending accounts for about one-third of the federal budget and pays for activities that require annual approval and appropriation of the amount to be spent. **Mandatory spending** accounts for the rest of the budget and pays for entitlements—payments that citizens are entitled to because of their age, income, disability, or military service—and interest on the federal debt.

The distinction between discretionary and mandatory spending is key. Discretionary spending accounts for only about one-third of all federal spending (although it can reach as high as 38 percent in some fiscal years). This amount is what the president and Congress must decide to spend in the next year, which they do by means of 13 annual appropriations bills, which Congress passes and the president signs. These bills allocate money to activities such as the FBI, Coast Guard, housing, education, space programs, highways, defense, and foreign aid.

Mandatory spending accounts for about two-thirds of federal spending and is authorized by permanent laws, not by the 13 annual appropriations bills. These include entitlements, such as Social Security, Medicare, veterans' benefits, and the Supplemental Nutrition Assistance Program (food stamps). They are called entitlements because citizens are entitled to the benefits based upon their age, income, military service, or other criteria (and, usually, the fact that they and their employers paid taxes to fund the programs). Mandatory spending also includes interest on the national debt.

Mandatory spending could be changed by changing the laws that govern the entitlements; otherwise, that money has to be spent according to the law. Changing the laws regarding entitlements is politically quite difficult. Meanwhile, annual appropriations, especially for activities such as defense and education, are not truly discretionary. The allocation of that spending may be up for debate—foreign aid, for example, is usually controversial—but huge sums for discretionary spending always wind up in the budget.

The federal government's fiscal year begins on October 1 and ends on September 30. During the fiscal year, the relevant government agencies spend and disburse the budgeted money. As they do, the agencies—OMB, congressional committees, and General Accounting Office (GAO)—all monitor the amounts spent and the effectiveness of the programs being funded. (The GAO is the main auditing department of Congress.)

Where It Comes From: Composition of Receipts

The federal budget is managed like most household and business budgets: money comes in from various sources of revenue and goes out to pay various expenses. If revenue does not cover the expenses in a given period, the household or business borrows the money to meet the expenses.

Increasing levels of debt usually indicate a need for a course of action other than continued borrowing. Economically, increasing taxes can make sense, as we'll see in Chapter 13. Politically, it can mean professional suicide for the president and legislators. It's the old story: everyone wants to go to heaven, but nobody wants to die. People want government services, but they don't want to pay for them.

ECONOTIP

The percentage of government receipts from various sources varies with economic conditions and policy changes. Also, when you see budget numbers in the press or at the White House website, bear in mind that administrations may use optimistic economic forecasts, which can lead to overstated tax receipts and understated deficits.

Income taxes on individuals account for about 45 percent of total federal revenue. That percentage may sound low to you, but payroll taxes, which are paid by individuals and businesses, account for another 35 percent. Payroll taxes include taxes for Social Security, Medicare, and unemployment insurance. That brings total revenue from income and payroll taxes to about 80 percent.

Corporate income taxes contribute about 10 percent of total revenue. The other 10 percent comes from excise taxes, estate and gift taxes, customs duties, and miscellaneous revenues, such as fines. Figure 12.2 shows the breakdown of federal revenues by source for 2010 and projections for 2020.

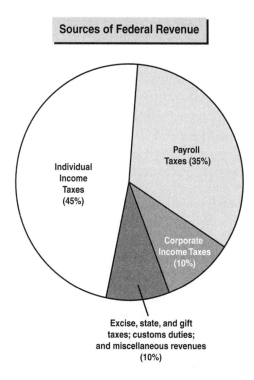

Figure 12.2

Where It Goes: Composition of Expenditures

Recall that two-thirds of the federal budget is spent on entitlements and other mandatory programs. Of these mandatory expenditures, the largest one is for Social Security, which accounts for about 20 percent of total federal expenditures. The next largest mandatory expenditure is for Medicare (12 percent) and Medicaid (8 percent), which add up to 20 percent of total federal expenditures. So about 40 percent of the federal budget is going to Social Security and subsidized health care. Other *means-tested entitlements* and mandatory payments and *net interest* on the federal debt add up to another 22 percent. So the 40 percent for Social Security and subsidized health care and the 22 percent for other entitlements and net interest equal about 62 percent of total expenditures.

> **ECONOTALK**
>
> **Means-tested entitlements** are those that people are eligible for only if they meet certain criteria, which usually have to do with income, age, assets, and other measures of a person's financial and living condition. **Net interest** is the interest paid out on government securities, minus interest earned. The federal government earns interest on loans it extends domestically (such as student loans) and to foreign governments, and on its holdings of foreign government bonds. (The U.S. government does not usually buy corporate stocks and bonds.)

Figure 12.3 (on the next page) shows the breakdown of federal expenditures for 2010 and projected expenditures for 2020.

Here's why it's so difficult to reduce federal expenditures. The entitlements are mainly agreements between the government and certain blocks of citizens to provide retirement or disability income (in the case of Social Security) or assistance for people who need health care (in the case of Medicare and Medicaid) or food (in the case of the Supplemental Nutrition Assistance Program). These are difficult areas in which to reduce spending.

How discretionary is discretionary spending? The United States cannot decide to spend nothing on defense for a year or two. As for nondefense spending, programs such as government-financed research in science and technology require ongoing support or they will fall apart. The same goes for programs that support education, transportation, and law enforcement.

Mandated payments have to be funded unless Congress changes the laws governing the entitlement programs, Social Security, and Medicare. Add Defense, Homeland Security, Agriculture, and the other departments, and you've got a huge budget that's extremely difficult to reduce.

The president and legislators—and lobbyists—do argue over allocations for certain programs within the departments, such as specific weapons systems or housing or education initiatives. And the president and Congress do reallocate priorities, as when President Reagan called for significantly increased defense spending. Also, President Obama's projections call for lower appropriations for defense and nondefense spending (as a percentage of the budget) by 2020.

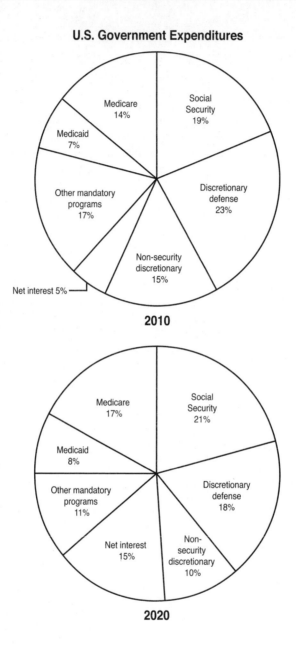

Figure 12.3

(Source: Office of Management and Budget)

Yet no one seems capable of stopping the growth of the federal budget, mainly because no one wants their government benefits (or contracts) reduced. Meanwhile, government also includes state and city expenditures, and many state expenditures are funded partly by federal tax dollars. In fact, most Americans agree—even if they think they don't—that government at various levels should represent about 25 to 30 percent of the economy, which it does in most years. That percentage has remained fairly steady over the past few decades. The problem is that we have not been paying for it as we spend it.

Whether the current system is fair is debatable. Some observers feel it may be a bit too progressive, given that at least 40 percent of the populace pays no income taxes. However, those people do pay payroll taxes and sales taxes, so technically they are taxpayers. Other observers feel that high marginal tax rates discourage entrepreneurial behavior and still others see corporate taxes as a deterrent to business activity. High income and corporate taxes may encourage noncompliance with tax laws rather than discouraging entrepreneurial activity. Those who favor corporate income taxes note that corporations benefit from government services and should therefore pay taxes.

The problem remains unsolved: people don't want to pay for the government services they want. This has led to one of the key issues in funding the U.S. government—concerns about the viability of Social Security and Medicare.

The Biggies: Social Security and Medicare

Social Security and Medicare (and Medicaid, which I'll lump in with Medicare in this discussion) each account for about 20 percent of federal expenditures. However, Social Security tax payments go into the general revenue fund and are used to fund programs other than Social Security. For the past several decades, the workforce has been larger than the retiree population, and payments into the system have exceeded benefits paid out, creating a Social Security surplus. That surplus is the amount in a given fiscal year by which the amount collected in Social Security taxes exceeds the payments to beneficiaries. This raises the subject of the *Social Security Trust Fund*, a topic of great confusion and controversy. An identical dynamic has been going on in the Medicare program, which also maintains a trust fund.

ECONOTALK

The **Social Security Trust Fund,** created in 1983, is an accounting convention used to track the money collected as Social Security taxes but spent on other programs. The fund holds U.S. bonds, which are essentially IOUs written by the U.S. government to itself and are not negotiable on the open market. It is not a trust fund in the usual sense of the term, with money invested in marketable securities.

The Social Security Trust Fund

Social Security has always been a pay-as-you-go program, with taxes on workers used to pay the beneficiaries. That works as long as there are enough workers to fund current retirees' benefits. But in the early 1980s, officials foresaw the day when there would not be enough workers to support the retirees.

The National Commission on Social Security Reform was created in 1983 to examine Social Security funding. This commission was headed by future Federal Reserve chairman (and future opponent of taxes) Alan Greenspan and is known as the Greenspan Commission. This commission recommended raising the Social Security tax, with the provision that the surplus funds go into a trust fund to secure the benefits for those paying into the Social Security system.

The Social Security Trust Fund does have assets: treasury bonds in the amount that the Social Security program has loaned to the federal government each year—the Social Security surplus. In other words, the Social Security surplus funds go into general revenue with the rest of your taxes and are *spent by the federal government every year.* In return, the government issues special, non-negotiable Treasury bonds to the trust fund. In the years since the fund was created, it has accumulated over $2 trillion in government bonds.

However, the Social Security Trust Fund does not fund anything. It is simply a claim maintained by a federal program against future revenues or future debt sold to the public. Those who believe in the financial viability of the trust fund point out that the features of the Social Security program—the terms of eligibility and the benefits—are set by law, and that is true. However, that law can be changed by Congress.

Those who see the Treasury bonds in the trust fund as real assets are correct—they *are* U.S. government bonds. But those bonds do not represent actual money saved and invested, as securities in a private pension fund or a true trust fund would.

All of this gives rise to one of the largest questions in public finance: is Social Security headed for a crisis?

Social Security Crisis—Coming or Not?

First, what do we mean by Social Security crisis? A few people define it as the point where the Social Security program starts collecting less in taxes than it pays out in benefits. That's the year when Social Security no longer operates on a pay-as-you-go basis. In its annual Performance and Accountability Report for 2009, the Social Security Administration (SSA) puts that date at 2016, one year sooner than the estimate in its 2008 report. Thus, in 2016 the Social Security program will need to redeem bonds—the government will have to start paying them back—to make up the shortfall between Social Security taxes collected and benefits to be paid. (What occurs at that point might be termed the Social Security deficit.)

Other people define the crisis as the point where the Social Security Trust Fund itself runs out of Treasury bonds to redeem. This is the point at which the program is insolvent—when it is unable to pay its obligations as they come due. The same 2009 SSA report projected that the trust fund will be exhausted in 2037. That means that at *current* tax rates and benefit levels, the fund would be depleted in 2037.

The actual crisis occurs if, or when, increased taxes or debt become a drag on the economy or when investors start demanding onerous interest rates on Treasury securities. No one can forecast those dates, because they depend on the growth and performance of the U.S. economy. The government knows that benefits can be paid only by redeeming the bonds and that the trust fund is an accounting convention. So reform of the program is almost a certainty in the not-too-distant future.

No one seriously posits that the U.S. government will default on its Treasury obligations, let alone go broke. Viability, of a sort, until 2037 is more or less assured. But those who say there's no need for reform either don't understand the nature of the trust fund or are unaware that benefits must be paid in cash, not in non-negotiable Treasury bonds. In truth, the 1983 Social Security solution did nothing to shore up Social Security. It was essentially a tax increase, and the proceeds went into the general revenue fund in exchange for Treasury bonds that were not even sold to investors.

Voters who believe that their benefits are secure are counting on one or both of two things: first, that legislators will not vote to raise the age of eligibility, lower benefits, or means-test eligibility; second, that economic and productivity growth will fund future benefits even with a workforce that will be significantly smaller than the number of retirees. However, neither of those are sure things, or even likely.

Government Agencies That Affect the Economy

Virtually every government agency affects the economy by its very existence, by doing its work, and by keeping people gainfully employed. But some government entities exist mainly to deal with the nation's business, economic, and financial matters. Here we briefly examine the most important ones.

The Treasury (www.ustreas.gov)

The Department of the Treasury was established by an act of the first Congress and has been overseeing the nation's money ever since. Key areas of the department include the following:

- **Internal Revenue Service:** Assesses and collects taxes within the country and is the largest of the Treasury's bureaus

- **Office of the Comptroller of the Currency:** Regulates and supervises national banks

- **Bureau of Printing and Engraving:** Designs and manufactures U.S. currency

- **U.S. Mint:** Designs and manufactures coins

- **Bureau of the Public Debt:** Borrows money to finance the deficit and administers the public debt

- **Financial Management Service:** Receives and distributes public funds, maintains government accounts, and prepares reports on the government's finances

Along with a few other bureaus, the U.S. Customs Service, the Secret Service, and (of all things) the Bureau of Alcohol, Tobacco, and Firearms also come under the Treasury Department. (Alcohol and tobacco are heavily taxed, but how do guns figure in this?)

Department of Commerce (www.commerce.gov)

Established by an Act of Congress in 1903, the Department of Commerce deals with commercial and industrial matters within the nation's borders. Significant areas include:

- **Bureau of Economic Analysis:** Compiles and analyzes economic data for the government and the public, with assistance from the Economic and Statistics Administration

- **Census Bureau:** Compiles and analyzes demographic data on the population

- **Patent and Trademark Office:** Ensures that inventors can register and benefit from ownership of their inventions

- **Economic Development Administration:** Stimulates job, commercial, and industrial growth in economically distressed areas

- **Small Business Administration:** Promotes the formation and sound management of small business

- **Minority Business Development Agency:** Promotes formation of minority businesses

- **International Trade Administration:** Encourages and monitors export and import activity

Federal Reserve (www.federalreserve.gov)

The Federal Reserve (the Fed) regulates the banking system, implements monetary policy, maintains the stability of the financial system, and provides certain services to financial institutions. The Fed is so important to the U.S. economy that it is discussed in depth in Part 4.

Council of Economic Advisors

The President's Council of Economic Advisors (www.whitehouse.gov/administration/eop/cea/) is a team of three professionals from the worlds of business, finance, and economics appointed by the president and served by a staff of economists and statisticians. The council monitors and interprets economic developments in the nation, appraises the effects of various programs, and advises the president on economic policy.

Regulatory Agencies

Federal regulatory agencies, such as the Federal Aeronautics Administration, the Food and Drug Administration, the Federal Communications Commission, among many others, affect segments of the economy by virtue of the roles they play in important industries. Essentially, these agencies oversee their respective industries and try to balance the industry's interests against those of the public and the economy.

State and Local Governments

Finally, state and local governments work to ensure that their economies remain robust. Through the power to tax, spend, regulate, and support programs that benefit education and the industrial infrastructure, these governments strongly affect business and household formation, employment, construction, and other key economic activities.

In the Great Recession and its aftermath, most state and many local governments faced serious financial challenges. The situation regarding increasing taxes and decreasing services at the state and local levels resembles that at the national level. Nobody wants to do either. But states and cities cannot print money and do not have virtually unlimited access to the debt markets. They must be more realistic about raising taxes, cutting services, and avoiding debt and must manage their budgets far more aggressively. When they do raise or reduce taxes, the effect is similar to that at the national level but on a far smaller scale. We learn about the effect of changes in taxes in Chapter 13.

Government: The Enemy?

Although it's fashionable to knock the government, the U.S. economy wouldn't be the powerhouse that it is without it. Aside from the government's share of GDP, economic policies have clearly contributed to the stability and growth of the U.S. economy.

Moreover, in a democracy, people get the government they vote for. Thus, if the government appears to be at odds with itself, perhaps society is at odds with itself. If elected officials won't discuss economic realities honestly, perhaps voters have given them no incentive to do so. Fortunately, the U.S. economy appears to be sound enough to absorb these imperfections and still provide one of the highest standards of living in the world.

The Least You Need to Know

- All government spending amounts to about 28 percent of gross domestic product (GDP). Of that 28 percent, about 16 percent goes to federal programs, and 12 percent goes to state and local programs.
- Discretionary spending accounts for one-third of the federal budget and requires annual appropriation of the amount to be spent. Mandatory spending accounts for the remaining two-thirds of the budget and pays for entitlements and interest on the federal debt.
- Although elected officials talk about cutting taxes and reducing spending, either is extremely difficult to do because the taxes and spending pay for programs that people want—even if they don't want to pay for them.
- The Social Security system will face a crisis when the baby boomers retire and payroll taxes will no longer cover the payments to beneficiaries.
- The real issue between the government and citizens is the mix of public and private goods society wants.

Fiscal Policy and Economic Growth

In This Chapter

- Goals of fiscal policy
- How fiscal policy works
- The record of tax, spend, and borrow

Although two-thirds of the federal government's expenditures are mandatory and many of the discretionary expenditures are not all that discretionary, government expenditures strongly influence the direction of the economy and the pace of growth. Much of that influence is long term. For instance, Social Security and the U.S. military didn't grow to their mammoth proportions in a few years, but rather over many decades. Yet even in a given year, U.S. government spending can influence economic growth.

Moreover there are decisions about taxes, which may be even more important. Cutting taxes is popular, so elected officials are always happy to talk about it and fairly often actually do it (as President Kennedy did in 1963, President Reagan did in 1981, and President George W. Bush did in 2001, 2002, and 2003). Officials also occasionally raise taxes, which can affect the economy—and their careers.

This chapter examines fiscal policy—the budget decisions of the federal government—and its consequences. It also covers deficit spending and the national debt, both of which have been major topics in the public discussion about the economy.

ECONOTIP

Any fiscal policy—spending or tax increases or decreases—will generate both positive and negative impacts. The question is which impacts are greater and cause the most benefit given the state of the economy and the needs of the people in it.

Government's Unique Situation

As you know, if any element of the C + I + G + (Ex – Im) formula increases, then gross domestic product (GDP)—total demand—increases. If the *G* portion— government spending at all levels—increases, then GDP increases. Similarly, if government spending decreases, then GDP decreases.

When it comes to financial management, four characteristics of the government set it apart from households and businesses (the *C* and *I* in the formula):

- **Government has the power to tax, which gives it greater control over its revenue.** Federal, state, and local governments can mandate higher taxes and increase their revenues. Households and businesses have the more difficult task of selling their labor, goods, and services in order to raise revenue.

- **By increasing or decreasing taxes, the government affects households' level of disposable income (after-tax income).** A tax increase will decrease disposable income, because it takes money out of households. A tax decrease will increase disposable income, because it leaves households with more money. Disposable income is the main factor driving consumer demand, which accounts for two-thirds of total demand.

- **The federal government can finance budget deficits by borrowing in the financial markets.** Investors consider U.S. government bonds to be risk-free, because they are backed by the taxing power of the government. States and cities also issue bonds to finance deficits. These bonds, however, are considered riskier because the *tax base* of the state or city could erode.

- **The federal government—and only the federal government—can *print more money.*** Like raising taxes, this has potential economic consequences (in the form of higher inflation) as well as political consequences. Nevertheless, the federal government does have that option, which is certainly not open to households and businesses.

ECONOTALK

The **tax base** in a nation, region, state, or city is the number of workers and businesses who can be taxed. The term usually refers to income taxes, but in the case of states and cities, it also refers to sales and property taxes.

The term *print more money* doesn't really mean that the government just prints money. In fact, some people say that the government is printing money when it is only borrowing it by selling bonds to investors or other governments. That is not printing money.

When the government (that is, the U.S. Treasury) issues bonds to itself (purchased by the Federal Reserve), it is printing money. But even then the Fed is not literally printing money. Instead it creates the money through the banking system, as explained in Part 4.

These unique characteristics set the government apart from the other players in the economy. They also position the federal government to formulate and implement economic policy.

Fiscal Fundamentals

Fiscal policy is the general name for the federal government's taxation and expenditure decisions and activities, particularly as they affect the economy. (Monetary policy refers to policies that affect interest rates and the money supply.)

Figure 13.1 (on the next page) shows how C + I + G add up to determine the equilibrium level of GDP. (For convenience, we're assuming that net exports [Ex – Im] are zero.) Line C represents consumption by consumers. Line C + I represents consumption by consumers plus investment by businesses. Line C + I + G represents consumption plus investment plus government spending.

The 45-degree line shows all the points at which total spending equals gross domestic product. At any point on that line, the quantity demanded by the households, businesses, and government in the economy (total spending) equals the amount being produced (GDP). Whenever total demand equals total spending, the economy is in equilibrium.

Where is the actual equilibrium point for the economy? Where the total demand of households, businesses, and government—C + I + G—equals their production. That equilibrium point occurs where the line C + I + G intersects the 45-degree line. At that point, which is point E on the chart, total spending (total demand) and total production (GDP) are equal.

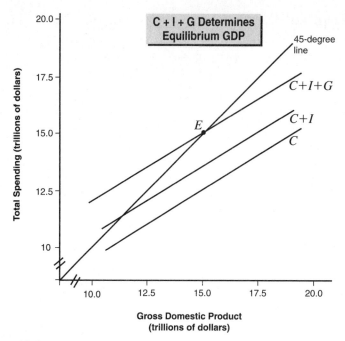

Figure 13.1

What About Taxes?

Figure 13.1 ignores taxes, but they are a crucial element in fiscal policy. Taxes lower households' disposable income. The amount collected in taxes doesn't find its way into consumption (C), but if the government spends every dollar that it collects in taxes, then that amount does find its way into total demand through government expenditures. When that occurs, the GDP remains unaffected by taxes. The size of the economy is the same whether people choose to produce and consume private goods (sportswear) or public goods (army uniforms). The mix of goods doesn't affect the level of GDP, as long as the total amount spent on them doesn't change.

What happens when the government collects more in taxes than it spends? Total spending—and therefore the equilibrium level of GDP—decreases. Suppose that the money for army uniforms is collected but not spent. In that case, there's no need to manufacture the uniforms, no need to staff the uniform factory, and no need to pay the workers, who now have less income to devote to consumption.

In general, when the government brings in more in taxes than it spends, it reduces disposable income and slows the growth of the economy. So the fiscal policy prescription to stabilize an overheated economy is higher taxes.

In times of inflation—when too much demand is bidding up prices—a tax increase, coupled with no increase in government spending, will dampen the upward pressure on prices. The tax increase lowers demand by lowering disposable income. As long as that reduction in consumer demand is not offset by an increase in government demand, total demand decreases.

A decrease in taxes has the opposite effect on income, demand, and GDP. It will boost all three, which is why people cry out for a tax cut when the economy is sluggish. When the government decreases taxes, disposable income increases. That translates to higher demand (spending) and increased production (GDP). So the fiscal policy prescription for a sluggish economy and high unemployment is lower taxes.

Spending policy is the mirror image of tax policy. If the government were to keep taxes the same but decrease its spending, it would have the same effect as a tax increase, but through a slightly different channel. Instead of decreasing disposable income and decreasing consumption (C), a decrease in government spending decreases the G in C + I + G directly. The lower demand flows through to the larger economy, slows growth in income and employment, and dampens inflationary pressure.

Likewise, an increase in government spending will increase G and boost demand and production and reduce unemployment.

Those are the fundamentals of fiscal policy, and they are summed up in Figure 13.2.

	Fiscal Policy Prescriptions	
	Taxes	Spending
Overheated Economy (high demand and inflation)	Increase	Decrease
Sluggish Economy (low demand and high unemployment)	Decrease	Increase

Figure 13.2

To dampen economic growth and inflationary pressure, the government can increase taxes and keep spending constant, or decrease spending and keep taxes constant. To stimulate growth and reduce unemployment, the government can decrease taxes and keep spending constant, or increase spending and keep taxes constant.

Finally, the government can pursue its fiscal policy objectives more aggressively by simultaneously adjusting both taxes and spending. For instance, in a sluggish economy, the government could decrease taxes *and* increase spending at the same time. Each could be adjusted either by small amounts, so that neither taxes nor spending are changed too radically, or by large amounts to deliver a stronger dose of fiscal stimulus. Similarly, in an overheated economy, the government could increase taxes *and* decrease spending, if it wanted to dampen growth (and enrage voters).

THE REAL WORLD

The political dimensions of fiscal policy tend to contribute to confusion. Conservatives lobby hard for reductions in taxes without discussing ways to reduce spending. Why? Because nobody wants to see their government services cut. Liberals argue for increases in government services without mentioning that they will increase the deficit or taxes.

It takes no imagination or political courage to sell lower taxes or more free services to voters who have no understanding of economics. But it works—and the United States has the national debt to show for it.

After the economic difficulties of the 1970s and the sharp recession brought about by the Federal Reserve in the early 1980s, the United States took a new approach to encouraging economic growth: constant fiscal stimulus coupled with relatively loose monetary policy. The fiscal stimulus (tax cuts and deficit spending) led to the towering levels of federal debt that the United States has piled up (discussed later in this chapter). The loose monetary policy led to the 1990s run ups in dot-com and tech-stock prices, and the 2000s run-up in housing prices. Constant fiscal and monetary stimulus are not recipes for sustainable long-term economic growth.

Other Issues in Fiscal Policy

To keep things simple, the previous section omitted three other aspects of fiscal policy: the automatic stabilizing influence of fiscal policy, the multiplier effect, and the propensity to spend or save.

First, fiscal policy exerts an automatic stabilizing effect on the economy, even when the government makes no explicit changes in its tax or spending plans.

When the economy contracts, tax receipts automatically decrease (because incomes decrease). This effect is magnified by progressive taxation, our system of applying higher tax rates to higher incomes. Workers who are laid off or lose their overtime pay automatically fall into a lower tax bracket. Their lower tax bills will partially offset the effect of their lost income. Similarly, when incomes rise, particularly during inflation, *bracket creep* pushes people into higher tax brackets. The higher taxes they pay takes money out of their pockets—money they can no longer use to bid prices up even higher.

ECONOTALK

Bracket creep occurs when inflationary pressure increases wages and pushes a worker into a higher tax bracket. This puts a double whammy on the worker, who loses purchasing power—wage-push inflation often increases prices faster than wages—and pays more in taxes. But it helps keep inflationary pressures under control.

Government spending also acts as an automatic stabilizer, especially during downturns. The federal government tends to maintain its general level of spending during recessions, which ensures a solid baseline level of demand from the *G* in C + I + G. Also, programs of unemployment insurance and public assistance help to ease the burden of tough times on households. (This was the case in the 2008–2009 recession, although extensions of the benefits periods had to be legislated and re-legislated.)

Second, the multiplier (covered in Chapter 7) will boost the effect of an increase or reduction in taxes or spending. For instance, an extra dollar of government spending will flow through the economy and, by being repeatedly re-spent, will magnify the stimulus provided by that incremental dollar. Likewise, a dollar of reduced spending will take a dollar out of the economy, and the multiplier applies to that as well.

Finally, like the multiplier, the propensities to spend and to save are at work. If the government reduces taxes to stimulate consumption, but households save the money rather than spend it, consumption will not rise, nor will investment. If people save the money, they are sitting on their wallets and consumption remains low. If consumption is low, businesses won't invest. In the 1990s and 2000s, this was a problem in the application of fiscal stimulus in Japan, where people tend to save increases in income.

THE REAL WORLD

The propensity to spend or to save can alter the effect of fiscal policy. President George W. Bush's reduction in income taxes generated controversy; critics noted that over 50 percent of the cuts went to the wealthiest 1 percent of taxpayers. But if the goal was to stimulate savings—rather than consumption— that may not have been a bad thing. Wealthy households have a higher propensity to save, so giving a disproportionately large share of the tax reduction to them could have stimulated savings and, by extension, investment.

If, however, the goal was to stimulate consumption, more of the tax cuts should have gone to lower income households. Actually, the only clearly articulated goal was to reduce taxes, and factors such as the housing boom and bust obscured the effects.

Of Deficits and Debt

Aside from taxes, few topics in economics excite more emotion than *deficit spending* and the national debt. Citizens decry the fact that the government spends more money than it takes in (at least, when the party they oppose is doing it), but they blanch at the idea of decreased services or increased taxes. Each of the two major political parties accuses the other of fiscal irresponsibility, and they are both correct.

ECONOTALK

Deficits occur when government expenditures exceed revenues. The practice of maintaining or increasing expenditures when revenues will not cover them is called **deficit spending.** Surpluses occur when government revenues exceed expenditures.

As of 2010, the national debt totaled about $13 trillion—a lot of money. Of that amount, $8.4 trillion was held by the private sector and $4.5 trillion was held in government accounts. I'll discuss the growth of the deficit later in this chapter. First, however, let's look at the two prevailing views of deficits and the national debt. One is that deficits and debt harm the economy, the other is that they don't matter.

I am lumping the two issues—deficits and the national debt—together in this discussion. This is proper given the reality of the federal budget, which ran a deficit for all but five years from 1960 to 2001 (1969 and 1998–2001). Continual deficit spending has created the $13 trillion U.S. national debt.

However, it would also be proper to treat the deficit and national debt separately. That's because a person could believe in the value of countercyclical deficit spending but not believe in accumulating a large national debt. In other words, the government could run deficits in years that required economic stimulus, and pay that debt down with surplus revenues in years of expansion. But unfortunately, that has not been the policy.

Stay Out of Debt!

People who believe that deficits and the national debt do matter point out that:

- Continual deficit spending displays lack of fiscal discipline on the part of the government and on the part of the citizens, who want government goodies without having to pay for them.

- This lack of fiscal discipline spills over into the private sector, where households and businesses have become addicted to debt.

- Interest payments on the national debt represent a substantial claim on tax revenues that could be better spent on other things.

- Future generations will bear the burden of today's debt and either have to pay the interest on it or pay down the principal, or both.

- Deficit spending and high debt limit the government's fiscal policy options: if deficit spending is the norm, how much more (deficit) spending will be needed to stimulate a sluggish economy?

- Foreign entities now hold about $3 trillion of U.S. government securities. If their willingness to buy or hold that debt diminishes, we would have to absorb it.

These points are hard to contradict, except perhaps for the last one: foreign entities seem to enjoy the safety, liquidity, and interest rates provided by U.S. government securities.

No, Debt's Okay!

The arguments in favor of continued deficit spending and high national debt are:

- The size of the national debt or budget deficit is not an indicator of the condition of the economy. Other factors, such as growth, productivity, employment, and price stability are all more important. The entire issue is one of politics, not economics.

• We owe the debt to ourselves (mostly) and therefore should not be overly concerned about paying it back. Also, we pay the interest on the debt mainly to ourselves, and that money remains in the economy.

• Although the burden of the deficit is passed on to future generations, so are the Treasury securities and, more important, the assets financed with the debt.

• The deficits and the national debt have not grown substantially relative to other measures of the economy's magnitude, including GDP, total income, and total assets in the economy.

• Paying down the national debt is not something the nation has to do because the debt can be rolled over indefinitely—that is, continually refinanced by issuing new government securities.

• Deficit spending has helped the nation to establish a solid baseline level of demand and has contributed to the outstanding U.S. record of economic growth.

Economists' Two Cents' Worth

Elected officials, candidates for office, and the public tend to move between the two poles. Economists themselves view the issue as quite complex, but on balance generally believe that:

• Future generations bear an unfair burden if the debt being passed on to them is not accompanied by a corresponding level of productive capital in the form of roads, water treatment systems, and other public infrastructure.

• Debt in foreign hands sends money out of the country, but this may be offset if the debt is used to finance infrastructure that produces additional income.

• We make the interest and principal payments (mostly) to ourselves. However, these amount to transfer payments when the people paying the taxes are not the same as the people holding the securities and receiving the interest and principal payments.

- Indefinite and unbridled deficit spending can lead to inflation and, potentially, economic instability. It can undermine credibility in the government's ability to manage the economy.

The Nobel Prize–winning economist Milton Friedman (who you will meet in Part 5) said it best: "There is no such thing as a free lunch." Is it conceivable that each generation of citizens could consistently demand more public goods and services than they are willing to pay for and generate no economic consequences? Doesn't the situation looming ahead for Social Security (described in Chapter 12) indicate that even the government can run out of rope? Might an aging population find itself unable to handle the level of debt the nation continues to incur? Also, how much of that debt has gone into productive plant and equipment? Our review of the budget in Chapter 12 showed that most of the budget, if not the deficit, is in fact not going into productive plant and equipment.

Also if interest rates increase, won't the interest payments on the national debt—which in most years consumes 5 to 8 percent of the budget—rise? In the economically difficult late 1970s, they accounted for 14 percent of the federal budget. In 2010, the Congressional Budget Office forecasted a return to that exact percentage for the 2020 U.S. federal budget.

THE REAL WORLD

Given the difficulty of reducing government spending, the political right conceived a plan to starve the beast as they put it—to run up so much debt that it became impossible for the government to keep piling up debt.

The effect has been to call into question the long-term creditworthiness of the U.S. government in some quarters, or at least the wisdom of deficit spending. However, although it resisted expansion of health-care coverage in 2009 and 2010, the right has not suggested reducing Social Security, Medicare, military, or other major expenditures. The main result of this plan has been towering debt—and Republican opposition to deficit spending when Democrats do it.

A Look at the Recent Record

The table on the following page provides some perspective on how the U.S. national debt reached $13 trillion.

U.S. National Debt and Percent Increases 1950-2008

Year	National Debt	Percent Increase
1950	$257 billion	
1960	$286 billion	11
1970	$371 billion	31
1980	$908 billion	145
1990	$3.2 trillion	252
2000	$5.7 trillion	78
2010	$12.9 trillion	127

Source: U.S. Treasury

From 1970 to 2000, the national debt rose from $371 billion to $5.7 trillion, a more than 13-fold increase in 30 years. In the preceding 30 years, which included World War II and the mobilization for the war in Vietnam, the national debt rose from $43 million to $389 million, an 8-fold increase. From 2000 to 2010, after a bit of moderation in the 1990s, the national debt more than doubled, to $12.9 trillion.

The largest sustained rise in the national debt occurred from 1980 to 1992, when it rose from $930 million to $4 trillion. Ironically, this is the period of the administrations of Ronald Reagan (1980–1988) and George H. W. Bush (1988–1992)—ironic because Republicans had long been associated in the public mind with fiscal responsibility. Indeed, President Reagan regularly spoke of "those tax-and-spend Democrats." The program of his administration was to spend and borrow after cutting taxes. As a result, the national debt tripled during his two terms. Yet President Reagan's strategy for igniting strong growth worked.

As I mentioned earlier, the 1970s had been a period of stagflation: slow growth along with high unemployment, high interest rates, and high inflation. The economic stimulus provided by President Reagan's tax cut in August 1981—which scaled back marginal tax rates by 25 percent over three years—clearly set the economy on a growth trajectory.

But it also set the national debt on a growth trajectory. The debt rose from $908 billion in 1980 to $2.6 trillion in 1988. Some observers point out that this doesn't matter because, after the tax cut, government tax receipts doubled from about $500 billion to $1 trillion from 1980 to 1990, due to the higher income in a growing economy. But whatever the increase in tax receipts, it clearly did not come near to covering the increase in government spending—for which each party blames the other.

THE REAL WORLD

Around 1980, the notion of supply-side economics became popular in some circles. Its central idea is that tax cuts cause economic growth (without deficits) by stimulating investment. Entrepreneurs and executives invest the tax savings in capital equipment, which increases the supply side of the economy—hence the name supply-side economics. The economy grows and tax receipts rise, which eliminates the deficit.

Supply-side economics was promoted by conservative journalists rather than mainstream economists. Many partisans still argue that supply-side economics worked—despite the huge deficits it created and its being disavowed by David Stockman, who was President Reagan's budget director and a main promoter of the program.

Essentially supply-side economics places too much faith in the ability of tax cuts to increase investment. In practice, tax cuts have failed to boost economic growth to the point that higher tax receipts lower the budget deficits. Also, if consumers aren't buying, an increase in investment isn't going to get them to start. They have to be hired first, which they won't be until consumption starts growing. So rather than directly boost investment, the 1981 tax cut probably boosted consumption.

Democrats enjoy taking credit for the slower growth of the national debt from 1992 to 2000, President Clinton's administration. During that period, the debt increased from $4.1 trillion to $5.7 trillion, or by 39 percent, well under the almost 300 percent of the Reagan administration. However, the Clinton administration had two things going for it: first, from 1992 onward, the economy grew even more rapidly than it did in the 1980s. Tax receipts rose dramatically, generating budget surpluses from 1998 through 2001. Second, inflation and interest rates remained at historical lows, and the monetary policy that partly engineered that phenomenon clearly contributed to the length and growth rate of expansion.

The Clinton administration also benefited from a new focus on fiscal discipline in both parties, prompted by the deficits of the 1980s. Groups like the Concord Coalition and individuals like Ross Perot—who based his quixotic presidential campaign on deficit reduction—were emblematic of this concern. In 1990, President George H. W. Bush even agreed to a tax increase. It was politically difficult given his famous campaign promise: "Read my lips: no new taxes." Recession followed in 1991, and given the reaction of the public, candidate Clinton won the presidency in 1992.

Some observers trace the expansion of the 1990s to President Clinton's tax *increase* in 1993, which boosted rates on the wealthiest households. The credit may be misplaced, yet the tax increase certainly didn't hurt the economy—and may well have helped.

Wait! How could a tax *increase* help a recovery? Isn't a tax increase supposed to cool a recovery by lowering disposable income? Ordinarily, yes. However, with the deficits and debt at high levels, some economists believe that crowding out and high interest rates hampered the growth of investment at the time. Crowding out occurs when government borrowing makes it harder for the private sector to obtain funds. The resulting competition for the nation's savings also increases interest rates.

The logic of the 1993 tax increase bolstering the expansion is that the financial markets saw it as a harbinger of declining deficits and lower interest rates. Indeed, deficits and interest rates both did decline in the mid- to late 1990s, and investment soared to record levels. It's quite possible that the financial markets and the business community responded positively to the tax increase. Again, it certainly did not hamper the recovery.

The Boom and Bust of the 2000s

After a mild, 11-month recession that began in 2001, the U.S. economy entered a 6-year expansion, presided over by George W. Bush, the son of the 1-term George H. W. Bush who preceded Clinton. This expansion was fueled by the fiscal stimulus of decreased taxes and higher spending (for instance, for the wars in Iraq and Afghanistan and the Medicare prescription drug program) and the monetary stimulus of relatively low interest rates (explained in Part 4). The tax reductions under George W. Bush reignited the trend of sharply rising deficits, after they abated under Clinton.

This, along with very lax mortgage-lending policies by private- and public-sector lenders and the packaging of subprime mortgages in securities sold in the global financial markets, fueled a housing boom and home-price bubble that burst in 2007. As a result, the financial markets went into disarray, banks stopped lending, consumers cut their spending, and businesses laid off workers and reduced investment.

To counter the resulting economic recession (and to restore confidence in the banking system), the U.S. government provided both fiscal and monetary stimulus under presidents Bush and Obama. This included direct financial support of some banks (the bailouts) and of auto companies General Motors and Chrysler, increased unemployment benefits, tax cuts, infrastructure spending, federal aid to states, and a federal funds rate of virtually zero. (See *The Complete Idiot's Guide to the Great Recession*, also written by me, for a full account.)

> **ECONOTALK**
>
> The federal funds rate (or fed funds rate) is the rate that the banks charge one another on overnight borrowings of excess reserves. Federal funds are deposits banks make into the Federal Reserve System to meet their reserve requirements. Excess reserves are funds beyond those needed by a bank to meet its reserve requirements (as explained in Part 4).

As I mentioned, tax receipts naturally decrease in a recession. That, coupled with the increased spending, generated a federal budget deficit of $1.3 trillion in fiscal 2010 alone. That in itself would not be a problem if the previous administration hadn't also run up huge deficits. The U.S. government did not have the option of letting the economy sink into a depression or letting millions of households go without any income whatsoever. Yet that necessary deficit spending followed years of deficits during good economic times and thus contributed to already high levels of debt.

So Who's Right About Fiscal Policy?

Did the tax cut of 1981 lead to the deficits of the 1980s and the need to raise taxes in 1990 and 1993? Did the 1981 tax cut also lead to the expansion of the 1980s? Did the tax increases of 1990 and 1993 help bring about the 1990s expansion? Did the deficit spending of the early to mid-2000s contribute to that decade's boom? Did that spending also add unnecessarily to the national debt?

I believe the answer to all those questions is yes. But I also believe that other factors helped the expansions of the 1980s, 1990s, and 2000 along, which together amount to one long, 25-year-plus expansion. The period from 1982 to 2000 was a long boom interrupted by a recession in 1991 and an even milder one in 2001.

By other factors, I mean the natural business cycle and long-term population trends. After the depressed demand of the 1970s, the economy was poised for expansion due to pent-up demand. The early 1970's tripling of gasoline prices had to be absorbed, and that did happen, but it hobbled growth in that decade. In the 1980s, that pent-up demand was released.

In addition, baby boomers had to find employment, get married, buy condos and houses and furniture and appliances, start purchasing new cars, have children, go to

Disney World, buy computers and software, join health clubs, get hair transplants, use health-care services, and make their contributions to production and consumption. They did, and it helped to drive the 25-year boom.

However, such factors give neither political party credit for economic genius. In truth, each major party has good and bad economic policy prescriptions. Also, the hurly-burly of politics is a better place than most to hash out the economic questions facing U.S. society. Fortunately for all of us, there is a less politically charged and equally useful tool for keeping the economy on a long-term, low-inflation, low-unemployment growth trajectory. That would be monetary policy, which we take up in Part 4.

The Least You Need to Know

- Fiscal policy refers to changes in the federal government's taxation and expenditure decisions and activities aimed at achieving certain economic goals. (Monetary policy refers to the pursuit of those goals by changing interest rates and the money supply.)

- In a sluggish economy, fiscal policy calls for a decrease in taxes or an increase in government spending, or both. In an overheated economy, fiscal policy calls for an increase in taxes or a decrease in spending, or both.

- People who oppose high deficits and federal debt believe that they indicate lack of fiscal discipline, that money paid in interest could be better spent on other things, and that future generations will unfairly bear the burden of interest and debt payments.

- People who believe that high deficits and debt don't matter believe that they are not indicators of the condition of the economy. They hold that we're paying the interest and principal to ourselves, that future generations will inherit the assets financed with the debt, and that deficit spending helps to keep the economy growing.

- Economists believe that future generations bear an unfair burden if the debt being passed on to them is not accompanied by a corresponding level of productive capital.

- Each political party has good and bad economic policy ideas, but neither party wants to deliver bad news to voters, who'd rather not hear it anyway.

Money, the Banking System, and Policy

Another realm of government economic activity exists apart from taxes and spending and deficits and debt. This involves the nation's money supply and its banking system. Compared with fiscal policy and its decisions about taxes and spending, the level of interest rates and the supply of money can be somewhat remote subjects.

They are not, however, remote in their effect on the economy. In fact, monetary policy is in some ways a more useful and powerful tool for achieving the goal of high employment and low inflation. Certain monetary policy measures can change the growth rate, and even the direction, of the economy.

They can also be implemented more quickly than fiscal policy because they do not require legislation or approval from Congress or even a directive from the president. This is the advantage of having the Federal Reserve System, a central bank that formulates and implements monetary policy more or less apart from political considerations. Some would say that the central bank is in fact political—and to an extent it is, but not when compared with taxing and spending, which is the purview of actual politicians.

This part of the book covers monetary policy and the Federal Reserve System, the U.S. central bank, which is the institution responsible for formulating and implementing that policy. Here the reasons for the movement of interest rates, the relationship between the banking system and the economy, and the workings of monetary policy itself will all become clear.

The Color—and Velocity—of Money

In This Chapter

- Definitions of money
- How money fuels the economy
- Interest rates and credit

It's been said that the most confusing thing in the world to an economist is a $10 bill lying on the sidewalk. He doesn't know whether to pick it up, leave it to be found by someone with a higher propensity to spend, or convert it into pesos.

Indeed the topic of money is far more complex to an economist than it is to a business person, consumer, or taxpayer. That's good, because in a modern economy, money takes many forms and behaves in ways that profoundly affect growth, employment, and prices. The better an economist understands the forms that money takes and the ways in which it behaves, the better she will understand our economy. The same goes for us.

This chapter puts money, in all its forms, under a microscope. It defines money and the money supply and shows how money serves as the lifeblood of the economy. It also explains the basic theories of monetarism.

What Is Money?

In Chapter 1, you learned that virtually all economic activity occurs in the form of transactions in which goods or services are exchanged for money. No money, no transactions. Wages, prices, taxes, spending, deficits, surpluses, and debt are all expressed in money.

That's what we mean when we say that money is a medium of exchange. It facilitates exchanges. The alternative is a barter economy, in which people exchange goods and services for goods and services. In a barter economy, people spend a lot of time facilitating exchanges, because an exchange can occur only when each party has what the other one wants.

Barter is so inconvenient that early societies soon came up with mediums of exchange. Gold, silver, furs, and many other substances have been used as money. Money might have intrinsic value—as in the case of furs, which can be used to keep you warm—but it doesn't have to have any intrinsic value. Money might also *represent* something that has intrinsic value, such as gold, which can be used to make tableware or to fill dental cavities. In that case, money, in the form of paper currency, is said to be backed by gold, and the economy is said to be on the *gold standard.*

ECONOTALK

In a nation with currency on the **gold standard,** the currency represents a certain amount of gold deposited in the nation's treasury. Typically, the currency can be converted into a defined amount of gold, and gold can be converted into the currency. For decades, the U.S. dollar was worth ⅓₅ of an ounce of gold, and gold was priced at $35 an ounce.

The United States was on the gold standard for much of the last century but abandoned it in August 1971, when President Nixon formally ended the convertibility of U.S. currency into gold.

Doing away with the link between the dollar and gold gave both the U.S. economy and the international monetary system, which you'll learn about in Part 5, much greater flexibility. This flexibility has its downside as well as its upside, as you will also see.

Today, dollars are backed by the full faith and credit of the U.S. government, as the saying goes. With the power to tax individuals, businesses, and imports—among other things—in the world's largest economy, there's a lot of faith and credit backing the dollar. However, the currency can no longer be exchanged for gold. Which brings us to money's true nature: it has value because people will accept it in exchange for goods and services, and they accept it because they know they will also be able to exchange it for goods and services.

Indeed, in most economies in the world today, the money is what is known as fiat money. Fiat money has value because the government has decreed that it is legal tender for settling transactions and paying debts and taxes. In other words, the government has decreed that it is the official medium of exchange in the economy.

Aside from functioning as a medium of exchange, money also serves as a unit of value—a single measure for assessing the value of all the various goods and services produced and sold in an economy. Money is also a store of value—a way of accumulating wealth so it can be used at a later date. Stocks and bonds serve a similar function because they can be quickly converted to money. But money already is money, the most readily available form of wealth.

The Money Supply

Economists have many definitions of money, or, more accurately, the money supply. The money supply includes money as we usually think of it plus various bank deposits and financial instruments. These deposits and instruments have one thing in common: they are *liquid assets*. A liquid asset is one that can readily be converted into currency.

The terms *liquid assets* and *near money* invariably mean short-term assets. For instance, a demand deposit (that is, a checking account) can be accessed almost instantly. It is therefore more liquid than a six-month certificate of deposit.

ECONOTALK

Liquid assets are assets that can be quickly converted to money. These include short-term government securities and a variety of other financial assets. Liquid assets are also referred to as **near money.**

Economists break the money supply into four groups based on how accessible they are, as follows:

M-1 Currency in circulation

Commercial bank demand deposits (checking accounts)

NOW accounts and ATS accounts

Credit union share drafts

Mutual savings bank demand deposits

Traveler's checks

M-2   All M-1 assets

Overnight repurchase agreements of commercial banks

Overnight Eurodollars

Savings accounts

Time deposits (certificates of deposit) under $100,000

Money-market mutual-fund shares

M-3   All M-2 assets

Time deposits over $100,000

Term repurchase agreements

L   All M-3 and other liquid assets such as:

Treasury bills

Savings bonds

Commercial paper

Bankers' acceptances

Eurodollar holdings of U.S. residents

A few of these terms are probably unfamiliar, so I'll define them here:

- **NOW Accounts and ATS Accounts** are Negotiable Orders of Withdrawal, which are interest-bearing checking accounts at banks and savings and loans, and Automatic Transfer from Savings accounts, which provide overdraft protection through transfers from saving accounts.

- **Overnight repurchase agreements** (repos) are overnight loans between corporations and banks. In this type of transaction, a company with excess cash buys a security from a bank with the agreement that the bank will buy it back the next day. The security is usually a government security. Both the bank and the company benefit. The bank has the use of the money, and the company gets a higher yield on its money than it would in a checking account.

- A **term repurchase agreement** is similar to a repo but with a longer term. For instance, the bank may agree to buy the security back in 14 days.

- **Eurodollars** are dollars in demand deposits in banks outside the United States (not just in Europe).

- **Money-market mutual-fund shares** represent money invested by mutual funds in short-term securities—usually short-term government securities. A mutual fund pools money from various investors and invests it in a designated type of security—for instance, a bond fund invests in bonds.

- **Treasury bills** are U.S. government securities with terms of one year or less.

- **Commercial paper** consists of short-term—2 to 270 days—obligations (basically IOUs) of large, extremely creditworthy corporations and banks. These are traded in the financial markets and give large institutions easy access to short-term borrowings.

- **Bankers' acceptances** are time drafts—checks payable at a specific time in the future—that have been accepted (or formally approved for payment) by a bank. Bankers' acceptances are used to finance import and export transactions.

Before 1980, the money supply was mainly thought of as currency and demand deposits. Since then, the definitions of money have expanded to cover new types of liquid assets and the increased amount of funds in these assets. There is still debate about the composition of the money supply, and economists have developed multiple definitions of the money supply. The proliferation of consumer credit gives them even more to worry about. Consider, for example, the liquidity that a credit card with an open $10,000 line of credit gives a person.

THE REAL WORLD

As you'll see in Chapter 15, money is created by increasing the money supply, mainly by banks extending credit in the form of various loans. Traditionally, and back in the 1950s and 1960s when monetary theory was being refined, these were personal loans or auto loans. That was before the explosion in credit cards and home-equity loans. Credit gives people money to spend, which increases economic growth, but with payments of interest and principal in the future.

Not all forms of credit are included in the basic monetary aggregates. M-1, M-2, and M-3 don't include credit cards, yet they are a form of money that can fuel spending. Thus, monetary policy is an imperfect tool and cannot be used to control the economy, only to influence it.

The Demand for Money

Money is both a medium of exchange and a store of value, which points to the two major types of demand for money. Transaction demand is the amount of money people need to conduct their exchanges in the economy. This includes demand for walking-around money for lunch and tickets to the movies as well as demand for money in checking accounts to pay the bills. Asset demand is the amount of money that people in an economy want to hold as money, usually in bank accounts or in the form of near money, such as shares in money-market funds.

Asset demand is motivated by people who save for unexpected contingencies and who would rather hold money than stocks or bonds. For example, when an investor says he has 40 percent of his portfolio in stocks, 40 percent in bonds, and 20 percent in cash, he is saying that 20 percent is in money-market funds, Treasury bills, or similar assets. People increase their holdings of cash when the stock market is shaky. During a bull market, most people who buy stocks are fully invested, meaning they are holding no cash in their portfolios.

Three forces mainly drive the demand for money: prices, incomes, and interest rates, as follows:

- When price levels rise, goods and services cost more, and people need more money to purchase them; therefore, demand for money increases. When prices fall, people need less money and demand for it decreases.

- When incomes rise, consumption rises and people spend more money. This, too, increases the demand for money. However, when incomes fall, so does consumption, and the demand for money decreases.

- When interest rates rise, demand for money decreases. That's because high interest rates increase the opportunity cost of holding (that is, not investing) money—the interest forgone. So people don't want to hold money. However, when interest rates fall, people are willing to hold money because the opportunity cost of doing so is low. Therefore, when interest rates fall, demand for money increases.

Of course, we all know that people's demand for money is literally unlimited. The supply, however, is not. That's one reason that money keeps changing hands.

In Circulation: The Velocity of Money

In 2001, M-1—the money used to purchase goods and services—amounted to about $1.1 trillion. In 2009, M-1 totaled about $1.6 trillion. M-1 represents a measure of the amount of money in the economy, and we know that money exists to facilitate transactions. We also know that the transactions in the economy add up to gross domestic product (GDP). If that's so, then what is the relationship between the stock of money as expressed by M-1 and GDP?

The stock of money constantly flows through the economy, circulating and repeatedly changing hands in transactions until the end of the year, when all those transactions add up to GDP. If GDP in 2001 was about $10 trillion and the stock of money was about $1.1 trillion, then how many times did the stock of money change hands in transactions? Put another way, how many times did the inventory of money turn over?

The answer is 9 times, because $10 trillion divided by $1.1 trillion equals 9. In this case, 9 is what economists call the *velocity* of money in 2001. Incidentally, the velocity hadn't changed substantially in 2009; that year's GDP of about $14 trillion divided by M-1 of $1.6 trillion also equals 9.

Stated mathematically:

Velocity = GDP ÷ M-1

ECONOTALK

The **velocity** of money is the average number of times that a dollar changed hands in the economy in a period of time. It is calculated by dividing GDP by the money supply as measured by M-1.

The velocity of money changes gradually over time with changes in interest rates and other factors. For instance, if interest rates rise, the velocity of money also rises because money flows into investments. That leaves a smaller M-1 to circulate through the economy, and a smaller amount of money must turn over more frequently to produce the same GDP. If incomes rise, the velocity of money also rises, because demand for money increases. When demand for money increases, the stock of money must turn over more frequently.

From the formula for velocity, it is also clear that if velocity increases and the money supply remains the same, then GDP will rise. Why? Because if we rearrange the velocity formula to solve for GDP we get:

$$GDP = M \times V$$

which means that GDP equals the money supply (using M instead of M-1, for simplicity) multiplied by velocity (represented by V).

GDP *must* equal the money supply times velocity because, by definition, GDP is the sum of all transactions, and transactions are facilitated by money changing hands. Indeed if we plug the real figures into the formula and round the results up to the nearest trillion, we get:

$$\$10 \text{ trillion} = \$1.1 \text{ trillion} \times 9$$

Economists became quite excited upon discovering the velocity of money. (Who can blame them?) They quickly built on the concept to create *monetarism*.

ECONOTALK

Monetarism is the school of economic thought that believes that economic stabilization and growth is best achieved by control of the money supply. Monetarists believe that central bank policies that influence interest rates and the availability of credit are the best tools for implementing economic policy.

The Equation of Exchange

As you know, GDP is the sum of the value of all goods and services produced and consumed in an economy, usually in a year. This means that GDP equals the price of all the goods and services produced in the economy multiplied by the quantity of all goods and services produced in the economy. Stated as a formula:

$$GDP = P \times Q$$

where P represents the average price level and Q represents the aggregate quantity of goods and services.

From this formula, the monetarists developed what is known as the equation of exchange. This equation relates the money supply and its velocity to the price level and the quantity of goods and services. Here's the equation of exchange:

$$M \times V = P \times Q$$

where M represents the money supply; V, the velocity of money; P, the average price level; and Q, the quantity of goods and services.

Economists point out that the equation of exchange is true by definition. In other words, the equation states that the number of times the money supply turns over has to equal GDP, because the stock of money must change hands a certain number of times in order to produce GDP. It also states that GDP has to equal the price of the goods and services multiplied by the quantity of goods and services, because the quantity of goods and services produced and purchased is valued by their total price. In other words, each side of the equation has to amount to GDP, even though they each get to the number by a different route.

With the equation of exchange in hand, the early monetarists developed the quantity theory of money, which states that the price level is determined by the money supply. If the money supply rises, then prices will rise; if the money supply falls, then prices will fall.

The quantity theory of money comes from rearranging the equation of exchange so that you are solving it for velocity:

$$V = \frac{P \times Q}{M}$$

This equation—velocity equals price times quantity, divided by the money supply—led to the quantity theory of money. Why? Because if V and Q are constant and the money supply rises, then prices will rise. The early monetarists assumed that V is constant because personal and institutional behavior remains essentially the same over time. They assumed that Q is constant because the economy is at the output level of full employment when inflation occurs. For the early monetarists, the link between the money supply and prices worked both ways. If the money supply falls, then prices will fall—but inflation (that is, rising prices) is usually a monetarist's main concern.

Modern Monetarism

The quantity theory of money was developed by the American economist Irving Fisher (1867–1947) in the early 1900s. Later economists—in particular, another American economist, Milton Friedman—recognized two problems in the quantity theory of money: first, velocity does not remain constant and, second, the economy is not always at full employment when inflation occurs.

Yet as these more modern monetarists updated the quantity theory of money, they came to the same basic conclusion as Irving Fisher: changes in the money supply are the most important factor determining the level of GDP. This is the central belief of monetarists. They also believe that the Federal Reserve should more or less limit its activities to permitting slow and steady growth in the money supply. (The updated theory acknowledges that velocity changes very gradually and that price levels can change even without full employment.)

ECONOTIP

The economist Milton Friedman helped foster the so-called Chicago School of Economics, which is characterized by an emphasis on mathematics, free market economics, and monetarism.

Friedman's thinking revolved around the role of incomes and consumption on the one hand and money and the banking system on the other. He believed that these factors were far more important to the economy than the government's role and that markets perform best when unfettered by regulation. Hence, he became identified as an anti-Keynesian as well as a monetarist. His books, such as *Capitalism and Freedom* and *Free to Choose,* both set forth his ideas and served as conservative credentials.

Although he worked at the U.S. Treasury from 1941 to 1943, Friedman spent his career in teaching, research, and writing on economics, based at the University of Chicago. He won the Nobel Prize in Economics in 1976, retired from teaching in 1977, and died in 2006 at the age of 94.

Monetarists generally don't believe in using monetary policy to try to alter the path of the economy. Most monetarists are economic conservatives who believe that the private sector will ensure steady economic growth and that this growth should be accommodated by steady, noninflationary growth in the money supply.

Some monetarists believe that the Federal Reserve and government efforts to fine-tune the economy generally do more harm than good. Some believe that the Fed touched off or worsened the Great Depression. All monetarists believe that the money supply, velocity, and interest rates exert the most important effects on economic growth and prices. Monetary theory would thus allow that the Fed probably contributed to the housing price bubble by keeping interest rates too low for too long during the expansion of 2002–2007, which increased the money supply. Indeed, this seems to have been a contributing factor.

Monetarists and Keynesians have often found themselves at loggerheads. Keynesians believe that changes in taxes and spending by the federal government are the preferred tool for stabilizing the economy during cyclical swings and for ensuring steady growth with high employment and low inflation. Monetarists believe that the money supply has more impact—or at least more potentially positive impact—on the economy than taxes and government spending, which they generally want kept to low levels.

Today, however, most economists believe in employing the most useful tactics of both fiscal policy and monetary policy in a given situation. This is not to say that strict disciples of the Keynesian and monetarist schools—as well as other truly outlandish schools—cannot be found. But today's economists, except those bound by ideology or political paymasters, consider every tool at their disposal when confronting complex economic issues.

Where We're Going

Despite the wish of strict monetarists for limited tinkering by the Federal Reserve, activist monetary policy has become an important tool in managing the economy. Particularly during the reign of Fed Chairman Alan Greenspan, the Fed aimed to use interest rates to generate soft landings as the business cycle turned downward. What the Fed proved less adept at (or less willing to attempt) was raising interest rates as the economy grew. Perhaps this was because inflation, the traditional main concern of central bankers during expansions, appeared to be under control. In any event, the Fed under Chairman Ben Bernanke, successor to Alan Greenspan, took a very aggressive role in countering the Great Recession of 2008–2009.

With an understanding of the money supply, the velocity of money, and their relationship to GDP, we're now prepared to learn how monetary policy works. Chapter 16 will show you how, but first Chapter 15 takes you into the Federal Reserve and the banking system, which is the medium through which monetary policy is implemented.

The Least You Need to Know

- The key requirement for money is that everyone in an economy accept it in transactions.
- Demand for money consists of transaction demand and asset demand. The demand for money is driven mainly by price levels, income, and interest rates. Demand for money rises when prices or incomes rise, but it falls when interest rates rise.
- Economists define the money supply in various ways. M-1, the most commonly used measure, includes currency, demand deposits, NOW and ATS accounts, credit union share drafts, and traveler's checks.
- The velocity of money is the number of times that the money supply changes hands, or turns over, in an economy in a year. It is calculated by dividing GDP by the money supply.
- Monetarists believe that changes in the money supply are the most important factor determining the level of GDP, and that the Fed should permit steady, noninflationary growth in the money supply.

The Banks' Bank: The Federal Reserve

In This Chapter

- The function of the Federal Reserve
- Key operating units of the Fed
- How the Fed influences the money supply
- How the Fed works with the banking system

You've probably heard of the Federal Reserve System before reading this book. The business news and even the general news regularly report on decisions the Fed makes regarding interest rates and the banking system, particularly during difficult economic times.

The Federal Reserve is so important to the economy that there's a whole cottage industry of Fed watchers within the business community. They monitor the Fed's moves, try to fathom the chairman's thinking, and develop forecasts of interest rates, money supply aggregates (M-1, M-2, and so on), and the growth of the economy.

This chapter takes you into the Federal Reserve System and shows you what it is, how it operates, and why it is so important.

A Bank for All Reasons

The Federal Reserve System is the central bank of the United States. The Fed oversees and regulates the commercial banking system and formulates and implements monetary policy. The goal is to keep the economy on a path of steady growth with low inflation and low unemployment.

The Federal Reserve was created by Congress with the passage of the Federal Reserve Act in 1913. This established the United States' central bank as the lender of last resort for banks in need of liquidity unavailable elsewhere. Establishment of the Fed aimed to shore up the strength of the banking system and the public's faith in the system. Until then, there had been recurring financial problems in the U.S. banking system, notably a wave of bank failures after the Panic of 1907.

Over time the Fed's role expanded. Today the Fed has four main responsibilities:

- Formulate and implement the nation's monetary policy

- Supervise and regulate banking institutions and protect the rights of consumers who use credit

- Maintain the stability of the financial system

- Provide certain financial services to the U.S. government, the public, financial institutions, and foreign government institutions

Later in this chapter, I'll discuss how the Fed fulfills these responsibilities. First, let's look at the structure of the organization.

THE REAL WORLD

The Fed takes its responsibilities seriously. During the financial crisis of 2007–2008, the Fed took aggressive action to provide liquidity (that is, cash and credit) to the banking system. To do so, it created several new classes of loans to enable banks to borrow so that they could issue commercial paper; extend credit through student, auto, and credit card loans; and borrow from the Fed itself. The Fed also kept interest rates quite low. Some criticized the Fed for these actions, but the Fed felt it had to act.

Structure of the Fed

The Federal Reserve System consists of a 7-member board of governors headquartered in Washington, D.C., and 12 regional Reserve Banks located in different U.S. cities. The members of the Board of Governors are appointed by the president, confirmed by the Senate, and serve 14-year terms. Each member comes from a different Federal Reserve District, the regions overseen by the 12 Federal Reserve Banks. The president appoints, and the Senate confirms, two of these seven members to be chairman and vice chairman of the Board of Governors, which amounts to chairman and vice chairman of the Fed.

The Fed Chairman is appointed by the president of the United States and usually confirmed by Congress with little controversy (compared with, say, a Supreme Court justice). The chairman serves a six-year term. The Fed Chairman as of this writing is Ben Bernanke, who was appointed by George W. Bush in 2004 and reappointed by Barack Obama in 2010. As noted, under Chairman Bernanke, the Fed intervened aggressively in the banking system in the 2008 crisis, and some senators disagreed with that action. In fact, 30 of the total of 100 voted against his reconfirmation.

Prior to Bernanke, Fed Chairman Alan Greenspan had held the post since being appointed by President Reagan in 1987. Although many saw Greenspan as an extremely effective Fed chairman for his first 10 years, his adherence to low interest rates is widely viewed as contributing to, respectively, the tech-stock bubble and the home-price bubble in the 1990s and 2000s.

The Board of Governors formulates monetary policy. The 7 board members represent a majority on the 12-member Federal Open Market Committee (FOMC). This committee makes the key decisions affecting interest rates and the availability of credit in the United States. (You'll learn more about the FOMC later in this chapter.)

The board also regulates and supervises banks that are members of the Federal Reserve System, *bank holding companies*, and international banks in the United States. Of the nation's approximately 8,000 commercial banks, about 2,400 are members of the Federal Reserve System. Banks chartered by the federal government—called national banks—must belong to the system, while those chartered by state governments may choose to belong to the system and use the Fed's services. Although member banks are less than half of those in the country, they control three-fourths of the nation's bank deposits.

ECONOTALK

Bank holding companies are corporations set up to own banks and other financial institutions such as finance companies and insurance companies.

The board plays a key role in maintaining the nation's inter-bank payment systems, which include the Fedwire and the Fed's automated clearinghouse (ACH). The Fedwire provides electronic funds transfer and payment services. These enable banks to move money and settle accounts for their customers and among themselves. The automated clearinghouse also processes electronic funds transfers, which enable banks to clear checks and settle accounts.

Finally, the Board of Governors, which meets several times a week, develops regulations governing consumer credit, such as the Truth in Lending Act and the Equal Opportunity Credit Act.

Federal Reserve Banks

The 12 Federal Reserve Banks are the operating arms of the Federal Reserve System. These are banks for banks set up and operated by the Federal Reserve System. They are located in Boston, New York, Philadelphia, Cleveland, Richmond, Atlanta, Chicago, St. Louis, Minneapolis, Kansas City, Dallas, and San Francisco. More Fed districts and banks are located east of the Mississippi due to the distribution of the population when the system was created.

Federal Reserve Banks influence the flow of money and credit in the U.S. economy. They hold the cash reserves of depository institutions and make loans to them. They move currency in and out of circulation and collect and process millions of checks each day. They provide checking accounts for the U.S. Treasury, issue and redeem government securities, and provide other services to banks.

THE REAL WORLD

As you probably know, very little money—as in currency—is actually moved from bank to bank. The vast majority of banking transactions occur through checks and electronic bookkeeping entries. This is probably the way your own personal financial transactions occur.

Think of the Federal Reserve Banks as 12 day-to-day operating centers of the Fed, each serving its own district and various government agencies. They operate check-processing services as well as the ACHs—computerized facilities for electronic exchange of payments among banks—that constitute the ACH system. In addition, they operate through a total of 25 Reserve Bank Branches.

Each Federal Reserve Bank is supervised by a board of nine directors who review their bank's finances, supervise internal audits, and bring an independent, regional perspective to the Federal Reserve System. The directors also appoint the Reserve Bank president, subject to the approval of the Board of Governors.

The Federal Open Market Committee

The FOMC is the key policymaking body in the Federal Reserve System and makes the key decisions regarding the Fed's open market operations, hence the name of the committee. Open market operations are purchases and sales of U.S. government and federal agency securities. I'll describe how these purchases and sales affect the money supply later in this chapter, but they are critical in implementing monetary policy.

The FOMC has 12 members—the 7 members of the Board of Governors and 5 Reserve Bank presidents. The president of the Federal Reserve Bank of New York is always on the FOMC. The other four seats on the committee are filled on a rotating basis by the presidents of the other Reserve Banks, who serve one-year terms.

By law the committee must meet at least four times a year in Washington. Since 1980, it has usually met eight times a year, or every five to eight weeks, on a scheduled basis. However, three unscheduled meetings were added in 2007, six in 2008, and three in 2009, reflecting the severity of the economic climate. At each meeting, the members vote on the monetary policy to be carried out until the next meeting. At least twice a year, the committee also votes on its long-run policy objective for growth in the money supply.

The financial and business communities monitor the outcomes of these meetings carefully. When you hear that "the Fed cut the fed funds rate yesterday" or "the Fed raised the discount rate" (I'll explain these rates in a moment), that decision was the result of a meeting of the FOMC. Of course, the Fed can choose not to change those rates, a move that holds its own significance.

ECONOTIP

At www.federalreserve.gov, you can obtain the schedule of the FOMC meetings and the official statements issued after the meeting and the meeting minutes.

A Bit of Background on Banking

The banking system makes it possible for the Fed to change the money supply. So before we look at how the Fed implements monetary policy, some background on the banking system is in order.

Banks in the United States, like banks everywhere, practice what is known as fractional reserve banking. Fractional reserve banking emerged when early bankers realized that only a small percentage of deposits would be withdrawn on a given day. For instance, if the bank had total deposits of $10 million, perhaps the most they would see withdrawn on a given day would be $1 million.

This would leave the bank with $9 million available to lend to borrowers. (Commercial and savings banks take deposits and loan them out at a higher rate of interest than that which they pay on deposits.) Depositors know their money is being loaned out, and they're comfortable with that. After all, they borrow money when they need it.

Note that there are two main types of banks: commercial banks and investment banks. Commercial banks are depository institutions. They accept deposits from customers (depositors) and loan most of the funds out to other customers (borrowers). Savings banks and credit unions also do this. Investment banks are not depository institutions. Instead, they accept funds from investors and then invest those funds in securities, such as stocks and bonds. Thus, investment banks put money at risk in the securities markets, where risks are typically higher than in lending. The two types of banks are essentially in two different businesses.

THE REAL WORLD

The Glass-Steagall Act, formally known as the Banking Act of 1933, prohibited financial institutions from engaging in both commercial banking and investment banking. This legislation was passed in response to abuses that led to the Crash of 1929 and instability in the financial system at the time. The act was repealed in 1999 by the Gramm-Leach-Bliley Act in response to financial services industry lobbying. Some observers believe that repeal helped to foster the financial crisis of 2007–2008, while others believe the crisis would have occurred anyway. After the crisis, there were calls for reinstatement of provisions similar to Glass-Steagall, but that did not occur.

Reserve requirements, which apply to commercial banks and not to investment banks, are funds—in the form of cash and other liquid assets—that a bank must, by law, keep in its vaults or on deposit with the nearest Federal Reserve Bank. The reserve requirement is a percentage of the bank's demand deposits and, occasionally, time deposits (that is, certificates of deposit). Currently the requirement is 10 percent of demand deposits.

If the Fed raises the reserve requirement, it will decrease the supply of loanable funds and slow the growth of the money supply. Why? Because funds in the vault or on deposit with a Federal Reserve Bank cannot be loaned out. Also, if the supply of loanable funds decreases, then their price—the interest rate—will increase. This is called tight monetary policy, and it is used to slow the economy down and combat inflation.

Conversely, if the Fed lowers the reserve requirement, banks have more money to lend. A lower reserve requirement increases the supply of loanable funds and speeds up the growth of the money supply. That's because having to keep less money in the vault or at the Federal Reserve Bank means more money available for banks to lend. If the supply of loanable funds increases, then interest rates decrease and demand for loans increases. This is called loose, or easy, monetary policy, and it is used to speed up the growth of the economy and combat unemployment.

ECONOTIP

The word reserve in Federal Reserve System refers to the fact that U.S. banks are required by law to keep funds—called reserves—in the form of cash or liquid assets either in their own vaults or on deposit with the nearest Federal Reserve Bank.

Funds that banks have on deposit with the Fed or in their own vaults above the amount of the reserve requirement are called excess reserves. Banks are free to lend excess reserves to their customers as well as to one another.

Monetary Moves

The Fed rarely changes the reserve requirement, but it is one of three tools it can use to implement monetary policy. All three monetary policy tools affect the level of reserves in the banking system and the supply of loanable funds. We'll look at the process of money creation later in this chapter. First, let's get familiar with the Fed's main tools of monetary policy:

- Open market operations
- Changes in the discount rate
- Changes in reserve requirements

We'll take these tools one at a time, but first a word of caution: although writers use the phrase *control the money supply*, the Fed doesn't really control the money supply, let alone the economy. Instead, using these tools, the Fed influences the demand for and the supply of funds that banks must have on deposit at the Federal Reserve Banks (that is, the amount of required reserves). This influences the federal funds rate, which in turn influences other interest rates, the availability of money and credit, and ultimately the economy. The Fed also uses these tools to influence the amount of excess reserves—that is, the amount of loanable funds—in the banking system.

ECONOTIP

Federal funds are funds deposited by commercial banks at Federal Reserve Banks. These include the required reserves and any funds beyond the required amount. Required reserves are amounts—expressed as a percentage of checking account deposits—that a bank must maintain in its vault or on deposit with the Fed.

Banks can lend excess reserves to each other on an overnight basis—at the fed funds rate—in order to meet their reserve requirements. The federal funds rate is the interest rate charged by banks for these loans. The federal funds rate is set daily by the market, not by the Fed. That makes it the most sensitive indicator of the direction of interest rates.

The Fed influences—it does not dictate or set—the federal funds rate. (We'll see how in a moment.) That's why an accurate news report will say that "the Fed is targeting a federal funds rate of 3 percent" or whatever. The Fed targets a fed funds rate. It does not set the rate.

Open Market Operations

Open market operations are purchases of U.S. government securities from financial institutions and sales of U.S. government securities to financial institutions by the Federal Reserve. Decisions about the purchase or sale of securities in the open market are based on a directive from the FOMC. The directive indicates the approach to monetary policy that the FOMC wants to pursue.

Open market operations enable the Fed to increase or decrease the supply of reserves in the banking system.

Sales of securities by the Fed decrease the supply of excess reserves. The money moves from the banks to the Fed when the banks pay for the securities. The banks get the securities, and the Fed gets the money. This takes money out of the banking system. Decreasing the supply of excess reserves decreases the supply of funds that banks have available to lend to one another to meet their reserve requirements. This raises the fed funds rate and slows the growth of the money supply.

Purchases of securities by the Fed increase the supply of excess reserves. The money moves from the Fed to the banks when the Fed pays for the securities. The banks get the money and the Fed gets the securities, which puts money—in the form of excess reserves—into the banking system. Increasing the supply of excess reserves increases the supply of funds that banks can lend to one another. This decreases the fed funds rate and speeds up the growth of the money supply.

The manager of the System Open Market Account and the staff of the Trading Desk (known as the Desk) conduct open market operations at the regional Federal Reserve Bank of New York. The actual transactions take three basic forms, depending on the Fed's objectives:

- Short-term repurchase agreements (RPs) are used when the Fed wants to add reserves to the banking system temporarily. RPs are the most common transactions at the Desk. In an RP, the Desk buys securities from the banks, which agree to repurchase them at a specific date and price. Upon repurchase, the reserves that were added to the system by the Fed's purchase are automatically subtracted.

- Matched sale-purchase transactions (MSPs) are used when the Fed wants to temporarily subtract reserves from the system. MSPs involve a contract for the Desk to sell Treasury bills to a bank, and a contract for the Desk to buy the bills back at a later date.

- Outright purchases or sales of securities by the Fed are used less often than RPs and MSPs. These transactions involve no agreement that reverses the transaction at a later date, so the effect on reserves is more permanent. (Again, the Fed's purchases of securities increase excess reserves, and sales of securities decrease excess reserves.) Outright purchases or sales are used to address a persistent need to increase or decrease reserves.

Open market operations occur every business day and give the Fed the most flexibility in implementing monetary policy. The Desk gathers information from securities dealers and large commercial banks, and data on bank reserves and on the Treasury's operations. With this information and through open market operations, the Fed keeps a finger on the pulse of the money supply and adjusts reserves accordingly.

Changes in the Discount Rate

Changes in the *discount rate* are used less often by the Fed. The discount rate is the interest rate that the Fed charges on loans to member banks. These loans are usually secured by government securities and other short-term paper and are used by the banks mainly to meet their reserve requirements.

These loans, which are made at the Fed's discount window (the department of the Fed that makes these loans), are a privilege rather than a right—one that the Fed traditionally discourages banks from using. (I say traditionally because, in the crisis of 2008, the Fed encouraged banks to borrow—not only at the discount window, but through the new loan facilities I mentioned earlier in this chapter.) To receive a discount window loan, the borrower must usually first use alternative sources of funds, such as the federal funds market. In a normal week, few banks borrow at the discount window. These loans provide a small fraction of the banking system's total reserves.

Therefore, although they affect the cost of funds borrowed at the discount window, changes in the discount rate are viewed in the business community more as indicators of monetary policy. Historically, the rate has changed infrequently and often remains the same even when monetary policy changes. Incidentally, if the discount rate is lower than the fed funds rate, the Fed does not allow banks to borrow at the discount rate and loan the money out at higher market rates.

ECONOTALK

The **discount rate** is the interest rate that the Fed charges on secured loans to banks that need to meet their reserve requirements. These loans are made at the Fed's discount window and are generally discouraged. (Banks must first use alternative sources of funds.) However, the Fed remains the lender of last resort for the banking system, which is one reason for the discount window and for the loan facilities the Fed created in the late 2000s financial crisis.

ECONOTIP

Current reserve requirements are low by historical standards. For instance, from 1937 to 1958, the required reserve ratio on deposits was 20 percent for banks in New York and Chicago, which were *central reserve cities* (a term no longer in use). Today, the requirement is 10 percent, having been reduced from 12 percent in April 1992 in order to put banks, in the Fed's words, "in a better position to extend credit."

Changes in Reserve Requirements

The Monetary Control Act (MCA) of 1980 authorizes the Fed's Board of Governors to impose a reserve requirement of 8 to 14 percent on demand deposits and of up to 9 percent on nonpersonal time deposits. There are other provisions of the act and other adjustments to the reserve requirements permitted, depending on a bank's level of deposits.

In practice, the relationship between reserve requirements and money creation is weak. The requirements apply mainly to demand deposits, leaving other accounts beyond the Fed's influence. Moreover, the Fed permits banks to acquire needed reserves from the money markets as long as they are willing to pay the prevailing federal funds rate. Therefore, the Fed rarely changes reserve requirements to implement monetary policy. The Fed retains the right to raise and lower reserve requirements, whether or not it regularly exercises that right. If indeed the Fed ever needs to administer strong monetary medicine, it is best that it have some on hand.

How Money Is Created

Here's the part of the book I know you've been waiting for: how money is created. It's a beautiful thing to see. Unfortunately, banks are the only outfits legally allowed to create money, and they do it under the auspices of the Federal Reserve.

By *money*, I mean deposits, not currency. Most money—most of M-1—exists in the form of deposits. When banks have reserves above the amount required by the Fed—excess reserves—they are allowed to create new deposits. These new deposits are created in the form of loans. So actually the term *money creation* in our economy means expansion of credit and debt.

No single bank can create money. Some people believe that one bank can take in new deposits and somehow lend out a multiple of that amount. That's not the case. A single bank can only lend out money that it has on deposit or buys in the money markets, also known as the credit markets. However, numerous banks and the banking system can together expand their loans at a multiple of the new reserves of cash, as you will see in a moment.

First, a few words about a bank's finances. When a bank accepts a deposit, it creates a liability for itself. In other words, the bank is liable for paying the depositor when he wants his money (in the case of demand deposits) or when the term of the deposit has expired (in the case of time deposits, such as six-month certificates of deposit, also referred to as CDs).

When a bank lends money, it creates an asset for itself. The bank is legally entitled to payments of interest and principal over the life of the loan. Indeed, that is how the bank earns its profit—by accepting deposits and making loans.

With that background in banking, let's look at money creation.

The Process in Action: First Round

Let's assume Mudpuddle National Bank has deposits totaling $10,000, a required reserve ratio of 10 percent, and $1,000 in reserves (which is 10 percent of $10,000). The reserves are the total of the cash in the bank's vault plus its deposits with the regional Federal Reserve Bank. The bank also has loans totaling $9,000.

Here is how Mudpuddle National's accounts would appear.

Mudpuddle National

Assets	Liabilities and Net Worth
Reserves $1,000	
Loans 9,000	Demand deposits $10,000

Let's also assume that the nation's money supply amounts to $1.2 million, which includes demand deposits of $1 million and currency of $200,000. Here's the composition of the money supply:

Nation's Money Supply

Demand deposits	$1,000,000
Currency	200,000
M-1	$1,200,000

Now let's assume that Harry Hobstweedle deposits $1,000 in cash into his checking account at Mudpuddle National. Here is the effect on the bank's accounts and on the money supply.

Mudpuddle National

Assets	Liabilities and Net Worth
Reserves $2,000	
Loans 9,000	Demand deposits $11,000

Nation's Money Supply

Demand deposits	$1,001,000
Currency	199,000
M-1	$1,200,000

At this point, there is no effect on the total money supply, only in its composition: $1,000 moved from currency into demand deposits.

The bank's accounts show $1,000 more in deposits—the liability that it must pay when Harry writes checks against that account—and an additional $1,000 in reserves, or cash in the vault. Here's a key point: some portion of those reserves are excess reserves, because the bank is only required to maintain reserves of 10 percent against the $11,000 in demand deposits.

If demand deposits are now $11,000 and the required reserve ratio is 10 percent, then the reserve requirement is now $1,100. That means that Mudpuddle National has excess reserves of $900 (which equals $2,000 in reserves, minus $1,100 in required reserves).

Excess reserves generate no interest income, so Mudpuddle National will loan that $900 to an eager borrower. Let's call her Samantha. To give Samantha the money she has borrowed, Mudpuddle National will create a demand deposit account for her (or give her a check drawn on Mudpuddle). The effect on the bank's accounts and on the nation's money supply will be as follows:

Mudpuddle National

Assets	Liabilities and Net Worth
Reserves $2,000	
Loans 9,900	Demand deposits $11,900

Nation's Money Supply

Demand deposits	$1,001,900
Currency	199,000
M-1	$1,200,900

At the bank, the cash is still in the vault, but a loan has been booked and a demand deposit has been created—both in the amount of $900, the amount of excess reserves (not a multiple of the excess reserves).

Yet, the nation's money supply has expanded! It has grown by $900 because of the demand deposit created to give Samantha her loan. As I pointed out, it is expanding credit—in this instance, extending the $900 loan—that creates money in our economy.

That completes the first round in the process of money creation. The money supply has grown by $900.

The Process in Action: Second Round

Samantha didn't borrow the $900 and agree to pay interest on it in order to let it sit in a checking account. Instead, she will quickly spend that money on whatever she borrowed it for.

Suppose she uses it to buy an antique clock from Theo. Theo will take Samantha's $900 check drawn on Mudpuddle National and deposit it into his account at InterTrust BankCorp. After the check clears, the effect on Mudpuddle and InterTrust will be as follows:

Mudpuddle National

Assets	Liabilities and Net Worth
Reserves $1,100	
Loans 9,900	Demand deposits $11,000

InterTrust BankCorp

Assets	Liabilities and Net Worth
Reserves +$900	Demand deposits +$900

There is no additional effect on the money supply at this point.

At Mudpuddle National Bank, when the check clears, Mudpuddle pays the liability of the $900 demand deposit created for Samantha, and does so by using the $900 that was held in its reserves. Samantha's $900 loan remains on Mudpuddle's books until it is paid.

At InterTrust BankCorp, demand deposits rise by the $900 Theo deposited from the transaction with Samantha, and InterTrust's reserves rise by $900.

What happens to complete this second round in the money creation process? InterTrust BankCorp will lend its excess reserves—in this case $810—to an eager borrower of its own. The $810 figure is the amount of InterTrust's excess reserves. (Multiplying the $900 increase in demand deposits at InterTrust by the 10 percent required reserve ratio yields $90. Taking the reserves of $900 and subtracting the required reserves of $90 yields $810.)

When InterTrust BankCorp lends that $810, it will create a demand deposit of $810 for the borrower. That will increase the money supply by $810, just as the first loan from Mudpuddle National increased the money supply by $900. And that completes the second round of money creation.

There will be a third round of money creation and a fourth round and a fifth round and so on until the banking system reaches a point of equilibrium. That point is reached when no bank in the banking system has excess reserves. The process of each bank lending its excess reserves will continue until that point is reached.

In our example, that point will be reached when each dollar of reserves is supporting $10 of deposits. In other words, ultimately, with the 10 percent reserve requirement in our example, the system will make loans that create new deposits until the new deposits reach 10 times the amount of the original new reserves added to the system. The system would ultimately create $10,000 in new deposits, because the initial increase in reserves was $1,000—the amount deposited by Harry Hobstweedle.

This is how the banking system creates money and how the money supply keeps expanding. Now it should be clear how a change in reserves—no matter which tool the Fed uses to bring it about—will affect the money supply. If the Fed creates excess reserves, banks will loan them and that will increase the money supply. Conversely, if the Fed decreases excess reserves, banks will curtail their lending, which will decrease the growth of the money supply. If tight monetary policy were pursued long enough, the money supply would contract as loans were paid off and not fully replaced by new loans.

Modern Money Creation

Central banking and a system of money creation gives modern capitalist nations a measure of control over their economies that would otherwise be impossible. Although the Federal Reserve System and the mechanisms of monetary policy are neither foolproof nor guaranteed to yield the intended results, they are dreams come true compared with the traditional alternatives. These alternatives were to have the health of banks depend on the faith of depositors and the skill and ethics of the bankers and to have the money supply depend on the amount of gold being discovered and mined.

As we will see in the next chapter, monetary policy has compiled a record that's as mixed as that of fiscal policy.

The Least You Need to Know

- The Federal Reserve System (the Fed) formulates and implements monetary policy, regulates banks, maintains the stability of the financial system, and provides services to financial and government institutions. The Fed must sometimes maintain stability by acting as lender of last resort to the banking system.

- The Federal Reserve System consists of the Board of Governors in Washington and 12 regional Federal Reserve Banks. The Federal Open Market Committee plays a key role in formulating monetary policy.

- The three main tools for implementing monetary policy are open market operations, changes in the discount rate, and changes in reserve requirements. Open market operations are by far the most important, but the loan facilities that the Fed created in response to the financial crisis of the late 2000s also proved important.

- Sales of securities in open market operations decrease the supply of excess reserves. Purchases of securities by the Fed increase the supply of excess reserves.

- Changes in the discount rate are relatively rare and mainly signal the direction of monetary policy. The Fed historically discourages banks from borrowing at the discount window.

- Money creation occurs by means of credit expansion as the banking system responds to changes in the level of excess reserves. Increased excess reserves mean increased lending activity and growth in the money supply. Decreased excess reserves mean decreased lending and slower growth in the money supply.

Monetary Policy: The Gas and the Brakes

In This Chapter

- How monetary policy is applied in practice
- How to become a skilled Fed watcher
- A look at the Fed's record

With a clear understanding of money and how it fuels the economy and of the Federal Reserve System and how it influences the growth of the money supply, you are prepared to see monetary policy in action. As I've mentioned, the Fed can implement monetary policy far more quickly than the president and Congress can agree on the budgetary provisions that constitute fiscal policy. So it's an extremely useful tool. In addition, the financial markets monitor every move the Fed makes (or chooses not to make), and they often respond even more rapidly to monetary policy than the banking system.

In this chapter, we complete our study of monetary policy by examining how it works in practice. You'll learn when monetary policy changes and what good (and harm) those changes have done in the past. And you'll learn about the unique role that the Chairman of the Federal Reserve System plays in the economy.

Monetary Policy in Action

In general, a policy acts as a framework for the appropriate action to take in a given situation. The government's economic policies aim to maintain a stable, growing economy with low inflation and unemployment. We've examined the fiscal policy actions that work toward those ends. In a sluggish economy, fiscal policy calls for a decrease in taxes or an increase in government spending, or both. In an overheated economy, fiscal policy calls for an increase in taxes or a decrease in spending, or both.

In a sluggish economy, monetary policy calls for an increase in the growth of the money supply, which occurs when the Fed targets a lower federal funds rate, buys securities through its open market operations, lowers the discount rate, or lowers reserve requirements. As I mentioned in Chapter 15, the Fed can also provide funds to the banking system through special loan facilities, as it did in the financial crisis of 2007–2008 and in the recession of 2008–2009.

In an overheated economy, monetary policy calls for a decrease in the growth of the money supply (or even a contraction in the money supply). This occurs when the Fed targets a higher fed funds rate, sells securities, raises the discount rate, or raises reserve requirements.

Ideally, monetary policy stabilizes the economy by cushioning the effects of the ups and downs of the business cycle. People in the financial and business communities often express it in the following ways (with well-mixed metaphors):

- When an expansion is underway and the economy and inflation begin to heat up, the Fed should apply the brakes. It should target higher interest rates and slower growth in the money supply. Thus the Fed is often accused of taking away the punch bowl just as the party gets going. Significantly, this occurred all too gradually during the expansion that lasted from 2001 to 2007.

- When a recession is on the way and the economy is cooling, the Fed should step on the gas—gently. That is the method by which the Fed can engineer what is known as a soft landing. Rather than aiming to reverse the downward cycle, the Fed lowers rates and increases the growth of the money supply enough so the economy does not sink deeply into recession. The exception is when a financial crisis, a prolonged recession, or even economic depression looms. In such cases, the Fed must take vigorous action to soften the downturn, usually in concert with expansive fiscal policy.

In general, monetary policy tries to work with the business cycle instead of fighting it. The goal is to minimize inflation on the upswings in the cycle and to moderate rising unemployment on the downswings. If the Fed tried to keep the economy constantly expanding, it would be fighting the natural ebb and flow of demand in the economy. As a result, monetary policy would stimulate the economy to grow beyond its natural long-run growth rate, which would generate inflation.

THE REAL WORLD

Central bankers are often characterized as inflation hawks, that is, as officials who prefer to keep inflation low, even at the cost of higher unemployment. There is some truth to this characterization.

However, in the developed world, inflation remained low during the 1990s and 2000s. Theories regarding this include increased use of cheaper labor in developing nations, productivity gains due to new technology, and changes to the way U.S. inflation was calculated. Each played a role, but it's possible that excessive public debt and monetary expansion in developed nations could reignite inflation in the years ahead.

Factors Affecting Monetary Policy

Although markets respond quickly to changes in monetary policy, there's a lag between the time policy is set and implemented and the time it affects the economy. In addition, the effect of a policy change is by no means certain. For example, in May 2000, the fed funds rate stood at 6.5 percent. By November 2002, the Fed had lowered it to 1.25 percent—the lowest level in four decades! Yet economic sluggishness persisted throughout the 12 rate cuts over that time frame, before growth strengthened in 2003 and 2004. Then, for much of 2008 and 2009, with an effective fed funds rate of 0 (the targeted rate was 0 to 0.25 percent, a record low), economic contraction and high unemployment prevailed. (In both cases, however, it is quite reasonable to believe that the economy would have been worse off without the rate cuts.)

Given the lag and uncertainty, the Fed must try to anticipate the path of the economy and the future effects of its actions. For example, if the Fed waits for an increase in inflation before raising rates, the inflationary momentum may already be underway. This would make it harder to diffuse the inflationary pressures and might cost more in lost jobs and output. This is why the Fed is (or used to be) accused of taking away the punch bowl as soon as the party—that is, an expansion—starts. Expansions can bring inflation, and the Fed wants to head it off before it starts. Given the tech stock and housing bubbles of the 1990s and the 2000s, it's possible that the Fed actually will take away the punch bowl when future expansions heat up.

Demand, output, inflation, and employment are also affected by forces outside the Fed's control. These include taxes and government spending at all levels, developments overseas, conditions in the financial markets, and new technologies. In 1997 and 1998, the economies of several East Asian nations slowed down significantly, which reduced their demand for U.S. products. This could have slowed the growth of the

U.S. economy, which exports huge amounts of goods. In the 1990s, heavy investment in personal computers, computer networks, and Internet-related technology began to pay off in terms of increased productivity. An increase in productivity enables the economy to grow at a higher rate without higher inflation. In the 2000s, the housing bubble was fueled by industry practices such as no income-verification loans and widespread subprime lending. The Fed has to factor developments like these into its policies.

Adding to these difficulties is the ever-changing composition of the money supply. So while the Fed still exerts a very real influence in the economy, a good portion of that influence is psychological rather than purely financial.

THE REAL WORLD

Stabilizing the financial system during times of stress stands among the Fed's key responsibilities. It generally does a good job of this. Such stress occurred after the stock market crashed in October 1987; during the international debt crisis in autumn 1998; after the terrorist attacks on September 11, 2001; and after the subprime mortgage loan crisis in 2007 and 2008.

In such instances, the Fed promoted the stability of the financial system by providing liquidity through open market purchases of securities and by extending discount window loans to banks. In addition, in the 2007–2008 crisis, the Fed created the loan facilities mentioned in Chapter 15 and explained later in this chapter and purchased troubled mortgage-backed securities from banks. When the Fed acts in this way, it supports the banking system and, by doing so, calms the markets.

How the Fed Gets the Word Out

The financial and business community closely monitors the Federal Reserve's view of the economy as well as its actions. The Fed employs several means of communicating with its various constituencies, the most important being the Monetary Policy Report to Congress, the Commentary on Current Economic Conditions (known as the Beige Book), and a statement that follows each meeting of the Federal Open Market Committee (FOMC):

- **Monetary Policy Report to Congress:** By law, the Board of Governors of the Federal Reserve must deliver a report to Congress two times a year on economic and financial developments and the nation's monetary policy. This testimony is delivered by the chairman of the Fed, usually in February and July. It includes a report on key economic variables, a review of the monetary policy measures taken since the previous testimony, and a forecast of economic growth. Highlights of this testimony are widely reported in the business news.

- **Commentary on Current Economic Conditions:** Eight times a year, the Fed publishes an informal survey by the 12 Federal Reserve Banks on current economic conditions in their districts. This report is commonly known as the Beige Book because of the color of its cover. The commentary gathers anecdotal information from the Bank presidents and branch directors. Other sources include interviews with key business executives, economists, and market experts. The Beige Book summarizes this information by district and industrial sector (agriculture, manufacturing, and so on).

- **Statements after FOMC Meetings:** After each FOMC meeting, the committee releases a statement announcing the targeted fed funds rate (or the lack of a new target, if there has been no change). The statement also describes the Fed's view of the economic picture and often comments on the risks to economic growth and, since March 2002, notes the vote of each member of the FOMC on monetary policy decisions.

The comments about economic growth are followed closely by the financial community and economists. The comments generally characterize the risks to the economy as positive, negative, or balanced. During and after the recession of 2008–2009, however, the statements followed a somewhat less formulaic approach. They commented more specifically on employment, lending, and housing conditions and on consumer and business spending trends.

THE REAL WORLD

The Fed now operates with far more transparency than it did in the past. Indeed, in a Joint Economic Committee Study in 1997, members of Congress specifically called for greater transparency and less secrecy in the Federal Reserve's conduct of monetary policy.

The Fed and its chairman are conscious that any statement they make may be viewed as prophecy, and the last thing they want to do is upset the markets. Instead, they want the markets to function as freely from direction by the Fed as possible.

Sometimes this desire has motivated the Fed to be secretive, but in recent years the Fed has become more open.

Leadership and Moral Suasion

The chairman of the Federal Reserve plays a very real leadership role in the U.S. and world economy. As part of the leadership role of the position, the Fed Chairman uses *moral suasion* as a policy tool—or rather he used to use it. In the 1960s and before, it was fairly common for the chairman of the Federal Reserve to urge banks to ease or tighten their lending policies, depending on the Fed's desires. Students of economics were taught that moral suasion was among the tools for implementing monetary policy, although a less powerful one than changes to interest rates or reserve requirements.

Today, however, the role of moral suasion appears to be diminished, perhaps because large companies rely far less heavily on banks for short-term funds. (The commercial paper market emerged in the 1970s.) Or perhaps in this age of hyper-coverage of business and economics by the media, the Fed would rather not put itself on the line in that manner. All of this said, the Fed chairman can move the markets—sometimes.

Let's Look at the Record

When the Federal Reserve was established in 1913, its main purpose was to prevent financial panics and runs on banks by acting as lender of last resort to the banking system. The Fed served this function by making loans to banks through the discount windows of the Reserve Banks. The Fed's limited charter, along with the gold standard, minimized the central bank's role in economic policy.

The Great Depression and the fiscal policy ideas of John Maynard Keynes prompted the government to take a more active role in managing the economy. After World War II, the Employment Act of 1946 required the federal government to "promote maximum employment, production, and purchasing power." This act didn't explicitly mention the Fed's role in this endeavor, and again, the Fed was somewhat constrained—relative to the leeway it has today—in influencing economic growth.

During the 1950s, annual inflation averaged about 2.2 percent as the economy expanded by an average of almost 3 percent a year and unemployment averaged 4.5 percent. The Federal Reserve was doing something right. For one thing, it established the overnight market in federal funds in the mid-1950s, which provided another, more flexible way to influence the money supply. In addition, the central bank deliberately focused on keeping inflation in check by raising rates in anticipation of increases in prices.

Inflationary pressures increased in the late 1960s due largely to budget deficits generated by spending on the Vietnam War and the Great Society social programs. As measured by the *consumer price index*, inflation averaged 4.3 percent from 1966 through 1969 versus 1.3 percent from 1960 through 1965. Unemployment averaged 4.8 percent for the decade, a modest increase over the 4.5 percent average of the 1950s. The prevailing view, especially among monetarists, is that the Fed failed to fight inflation vigorously as this decade of economic growth and deficit spending progressed.

Whether or not that is so, inflation rose to unprecedented levels in the 1970s due to continuing budget deficits and the tripling of oil prices. During this period, the Fed definitely didn't fight inflation actively enough. Both the *real* discount rate and the *real* fed funds rate were negative for most of the second half of the decade as inflation rose from 4.9 percent in 1976 to 13.3 percent in 1979. Meanwhile, the unemployment rate rose to an average of 6.2 percent for the decade.

 ECONOTALK

The **consumer price index** measures the increase or decrease in the price of a market basket of goods and services that a typical consumer purchases in the course of a month. A **real** interest rate is the rate under consideration—the discount rate, fed funds rate, or prime rate—minus the rate of inflation.

Beating inflation became the priority in the 1980s. The consumer price index rose by 13.3 percent in 1979 and by 12.5 percent in 1980. But the real fed funds rate was cranked up to the 7 to 9 percent range in those years, and inflation eased back to 8 percent in 1981 and dropped to 3.8 percent in 1982 and 1983. From 1984 through 1989, inflation averaged 3.7 percent. This occurred in an environment of vigorous deficit spending, showing that aggressive management of the money supply can indeed combat inflation. However, there may have been a price to pay in unemployment, which rose to an average of 7.3 percent for the decade (and exceeded 9.5 percent in 1982 and 1983).

The Fed continued to keep inflation at bay in the 1990s, when the consumer price index rose by an average of 2.9 percent for the decade and by just 2.5 percent from 1993 through 1999. In the early 2000s, it hovered around 2 percent, where it stayed for most of the decade. Unemployment averaged 5.5 percent from 1990 through 2001 and remained in that range until the onset of the Great Recession in 2008.

Over the past 50 years, judged by its goal of helping to maintain a growing economy with low inflation and low unemployment, the Fed succeeded in the 1950s and early 1960s. It failed in the late 1960s and the 1970s, succeeded in the 1980s on inflation but failed on unemployment in that decade. It succeeded on both counts from the 1990s until the late 2000s—that is, to the extent that the Fed can indeed be blamed or credited.

ECONOTIP

One major difficulty in judging the effectiveness of economic policy is that increases or decreases in output, unemployment, inflation, and other measures may or may not be directly attributable to the policy in question.

For instance, would the Fed have worsened matters by raising short-term rates in the 1970s to try to curb inflation? Maybe, maybe not. The prime rate and mortgage rates reached historic highs without curing inflation, so perhaps it wouldn't have helped. On the other hand, the Fed didn't inspire much confidence in the 1970s, so action might have helped. Was it monetary policy that created the expansions of the 1980s and 1990s? Or was it fiscal policy? Probably both. Did the easy-money policies of the Fed contribute to the dot-com and home price bubbles of the 1990s and 2000s? Quite possibly.

The Fed's Response to the 2008 Financial Crisis

As the financial markets were threatened in 2008 by the failure of Bear Stearns and market turmoil, the Fed (along with the U.S. Treasury) supported several major banking institutions. As the regulator of the banking system, the Fed took a number of other steps to address the crisis, the most significant being the following.

Lowering the Fed Funds Rate

Between June 2006—when the fed funds rate peaked at 5.25 percent—and December 2008, the Fed lowered the rate in 10 increments to virtually 0 (technically, between 0 and 0.25 percent). This was a first in Fed history, and it shows how desperate the central bank was to inject liquidity into the financial system and encourage banks to lend.

Providing Short-Term Loans to Banks

Apart from interest rates, the Fed has other policy tools to achieve its goals and to play its role of *lender of last resort*. I mentioned these loan facilities earlier in this chapter and in Chapter 15, and they include:

- **Term asset-backed securities loan facility,** which helps banks extend credit to households and small businesses by supporting securities collateralized by student, auto, and credit card loans, and loans guaranteed by the Small Business Administration.

- **Term auction facility,** under which the Fed auctions funds to banks as it did aggressively in 2008. These funds must be fully collateralized, and the rates are determined by auctions among the banks.

- **Commercial-paper funding facility,** which backs up U.S. issuers of commercial paper (unsecured short-term borrowings among major banks and corporations) by guaranteeing payment in the event of default. The commercial paper market is an essential source of credit for major banks and corporations in the economy, and the subprime crisis threatened the liquidity of this market.

ECONOTALK

The term **lender of last resort** refers to the entity that can supply liquidity—that is, money—to the banking system when the banking system has insufficient funds. During one banking crisis in the early 1900s, banker J.P. Morgan acted as lender of last resort, but that was before the Federal Reserve System was established.

These tools all aimed to put money into the banking system and thus to increase the supply of loanable funds. The Fed has policy tools beyond these and can add others as conditions warrant, as you can learn by visiting www.federalreserve.gov/monetarypolicy and clicking on *Policy Tools*.

The Fed's Expanding Balance Sheet

Many banks availed themselves of the loan facilities described previously. As a result, the Fed's balance sheet expanded significantly as the crisis unfolded. The Fed's balance sheet is, like any balance sheet, a snapshot of the entity's assets, liabilities, and net worth on a specific date. Over the course of the crisis, the Fed's balance sheet—generally measured by its total assets—more than doubled. Specifically, from the end of 2007 to the end of 2008, total assets rose from $915 billion to $2.3 trillion, an unprecedented increase.

Concerns about the Fed's balance sheet arise in thoughtful critiques of the government's response to the crisis. However, often left unexplained is the significance of the expansion in the Fed's positions and the potential positive or negative implications.

First, the significance. The goal of the Fed during the crisis was to provide liquidity to the banking system. It does this mainly by extending short-term loans to banks. Ordinarily it does so by creating new reserves—in essence a loan to each bank requiring one, against which the bank can lend to its customers. However, creating those reserves at the high level required in that crisis could have expanded the money supply too much, too fast and created inflationary pressures. So instead, the Fed started paying interest on reserves, which attracted—rather than created—reserves. It also sold holdings of Treasury securities and loaned the proceeds, which doesn't change the amount of money in the economy. The Fed created new assets in the form of its various facilities, again with the goal of providing liquidity while minimizing inflationary pressures.

All of these new assets expanded the Fed's balance sheet, with liabilities expanding as well. (To a bank, including a central bank, a loan to another entity is an asset—cash to be collected from a borrower—and a deposit is a liability—cash to be paid to a depositor.) For example, on the liability side of the balance sheet, deposits from banks rose from $20 billion at the end of 2007 to $860 billion at the end of 2008. Deposits from the Treasury rose from $16 billion to $106 billion, and a new Treasury Supplementary Financing Account added another nearly $260 billion. Those three liability items funded more than $1.2 trillion of the $1.4 trillion in assets added during 2008.

These moves by the Fed amounted to an unprecedented, extremely strong response to market concerns about bank liquidity. The strength of this response generated strong opinions regarding potential positive and negative implications.

On the positive side: although the strength of the Fed's response scared some observers (causing them to see the central bank as trying to ward off a depression), that response by the Fed was apparently called for, given the threat to the U.S. and global financial system. We know this because the Fed kept expanding its balance sheet, creating new facilities, and requesting more assistance from the Treasury over the course of the crisis. Central bankers do not expand their institutions' balance sheets for no reason; they do it in response to demand from the banking system. We can all take solace that the growth in the Fed's balance sheet not only ceased after the period of greatest threat to the financial system, but that contraction in the balance sheet occurred after the danger passed.

Also on the positive side, the Fed could readily unwind many of the assets it created to provide liquidity and thus contract its balance sheet. Most of the asset positions could be unwound, as long as it was neither premature nor too late. If the Fed's balance sheet were to contract prematurely and credit availability dried up, it could hobble the recovery. If the balance sheet were to expand too much for too long, it could allow credit to expand to the point at which inflation could be ignited.

On the negative side, some feared that the Fed *may* have created moral hazard, set the stage for inflation, or assumed inordinate risks in some cases, such as in purchasing mortgage-backed securities from banks. These fears were real but minor, particularly next to the prospect of the Fed doing too little to address the crisis. So much of what the Fed did centered on short-term assets and facilities that it did not really incur much long-term risk. It also did what it could to minimize inflationary pressures, as explained above. Finally, the Fed's purchases of risky assets, and specifically mortgage-backed securities—although they totaled in the billions—represented a small portion of its total assets.

So, both in times of crisis and in normal times, keep an eye on the Fed and you will have a good fix on monetary policy and, usually, on the general direction of the economy.

Fed Watching

Fed watching is the name given to the pastime of anticipating and understanding changes in monetary policy. Serious Fed watchers pour through the Fed chairman's testimony before Congress and the Beige Book at the Fed's website. Anyone with any interest in the direction of the economy will watch for changes in the targeted fed funds rate after a meeting of the FOMC. The schedule of meetings is posted at the Fed's website, as are the press releases of the statement issued after each meeting.

Most (but not all) Fed watchers believe that the Fed knows what it is doing, particularly because the Board of Governors and the FOMC have access to the best economic and financial data and information. Moreover, whether or not the Fed gauges the condition or future path of the economy correctly, monetary policy can amount to a self-fulfilling prophecy. If the Fed believes that inflationary pressures are rising, and as a result increases the targeted fed funds rate, the effect will be to slow the growth of the money supply and perhaps the growth of the economy. Conversely, if the Fed believes that the economy needs a boost, and as a result adopts a policy of easy money, the effect will be to increase the growth of the money supply and perhaps economic growth.

THE REAL WORLD

Some Fed watchers believe that the Fed considers the White House's stake in economic performance. Fed Chairman Alan Greenspan, who served from mid-1987 to early 2006, kept rates low through the tech stock and housing bubbles. That helped feed the growth—or apparent growth—of the economy under Bill Clinton and George W. Bush, which made Greenspan popular with those presidents. That's partly why some observers feel the Fed is politicized, implementing policies that may help the banking system and the political party at the helm, but with risk to longer-term economic prospects.

In the previous paragraph, the word *perhaps* is important. While people often speak of the levers of monetary policy—rates, reserves, and so on—there isn't a mechanical relationship between lower rates and higher growth or vice versa. Recent evidence of this occurred when the Fed reduced the fed funds rate to the 0 to 0.25 percent range for much of the Great Recession (its lowest level ever), and lending and economic activity both remained stagnant.

One issue complicating that situation was the fact that rates had been kept relatively low for much of the previous expansion. Given that, and the fact that deficit spending (also known as fiscal stimulus) continued throughout the expansion, both the Bush and Obama administrations were left with few policy options when the financial crisis and economic downturn did hit. Monetary stimulus can hardly be expected to work when interest rates were already relatively low.

So as you watch the Fed, watch with the knowledge that whatever the Fed does may or may not work as intended.

The Least You Need to Know

- Monetary policy tries to work with the business cycle instead of fighting it. The goal is to control inflation during expansions and to moderate rising unemployment during contractions.

- The Fed communicates by means of its Monetary Policy Report to Congress, Commentary on Current Economic Conditions (the Beige Book), and statements following each meeting of the Federal Open Market Committee—and through its website at www.federalreserve.com.

- The Fed helped to maintain a growing economy with low inflation and low unemployment in the 1950s and early 1960s, failed in the late 1960s and the 1970s, succeeded on inflation in the 1980s, and succeeded on both in the 1990s.

- During the financial crisis and subsequent severe recession of the late 2000s, the Fed acted aggressively to keep interest rates low and support the banking system—and thus the economy. The support for the banking system essentially worked, but the monetary stimulus proved less effective because rates were kept fairly low during the preceding expansion.

- Fed watchers believe that the Fed has superior economic and financial information and that monetary policy affects the economy. Therefore, they try to anticipate, or at least understand, the Fed's thinking and decisions.

The Global Economy

Like any economy, the global economy is a system in which transactions (exchanges of goods and services for money) take place—in this case, in the form of foreign trade and international finance. Several factors make these transactions more complicated than transactions in a national economy. These factors center on the many differences—in currencies, laws, languages, customs, and cultures—among nations.

In this part, we look at the workings of foreign trade, international finance, the global marketplace, and developing economies. We also touch upon topics such as globalization, trade blocs, and the capitalist trends that have emerged in China. Our goal in this part is to understand why nations do business—and refuse to do business—with one another and the transformative power of economics in the world today.

International Trade: Exports, Imports, etc.

In This Chapter

- Why nations import and export goods
- International trade agreements
- Protectionism and other trade policies

Up to now, we have left exports and imports—the final component of gross domestic product (GDP)—out of our analysis. Now it's time to bring them in. It's a potentially complex area, but this chapter will first show why nations export and import goods, and then examine barriers to trade and various steps governments have taken to lower barriers to trade.

Foreign trade isn't as emotionally loaded as say, taxes and government spending, but, like most topics in economics, it stirs the blood of people whose livelihoods and lifestyles are most affected by exports and imports. They have very real concerns, but those concerns are specific to their individual lives. Economists almost universally believe that foreign trade in a free global marketplace will create the greatest good for the greatest number of people.

Let's start with why economists would believe this.

Exports, Imports—Why Bother?

The fundamental reason for foreign trade is quite simple: some nations are better at producing certain things than others. This means that all nations will be economically better off if they specialize in what they do best and exchange a portion of what they produce for the goods of other nations who also specialize in what they do best.

In a way, the rationale for international trade follows the same logic that caused a worker in a medieval village to specialize in butchering, baking, or candlestick making, and then to exchange her goods with other specialists. International trade works the same way, only on a larger scale.

To illustrate this, let's suppose that there are only two countries on the planet—the United States and Japan—and they make only two products: food and personal computers. The following two tables show the production possibilities, per week, for each nation.

Table 17.1   U.S. Production Possibilities (in thousands per week)

Possibility	Bushels of Food	Personal Computers
A	0	12
B	3	9
C	6	6
D	9	3
E	12	0

Table 17.2   Japan's Production Possibilities (in thousands per week)

Possibility	Bushels of Food	Personal Computers
A	0	12
B	1	9
C	2	6
D	3	3
E	4	0

Figure 17.1 shows the production possibility functions of each nation. It is simply the graphic representation of the values in Tables 17.1 and 17.2.

Each nation can produce the same number of personal computers in a week. But the United States can produce three times as much food as Japan. In other words, if each nation chose to produce only computers, they would each produce 12,000, but if each chose to produce only food, the United States would produce 12,000 bushels and Japan would produce only 4,000.

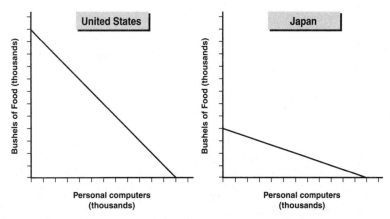

Figure 17.1

At first glance, it may seem as if the two nations—particularly the United States—have no reason to engage in foreign trade. After all, the United States is just as efficient at producing computers and three times as efficient at producing food. Why would the United States be interested in trade?

Here's where the notion of *comparative advantage* comes in. The United States can produce either food or computers at a one-to-one trade-off. In other words, if the United States chooses to produce another personal computer, it must give up one bushel of food. That bushel of food is the United States' opportunity cost of producing another computer.

However, if Japan gives up one bushel of food, it can produce three personal computers. The opportunity cost of producing personal computers in Japan is only one-third what it is in the United States. Japan sacrifices less food than the United States would in order to increase its production of personal computers.

The nation with the lower opportunity cost in producing a good has a comparative advantage in the production of that product. In this case, Japan has a lower opportunity cost than the United States in producing computers. The United States has what economists call an *absolute advantage* in producing food. The United States can produce 12,000 bushels of food per week while Japan can produce only 4,000. But absolute advantage doesn't necessarily indicate that a nation should export that product. That's because the nation might have to give up producing some of a product in which it has an even greater absolute advantage.

ECONOTALK

Comparative advantage arises for a nation when its opportunity cost of producing a good is lower than that of another nation. **Absolute advantage** arises when a nation can produce a good more cheaply than another nation. Comparative advantage, not absolute advantage, indicates which good a nation should export or import.

The British economist David Ricardo (1772–1823) developed the concept of comparative advantage to answer the question, "Which nation should specialize in producing which good?" He found that the nation having a lower opportunity cost than other nations in producing a product should specialize in that product, and he called that the principle of comparative advantage.

So in this example, even though the United States has the absolute advantage in producing food and is equally efficient at producing personal computers, Japan has a comparative advantage in producing personal computers. However, the United States also has a comparative advantage relative to Japan—in food.

Why? Because the United States only has to give up one personal computer to produce an additional bushel of food, while Japan must give up three computers. The United States faces a lower opportunity cost than Japan when it chooses to produce food instead of computers. That means that the United States should produce food and exchange it with Japan for computers.

So in our example and in theory, the United States would produce only food, Japan would produce only personal computers, and they would each exchange some of their production with one another.

ECONOTIP

The top 11 trading partners of the United States in 2009 were Canada, China, Mexico, Japan, Germany, the United Kingdom, South Korea, France, the Netherlands, Taiwan, and Brazil. This is based on U.S. Census totals of both imports and exports. These 11 countries account for 60 to 65 percent of U.S. import and export volume.

The Argument for Free Trade

Obviously, the example here is incredibly oversimplified. In the real world, scores of nations produce thousands of products, most with different cost structures and at different levels of efficiency. However, this simple example is the fundamental argument for free trade, which most economists support both in theory and in practice.

Economists support free trade because in general they want an economy, including the global economy, to deliver the greatest good to the greatest number of people. A look back at the example of United States and Japanese food and computer production will reveal the benefits of specialization and exchange.

If you pick any possibility from the range of production possibilities in Tables 17.1 and 17.2, you will see that the greatest total production of food and computers occurs when the United States produces only food and Japan produces only personal computers. The following table shows one example:

Table 17.3

	Food	Computers
Possibility C:		
United States	6,000	6,000
Japan	2,000	6,000
Total	8,000	12,000
Total production = 20,000 units		
With Specialization:		
United States	12,000	0
Japan	0	12,000
Total	12,000	12,000
Total production = 24,000 units		

Specialization generates the highest level of production of the two goods. Then, through trade, each nation can consume the amount of the good that it wants to consume. In this way, production is maximized because each nation is doing what it does most efficiently.

Again, this is an oversimplification. A range of issues, including transportation costs, quality, differences in domestic demand, and national security considerations are all left out of the analysis. Yet the very real principle of comparative advantage and the equally real benefits of trade form the basic argument in favor of free trade.

Unfortunately, numerous arguments—and measures—against free international trade have taken hold in the world.

Arguments Against Free Trade

Today, most arguments against free international trade are mounted by special-interest groups. Both labor unions and management oppose free trade when they believe— sometimes correctly, sometimes incorrectly—that it will make them worse off. What they conveniently ignore is that free trade will make everyone else better off.

It is true that if the U.S. auto industry loses 5,000 jobs to foreign competitors, those 5,000 workers and their households are worse off. However, the millions of other households that can purchase less expensive, more efficient vehicles from a wider range of choices are better off. The pain endured by one of those 5,000 households may well be greater than the benefit enjoyed by any given car-buying household. That is why labor unions fight so hard to keep their members' jobs. But an economist would argue that if another nation can make cars more efficiently, those U.S. auto-workers should move into another U.S. industry and let the whole population enjoy the benefits of free trade with the more efficient auto industry of another nation.

Special-interest groups put forth various arguments to support their view. Some arguments make a certain amount of economic sense, and others are incorrect or at least suspect. The truth, however, is that those asking for protection from free trade usually stand to benefit the most.

The arguments most often heard are:

- It's important to keep jobs in the United States.
- Low foreign wages are harming the U.S. economy.
- We don't want money leaving the country.
- National security is at stake.
- Other nations don't treat their workers fairly.
- Other nations are dumping goods in the United States and don't open their market to us.

Let's look at these positions one at a time.

Keeping jobs in the United States is important, but it's more important to keep jobs in industries in which we operate efficiently. Otherwise, we are subsidizing inefficiency, which hurts national productivity as well as consumers. If, indeed, another nation is more efficient—has a comparative advantage—in producing a product, it's generally in our interests to buy it from them.

As to the idea that we are exporting jobs when, say, U.S. auto manufacturers set up assembly plants in Mexico, the autoworkers' union has a point. But the same counter-argument applies. If Mexico is the least expensive place to assemble the vehicles, from an economic standpoint, that is where it should be done—as long as it can be done with the same level of quality.

The quality argument is often put forth as a reason to keep jobs in the United States. In reality, however, imported goods of inferior quality sell at lower prices, which reflects their quality and gives the consumer another choice. (Some people *like* cheap shoes.) Also, foreign producers have a good record of improving the quality of their goods to meet U.S. standards. The Japanese auto industry of the 1970s and 1980s provides an outstanding example of this. American producers in certain industries have done the same thing. For instance, over the past 25 years, the California wine industry has improved the quality of its wines to compete with imports from France. That created jobs in the United States' wine industry—and in trucking, warehousing, advertising, retailing, and restaurants (thereby employing otherwise unemployable wine stewards)—while combating imports of burgundy and Bordeaux.

Low foreign wages are harming the U.S. economy, and the United States has not done enough to remain competitive. If a low-wage foreign industry threatens a U.S. indus-try, it basically means that the foreign nation has a comparative advantage in that industry. The question is, what should the United States do to respond?

On one level, the argument that low foreign wages can harm a U.S. industry is bogus. What matters is not just the level of wages, but also the level of wages relative to the productivity of the workers. If a U.S. industry has high wages—say, quadruple the level of the foreign wage—but is six times more productive, that industry is still quite competitive with the foreign one. Productivity relates not only to the volume of goods but also to their quality. Germany, a relatively high-wage nation, has a strongly export-driven economy, thanks in large part to the high quality of its goods.

So the United States can increase its productivity and it can increase the quality of its goods, both of which it has done. Quality increased dramatically in the California wine industry but less so in automobiles. The United States can also try to contain its labor costs. A developed nation like the United States cannot really compete on labor costs with a very low-wage economy like China's—but it could adopt universal, taxpayer-funded health insurance, as every other developed nation has, and do more to contain increases in health-care costs. That would help to put U.S. industries on a more even footing with those of other developed nations.

THE REAL WORLD

The United States has in fact exported millions of manufacturing jobs over the past 25 years. That has hurt the U.S. economy because manufacturing jobs usually enable semiskilled workers (without college educations) to produce items of enough value to justify good wages. That is, the combination of capital (machinery) and labor boosts labor productivity and justifies a higher wage.

Observers who note that the U.S. economy has instead created millions of low-wage service jobs (in restaurants, retail, and hotels) have a point. But rather than governments trying to protect existing manufacturing jobs that natural market forces would eliminate, they should put public support behind developing an educated and trained workforce so more workers can produce higher-value goods and services in new or evolving industries such as information technology, health care, and clean energy.

We don't want money leaving the country may sound like a sensible argument when you look at the GDP formula. If we import more than we export, GDP is lowered. Doesn't that mean we are worse off? In a way, yes; but in a way, no.

The money-leaving-the-country argument goes all the way back to mercantilism, the economic theory that international trade generates wealth for a nation. The mercantilists believed that exports should be encouraged, imports should be discouraged, and gold should be hoarded. Mercantilism flourished in the 1600s and 1700s and fueled the worldwide exploration and imperialism of Western European nations in those centuries. However, as economic theory, mercantilism is dead.

Keeping money in the country is not a priority. We don't want exports to be high because they keep money in the country but because they fuel domestic production and incomes. If those incomes are spent on imports, that can be a very good thing for consumers. From the economists' point of view, the way to promote exports is not by limiting imports. Other nations will retaliate against protectionist policies, anyway. The way to promote exports is to be as innovative, productive, and efficient as we can be.

National security is at stake with regard to some industries. Defense is the best example of an industry that requires protection on the basis of national security. Steel may be another, but the steel industry has been only partly successful with this argument. Oil is another industry on which national security can depend, although, as a by-product of its support for the domestic auto industry, U.S. consumption of and dependence on foreign oil has been encouraged by the phase-out of fuel efficiency standards for passenger vehicles and low gasoline taxes (relative to those in Europe).

Although economists disagree about how best to protect industries on which national security depends, most agree that some industries warrant such protection. They also agree that some industries that have claimed this status, such as the American watch industry (I'm serious), probably do not warrant it.

Other nations' unfair treatment of their workers is a relatively new argument against imports, and it can be a tough argument both to document and deflect. It's hard to document because, as we've learned, everything is relative. The awful truth is that, bad as they are, jobs in sweatshops may still be the best way for people in poor nations to feed and clothe themselves. Limiting imports from these nations may hurt the very people we would be trying to help. These arguments are hard to deflect because the truth is that low-cost foreign production sites often don't meet reasonable health and safety standards.

Then there is the issue of child labor and forced labor, which virtually everyone sees as highly exploitative. UNICEF estimates that 158 million children from ages 5 to 14 are engaged in child labor. The International Labor Organization estimates that 218 million children from ages 5 to 17 are child laborers. The United States has funded and contributed to a number of efforts to prevent child labor and is the world's largest contributor to the International Program for the Elimination of Child Labor.

Several efforts to have other nations voluntarily comply with guidelines for eliminating child labor are underway. The United States devotes tens of millions of dollars annually to international programs to end abusive child labor. Also, in 1999, the United States ratified a new international initiative to eliminate child slavery, debt bondage, and forced labor.

In addition, the Child Labor Deterrence Act was introduced as a bill to the United States Congress in 1999, but it has yet to pass. However, in 1999, Executive Order #13126 prohibited federal agencies from buying products made with forced or indentured child labor. More recently, the Food, Conservation, and Energy Act, passed in 2008, established the Consultative Group to Eliminate the Use of Child Labor and Forced Labor in Imported Agricultural Products.

ECONOTIP

Even eliminating child labor is controversial because doing so can put children out of work in foreign economies, which can harm their families financially and force them into more hazardous or unhealthy forms of work.

Other nations dumping goods in the United States and keeping our imports out do give protectionists ammunition in their battle against free trade. Dumping occurs when a nation sells its goods in a foreign market at a price that is lower than its price in the domestic market or lower than it cost to produce. The objective is to drive the domestic producer out of the market—and out of business—and then to raise the price when the domestic competition is gone. Both dumping and protectionism by other nations can put the United States at a disadvantage.

Under current laws and trade agreements, dumping is illegal. If U.S. producers can prove that dumping is occurring, special duties can be added to the price of the goods being dumped. One reason that dumping occurs is that many foreign industries are subsidized by their government in ways that ours are not (although U.S. agriculture is highly subsidized, as is agriculture in most industrial nations). The steel industry is a good example of an industry that has won protection. In 2001, President Bush levied tariffs of up to 40 percent on certain types of steel imports. In 2009, President Obama levied tariffs starting at 35 percent on $1.8 billion of tire imports from China. Perhaps in retaliation, China began an investigation into potential U.S. dumping of chicken and automotive products.

When other countries practice protectionism, the preferred method is to work toward free—or at least fair—trade through a process of negotiation. These processes have been quite useful and have brought the world into an age of much freer international trade.

The Rise of China

China has developed into a significant global economic force over the past 20 years. Through a mix of high savings, investment in public projects, rapid industrialization, gradual adoption of capitalist-style economic incentives, and disciplined trade and foreign-exchange policy, the People's Republic of China has achieved double-digit GDP growth in most of the past decade, and close to it during the global recession of the late 2000s.

Much of China's growth has been export-led, and the United States is the nation's largest trading partner. However, China has also seen to its internal infrastructure and applied some $600 billion in economic stimulus, a good portion of it in the form of public projects, to support demand during and after the recession.

Perhaps most surprisingly, in 2010 China held about $1 trillion in U.S. Treasury securities—surprising because the United States, as the more developed and far larger ($14.3 trillion) economy, would normally be expected to be a net creditor of a less developed and smaller ($4.9 trillion) major trading partner like China. So there is some truth to the notion often cited in the media that the United States is borrowing from China to buy its products.

Indeed, China's exports of consumer goods to the United States have helped keep U.S. inflation low and spurred China's growth. However, tensions over trade and economic issues have occasionally increased between the two nations. The U.S. trade deficit with China (the excess of imports from China over exports to China) grew from about $83 billion in 2000 and 2001 to $268 billion (that is, over a quarter of a trillion) in 2008, and then eased back to $227 billion in 2009.

This deficit must be financed, as explained in Chapter 18, and financing it over the years has led to the $1 trillion in U.S. debt held by China. At one point in 2009, the overall high level of U.S. debt prompted a Chinese official to express concerns about the value of the dollar. The low U.S. savings rate must increase and consumption in China must increase even faster than it is (or its savings must decrease, or both) for this situation to change. That may or may not occur, and will probably take time, but it is certain that China—now the world's second largest national economy—has become a major player in the world economy.

Barriers to International Trade

Free trade refers to the elimination of barriers to international trade. The most common barriers to trade are *tariffs*, *quotas*, and *nontariff barriers*.

ECONOTALK

A **tariff** is a tax on imported goods, while a **quota** is a limit on the amount of goods that may be imported. Both tariffs and quotas raise the price of and lower the demand for the goods to which they apply. **Nontariff barriers,** such as regulations calling for a certain percentage of locally produced content in the product, also have the same effect, but not as directly.

A tariff is a tax on imports, which is usually collected by the federal government and which raises the price of the good to the consumer. Also known as duties or import duties, tariffs usually aim first to limit imports and second to raise revenue. A quota is a limit on the amount of a certain type of good that may be imported into the country. A quota can be either voluntary or legally enforced.

The effect of tariffs and quotas is the same: to limit imports and protect domestic producers from foreign competition. A tariff raises the price of the foreign good beyond the market equilibrium price, which decreases the demand for and, eventually, the supply of the foreign good. A quota limits the supply to a certain quantity, which raises the price beyond the market equilibrium level and thus decreases demand.

Tariffs come in different forms, mostly depending on the motivation—or rather, the stated motivation. (The actual motivation is always to limit imports.) For instance, a tariff may be levied in order to bring the price of the imported good up to the level of the domestically produced good. This so-called scientific tariff has the stated goal of equalizing the price and, therefore, leveling the playing field between foreign and domestic producers. In this game, the consumer loses.

A peril-point tariff is levied in order to save a domestic industry that has deteriorated to the point where its very existence is in peril. An economist would argue that the industry should be allowed to expire. That way, factors of production used by that inefficient industry could move into a new one where they would be better employed.

A retaliatory tariff is one that is levied in response to a tariff levied by a trading partner. In the eyes of an economist, retaliatory tariffs make no sense because they just start tariff wars in which no one—least of all the consumer—wins.

ECONOTIP

You may wonder why a nation would ever choose to use a quota when a tariff has the added advantage of raising revenue. The major reason is that quotas allow the nation that uses them to decide the quantity to be imported and let the price go where it will. A tariff adjusts the price but leaves the post-tariff quantity to market forces. Therefore, it is less predictable and precise than a quota.

Nontariff barriers include quotas, regulations regarding product content or quality, and other conditions that hinder imports. One of the most commonly used nontariff barriers are product standards, which may aim to serve as barriers to trade. For instance, when the United States prohibits the importation of unpasteurized cheeses aged less than 60 days, is it protecting the health of the American consumer or the revenue of the American cheese producer?

Other nontariff barriers include packing and shipping regulations, harbor and airport permits, and onerous customs procedures, all of which can have either legitimate or anti-import agendas, or both.

THE REAL WORLD

Before they formed the European Union (EU), European nations used many trade barriers and other forms of protectionism to favor their own industries and control imports. While some, such as the German beer purity law (the Reinheitsgebot, which dated from the 1500s), were rooted in tradition, others, such as some nations' laws about decibel limits on certain machines, were rooted in industry lobbying.

However, the EU did away with most barriers of this nature to allow for freer trade. Two of the major benefits were much easier movement of goods across borders and increased trade volume.

International Trade Agreements

Trade agreements regulate international trade between two or more nations. An agreement may cover all imports and exports, certain categories of goods, or a single category. The United States is currently engaged in over 300 trade agreements with various nations. However, several general trade agreements have shaped trade policy on broad levels.

The most important general trade agreement is called, simply enough, the General Agreement on Tariffs and Trade (GATT). GATT was signed in October 1947 to liberalize trade, create an organization to administer more liberal trade agreements, and establish a mechanism for resolving trade disputes. The GATT organization is small and located in Geneva. More than 125 nations have signed the general agreement, which originally was signed by 24 nations, including the United States. To a large degree, the role of GATT as an organization has been superseded by the World Trade Organization, which I discuss later in this section.

Since GATT was signed, several rounds of talks to liberalize trade have occurred. The most significant of these were the Kennedy rounds in the 1960s (which eventually led to a one-third reduction in tariffs) and, in the 1990s, the Uruguay rounds.

The Uruguay rounds dealt with general barriers to trade and the relatively new issues of intellectual property rights, fishing practices, and environmental concerns.

The Doha rounds (named for the city in Qatar) began in 2001 with the goal of further lowering tariffs and increasing trade volume. Related negotiations occurred in Cancun, Geneva, Hong Kong, Paris, and Potsdam. Progress has been made in areas such as licensing medications and protecting patents, but negotiations broke down over agricultural issues and the level of special treatment to be accorded to developing nations. Of course, international negotiations of this type usually progress slowly (or in fits and starts) and break down occasionally, only to be revived.

A major trend of the past 30 years has been the creation and growth of free trade zones among nations agreeing to form regional trade blocs. The agreements that create free trade zones all share the same aims: to liberalize trade, promote economic growth, and provide equal access to markets among the member nations.

The most significant free trade zones are the European Union (EU), the North American Free Trade Agreement (NAFTA), and the Association of Southeast Asian Nations (ASEAN).

In addition, the World Trade Organization (WTO) is a global organization, headquartered in Geneva, for dealing with trade between nations. Established in January 1995 by the Uruguay round negotiations under GATT, the WTO included 153 nations as of May 2010. The WTO administers trade agreements, provides a forum for trade negotiations and resolving trade disputes, monitors trade policies, and provides technical assistance and training for developing countries.

ECONOTIP

Check out the European Union official (English language) website at europa.eu/index_en.htm, the NAFTA website at www.nafta-sec-alena.org, the ASEAN site at www.aseansec.org, and the World Trade Organization website at www.wto.org.

Let's Trade

Despite calls for protectionism from those who stand to lose from free trade, the world has clearly been liberalizing trade policy, lowering barriers to trade, and forming regional trade blocs. As a result, international trade is freer than it has ever been. We can all thank economists for this. They are without a doubt the steadiest, strongest, clearest voices in favor of free trade.

U.S. tariffs stand at their lowest level in history. Before World War II they ranged up to 40 percent on some imports. Today, tariff revenues amount to less than 5 percent of import dollar volume, and many imports are exempt from tariffs and quotas. Nontariff barriers to trade have also been largely—but not completely—eliminated.

This does not mean that all is rosy in the world of foreign trade, nor does it mean that the United States always plays fair in the global marketplace. U.S. agricultural subsidies and textile tariffs, for example, sometimes hinder imports of food, cloth, and clothing from poor nations in order to protect these domestic industries. Nevertheless, the United States and the world in general are expected to continue on the path toward freer international trade.

The Least You Need to Know

- A nation has a comparative advantage in producing a good when its opportunity cost of producing it is lower than that of another nation. A nation has an absolute advantage when it can produce a good more cheaply than another nation can.

- Comparative advantage, not absolute advantage, determines which goods a nation should export and import. A nation should export goods in which it has a comparative advantage and import those in which it has a comparative disadvantage, vis-à-vis another nation.

- While some arguments against free trade are sound, others are mere excuses for protectionism put forth by those who would benefit most by limiting imports.

- The most significant trade agreements have been the General Agreement on Tariffs and Trade (GATT) and those that have produced the free trade zones of the European Union, NAFTA, and ASEAN.

- Over the past 30 years, trade policy has generally become more liberal across the world, and economists expect this trend to continue.

International Finance

In This Chapter

- Foreign exchange rates and how they work
- Trade deficits and their importance
- The international monetary system
- Why a strong dollar can be good or bad

In our discussion of foreign trade in Chapter 17, we left out one crucial element: how do buyers and sellers in different countries do business when they all use different currencies? When a giant bluefin tuna is packed in ice and flown from Cape Cod to Tokyo, the fishing boat captain wants to be paid in dollars. But the Japanese fishmonger has nothing but yen. That doesn't help the Cape Cod captain, who has to pay his crew and his bills in dollars. So the Japanese fishmonger must somehow pay for the tuna in dollars.

How are these problems resolved? What determines how many yen a dollar is worth? In other words, how does the foreign exchange system work?

This chapter answers these questions and explains the foreign exchange markets, balance of payments, International Monetary Fund, and what is meant by a *strong* or *weak* dollar.

About Foreign Exchange

As you know, money is anything that is accepted as a medium of exchange. In most of the world, people accept pieces of paper imprinted with pictures of national heroes or local wonders of nature as money. But in each nation, they accept different pieces of paper.

This means that if someone in the United States wants to buy something from someone in, say, Mexico, she must first exchange her local currency—dollars—for the currency accepted in Mexico—pesos. This *currency conversion* occurs at an *exchange rate*.

ECONOTALK

Currency conversion is the procedure of changing one currency into another currency. The **exchange rate** is the ratio by which one currency is converted into another. It is the price of one currency expressed in another currency. Exchange rates are necessary because currencies have different values relative to one another.

The exchange rate—the price of one nation's currency in terms of another nation's—is a central concept in international finance. Virtually any nation's currency can be converted into the currency of any other nation, thanks to exchange rates and the *foreign exchange market*. For instance, let's say the current exchange rate between the U.S. dollar and the Mexican peso is $1 to 10 pesos. This means that $1 will buy 10 pesos and that 10 pesos will buy $1. (I am ignoring transaction costs, such as the commission charged by the bank or foreign exchange broker who does the currency conversion.)

ECONOTALK

The **foreign exchange market** includes the importers, exporters, banks, brokers, traders, and organizations involved in currency conversion. The FX or FOREX market, as it is called, is not a physical place—though many participants work in offices and on trading floors—but rather the entire network of participants in the market.

Importers and exporters need foreign currency in order to complete transactions. Banks and brokers maintain inventories of foreign exchange (that is, various currencies) and convert currencies as a service to customers. Traders and speculators make (or lose) money on the movement of foreign exchange rates (which I'll describe later). As you will see, central banks also play a role in the foreign exchange market.

Types of Exchange Rates

Foreign currency exchange rates have historically been determined in three different ways:

- Fixed rates

- Floating (or flexible) rates

- Managed rates

With a fixed exchange rate, the value of the currency is determined by the nation's central bank and held in place by central bank actions—mainly the purchase and sale of the currency. Another way to fix exchange rates, which has been used by the United States and other nations in the past, is to tie currencies to the gold standard. If all the currencies in the exchange rate system have a value pegged to gold, it is a simple matter to convert the currencies to one another according to their value in gold.

Floating exchange rates are determined by the market forces of supply and demand. We will examine these forces in this chapter. Essentially, if demand for a currency increases, the value of that currency in terms of other currencies increases. If demand for the currency decreases, then the value of the currency decreases.

Managed exchange rates are influenced by nations' central banks but are not targeted to a fixed rate. In practice, the system of managed rates that we have today operates through the forces of supply and demand *and* is influenced by central banks. So we now have a mix of floating and managed rates, which is called managed float.

Foreign Currency Supply and Demand

The economic forces that determine foreign exchange rates are rooted in supply and demand, both of which are determined mainly by foreign trade activity. For instance, if Americans increase their demand for products from Mexico, Americans will need to buy more pesos in order to buy those Mexican products. Thus an increase in U.S. demand for Mexican imports will increase the demand for pesos. The dynamics are illustrated in Figure 18.1 (on the next page).

An increase in the demand for any item, including currency, will increase its price. As we see in Figure 18.1, that is the case when Americans demand more pesos. The increase in the demand for pesos from $10 billion to $12 billion increased the price of pesos. Where $1 used to buy 10 pesos, after the increase in U.S. demand for Mexican imports—from $10 billion to $12 billion of Mexican goods—it takes $1.20 to buy 10 pesos. Put another way, a peso that used to cost 10¢ costs 12¢ after the increase in demand.

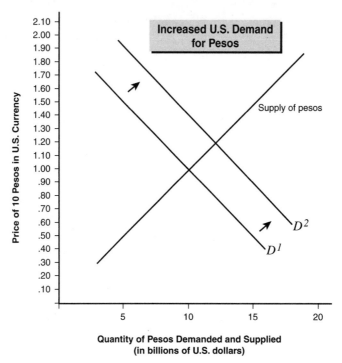

Figure 18.1

In this situation, the dollar is said to have depreciated against the peso. Other ways of stating this are to say that the dollar lost value, lost ground, or weakened against the peso. This sounds worse than it is. All it means is that the United States demanded more imports from Mexico. But this kind of language is used for a simple reason: the dollar buys less than it used to in Mexico. After the increase in the peso-to-dollar exchange rate, it takes $1.20 to buy what $1 used to buy in Mexico.

ECONOTIP

Business news reporters often employ colorful but potentially confusing terms to describe economic events. When a reporter states that the "dollar rallied" in that day's trading, it means that the dollar (or whatever currency is being discussed) strengthened against most currencies or a major currency, such as the euro. When a reporter says there was a "sell off" of the dollar or that the dollar "was attacked," it means that the dollar weakened.

Given the law of supply and demand, this only makes sense. When Americans demand more Mexican products, they bid up the price of those products. When that occurs, the exchange rate mechanism adjusts itself to reflect that price increase. Therefore, the price of the peso, and thus of Mexican goods, rises.

Let's look at this from Mexico's point of view. If the dollar has depreciated—lost value, lost ground, and weakened—against the peso, then the peso has appreciated—gained value, gained ground, and strengthened—against the dollar. While this makes Mexico's products more expensive for Americans, it also makes U.S. products cheaper for Mexicans. The effects of the changes in two currencies mirror one another.

Effect on Imports, Exports, and GDP

Recall the formula for gross domestic product (GDP), C + I + G + (Ex – Im). The expression (Ex – Im) equals net exports, which may be either positive or negative. If net exports are positive, the nation's GDP increases. If they are negative, GDP decreases. All nations want their GDP to be higher rather than lower, so all nations want their net exports to be positive. (Of course it is not possible for all nations to have positive net exports, because one or more nations must import more than they export if the others export more than they import.)

Returning to our example of the United States and Mexico, here is the sequence of events I just described and the impact on trade and GDP:

- U.S. demand for Mexican imports increased.

- This increased U.S. demand for pesos.

- The increased U.S. demand for pesos raised the price of the peso in dollars.

- When Americans purchase more imports from Mexico—holding all else equal—U.S. net exports (and GDP and employment) will decrease.

- However, the change in the exchange rate will automatically correct this situation, because a) as the price, in dollars, of Mexican imports rises, U.S. demand for Mexican imports will fall, and b) as the price, in pesos, of U.S. exports to Mexico falls, Mexican demand for U.S. products will rise.

- When U.S. exports to Mexico rise (because they are cheaper), it will reverse the trend that began when U.S. demand for Mexican products increased. It will also reverse the effect on U.S. net exports, which will increase when exports to Mexico increase.

The price of the peso in dollars—the dollar/peso exchange rate—is determined by U.S. demand for Mexican goods and Mexican demand for U.S. goods. However, when the exchange rate changes, that affects the price of each country's goods. That price change affects each country's demand for the other's goods in ways that tend to reverse the initial trend.

This mechanism depends on floating exchange rates. If exchange rates are not permitted to respond to the forces of supply and demand, these automatic adjustments cannot occur. Given the high levels of international trade in the world today, and the managed float nature of exchange rates, the economies of most nations are intertwined in various ways. Let's examine some of those ways.

THE REAL WORLD

As the single largest foreign holder of the U.S. government debt and a major exporter to the United States, China has a vested interest in a strong dollar. In addition, China has adopted a policy of keeping its currency, the renminbi (also known as the yuan), at a fixed rate vis–à–vis the dollar. That means that, as the dollar fluctuates against other currencies, the renminbi also does, but its value against the dollar remains the same.

This has caused tension with the United States because, when tied to the dollar, the value of China's currency is not free to fluctuate in the ways described in this chapter. Thus the import/export dynamics described in this chapter are short-circuited, and China's exports to the United States tend to remain high because the dollar does not weaken against the renminbi.

The Balance of Payments

The balance of international payments, commonly known as the balance of payments, is the overall accounting of a nation's international economic activity. It is a statement summarizing the transactions that took place between a nation and the rest of the world, usually over a calendar quarter or year. It shows the sum of all the transactions between the individuals, businesses, and government agencies of the nation and those of the rest of the world.

Transactions are recorded as debits and credits in the balance of payments. Transactions that cause money to flow into the country (inflows) are credits, and those that cause money to leave the country (outflows) are debits.

For example, if the United States exports a cement mixer to Brazil, the transaction is a credit to the U.S. balance of payments and a debit to Brazil's balance of payments. If Malaysia borrows $1.5 billion from the U.S. government, the transaction is a debit to the U.S. balance of payments and a credit to Malaysia's. However, when Malaysia makes its first payment on the principal and interest on the loan, it is a credit to the U.S. balance of payments and a debit to Malaysia's.

The balance of payments statement divides international transactions into three accounts:

- **The current account** includes trade in goods and services; income receipts, such as dividends and interest; and unilateral transfers of assets, such as foreign aid.

- **The capital account** includes forgiveness of international debt, migrant transfers (goods or financial assets accompanying migrants into or out of the country), transfers of funds arising from gift and inheritance taxes, and uninsured damage to fixed assets.

- **The financial account** records trade in fixed assets such as companies and real estate; in financial assets such as stocks and bonds; in government-owned assets and foreign-owned assets in the United States; and in rights and intangible assets, such as mineral rights, copyrights, patents, trademarks, franchises, and leases.

Each of these three accounts is summed separately. The sum of the current account should balance with the sum of the capital account plus the financial account. Thus, the current account should balance out to zero against the capital and financial accounts. In practice, the balance is rarely exactly zero. This is due to statistical discrepancies, accounting conventions, and exchange rate movements that change the recorded value of transactions.

Why should the current account, which mainly represents imports and exports of goods and services, balance out to zero against the capital and financial accounts?

Because when the United States imports more goods and services than it exports, the result is a current-account deficit. The United States must finance that current-account deficit, either by international borrowing or by selling more capital assets than it buys internationally. Conversely, when the United States exports more than it imports, its trading partners must finance their current-account deficits, either by borrowing or by selling more capital assets than they purchased.

ECONOTIP

Check out the balance of payments at the Website of the Bureau of Economic Analysis at www.bea.gov/international/ and clicking on the desired links.

The U.S. current-account deficit is offset by the amount of foreign investment in the United States, which exceeds U.S. foreign investment. Although America does a lot of foreign investment, the rest of the world invests even more in the United States annually. So America's ability to attract foreign investment helps to finance its appetite for imports.

The United States has run a merchandise trade deficit since 1976, although it typically runs a surplus in services. Over the years, current-account deficits have generated the $3 trillion in U.S. Treasury securities that were held by foreign entities at the end of 2009. Increasing oil imports and federal budget deficits since the late 1970s are two key reasons for the balance-of-payments deficit. Also, the United States imports huge amounts of goods. This was partly the result of U.S. companies choosing to move manufacturing jobs to foreign locations with low production costs and U.S. consumers choosing to pay lower prices than they would have for U.S.–made goods.

Historical Highs

The current-account deficits of the 1980s and 1990s were considered high even back then. From 1980 through 1989, the cumulative current-account deficit totaled $846 billion, an average of $85 billion a year. From 1990 through 1999, the cumulative *trade deficit* totaled $1.1 trillion, an average of $105 billion a year. Until 1971, the United States had always run a current-account surplus—it had always exported more than it imported. So the reversal of that trend to deficits in 1971 was a surprise. (Since then, only 1973 and 1975 have been years of U.S. current-account surpluses.)

ECONOTALK

A **trade deficit** occurs when, during a certain period, a nation imports more goods and services than it exports. A trade surplus occurs when a nation exports more goods and services than it imports.

However, as high as the current-account deficits of the 1980s and 1990s seemed, they pale in comparison with those of the 2000s. For the nine years from 2000 through 2008, the cumulative current-account deficit totaled $5.1 trillion, an average of about $572 billion (or more than *half a trillion*) a year. That is five times the annual average of the 1990s.

The current-account deficit is financed through the financial account within the balance of payments. When other nations loan or invest more in the United States than the United States invests in those nations, the financial account runs a surplus. Despite the name, this surplus is not necessarily good. It means that the United States is in debt to or owned by foreign entities more than it has loaned to or invested in foreign entities. It means that foreigners own more U.S. financial securities or real assets (such as factories or real estate) than the United States owns in foreign nations.

The United States, the world's largest economy, has become a debtor nation. The United States is a net user of funds rather than a net supplier of funds—as it was before the 1970s. Normally, one would expect a wealthy, developed nation to be a net supplier of funds to less developed nations: a lender to and investor in other nations, and a collector of interest and dividend payments. Of course, the United States does lend to and invest in other nations, but not as much as other nations do in the United States.

Trade Deficits: Bad or Good?

As usual in economics, there are several different views of trade deficits. Depending on who you talk to, they are bad, good, both (depending on the situation), or immaterial. However, few economists argue that trade deficits are always good.

Economists who consider trade deficits to be bad believe that a nation that consistently runs a current-account deficit is borrowing from abroad or selling off capital assets—long-term assets—to finance current purchases of goods and services. They believe that continual borrowing is not a viable long-term strategy and that selling long-term assets to finance current consumption undermines future production. (If this reminds you of the discussion about federal budget deficits and the national debt, that's no accident. The mechanisms at work are similar.)

Labor unions oppose trade deficits because they believe that when imports exceed exports, jobs are being lost to overseas workers (or soon will be). On the surface, it seems a reasonable argument, but the data on trade deficits and unemployment don't support it. In the late 1990s, when the trade deficit reached then-record highs, unemployment dropped to its lowest level in three decades. However, union jobs were undoubtedly lost.

Some economists who oppose trade deficits see them as a symptom, rather than a cause, of trouble: specifically, bad central-bank policy. They believe that trade deficits arise from loose monetary policy. A rapidly growing money supply boosts demand, including demand for imports. This has two effects: first, it generates inflationary pressure, some of which is exported to other nations in the form of higher prices over there. Second, it directs too much investment in other nations into export industries. These nations' economies then suffer when America hits a recession and imports less.

Economists who consider trade deficits good associate them with positive economic developments—specifically, higher levels of income, consumer confidence, and investment. They argue that trade deficits enable the United States to import capital to finance investment in productive capacity. Far from hurting employment, they believe that trade deficits financed by foreign investment in the United States help to boost U.S. employment.

Some economists see trade deficits as mere expressions of consumer preferences and as immaterial. These economists typically equate economic well-being with rising consumption. If consumers want imported food, clothing, and cars, why shouldn't they buy them? That range of choices is part of a successful economy.

Perhaps the best view of trade deficits is the balanced view. If a trade deficit generates borrowing to finance current consumption rather than long-term investment, results from inflationary pressure, or erodes U.S. employment, then it's bad. If a trade deficit fosters borrowing to finance long-term investment or reflects rising incomes, confidence, and investment—and doesn't hurt employment—then it's good. If a trade deficit merely expresses consumer preferences rather than these phenomena, it is immaterial.

But what about the effect on GDP? Shouldn't Americans worry when net exports are negative and GDP is smaller than it otherwise would be?

Most mainstream economists believe that because the current-account deficit is offset by foreign investment in the United States, the effect on GDP is negligible. The size and productivity of the U.S. economy and the security of the U.S. dollar make investments in U.S. productive capacity and in U.S. corporate and government securities quite attractive. So as long as the trade deficits are financed by foreign investment and the dollar is not overly weakened by them, then GDP will be fine.

However, to the extent that the foreign investment has been financing consumption rather than infrastructure improvements and expansion of U.S. industrial capacity, trade deficits could be harmful. Anytime a nation, company, or household is using long-term debt to finance current consumption, it is creating future imbalances and, to some extent, undermining its future ability to produce and consume. Thus the trade deficit in and of itself is not necessarily bad, but continually borrowing and not having increased productive capacity to show for it is certainly not good.

The International Monetary System

The rules and procedures for exchanging national currencies are collectively known as the international monetary system. This system doesn't have a physical presence, like the Federal Reserve System, nor is it as codified as the Social Security system. Instead, it consists of interlocking rules and procedures and is subject to the foreign exchange market and therefore to the judgments of currency traders about a currency.

Yet there are rules and procedures—exchange rate policies—that public-finance officials of various nations have developed and, from time to time, modify. There are also physical institutions that oversee the international monetary system, the most important of these being the International Monetary Fund.

Exchange Rate Policies

In July 1944, representatives from 45 nations met in Bretton Woods, New Hampshire, to discuss the recovery of Europe from World War II and to resolve international trade and monetary issues. The resulting Bretton Woods Agreement established the International Bank for Reconstruction and Development (the World Bank) to provide long-term loans to assist Europe's recovery. It also established the International Monetary Fund (IMF) to manage the international monetary system of fixed exchange rates, which was also developed at the conference.

The new monetary system established more stable exchange rates than those of the 1930s, a decade characterized by restrictive trade policies. Under the Bretton Woods Agreement, IMF member nations agreed to a system of exchange rates that pegged the value of the dollar to the price of gold and pegged other currencies to the dollar. This system remained in place until 1972. In 1972, the Bretton Woods system of pegged exchange rates broke down and was replaced by the system of managed floating exchange rates that we have today.

The Bretton Woods system broke down because the dynamics of supply, demand, and prices in a nation affect the true value of its currency, regardless of fixed rate schemes or pegging policies. When those dynamics are not reflected in the foreign exchange value of the currency, the currency becomes overvalued or undervalued in terms of other currencies. Its price—fixed or otherwise—becomes too high or too low given the economic fundamentals of the nation and the dynamics of supply, demand, and prices. When this occurs, the flows of international trade and payments are distorted.

In the 1960s, rising costs in the United States made U.S. exports uncompetitive. At the same time, Western Europe and Japan emerged from the wreckage of World War II to become productive economies that could compete with the United States. As a result, the U.S. dollar became overvalued under the fixed exchange rate system. This caused a drain on the U.S. gold supply, because foreigners preferred to hold gold rather than overvalued dollars. By 1970, U.S. gold reserves decreased to about $10 billion, a drop of more than 50 percent from the peak of $24 billion in 1949.

In 1971, the United States decided to let the dollar float against other currencies so it could find its proper value and imbalances in trade and international funds flows could be corrected. This indeed occurred and evolved into the managed float system of today.

A nation manages the value of its currency by buying or selling it on the foreign exchange market. If a nation's central bank buys its currency, the supply of that currency decreases and the supply of other currencies increases relative to it. This increases the value of its currency. On the other hand, if a nation's central bank sells its currency, the supply of that currency on the market increases, and the supply of other currencies decreases relative to it. This decreases the value of its currency.

THE REAL WORLD

Private-sector foreign-currency traders buy and sell currencies with the goal of making money on foreign exchange rate movements. They make their judgments based on the economic fundamentals of the nation behind the currency. They also look at trends in the supply and demand of the currency. They want to buy currencies that will appreciate and avoid those that will depreciate. Like stock investors, they want to buy low and sell high. But these folks are not investors. They are traders with investment horizons often measured in hours or even minutes.

Many FX traders engage in arbitrage, the practice of profiting from the differences in price when the same currency (or security or commodity) is traded in more than one market. For instance, if an arbitrageur can buy yen with dollars more cheaply in Tokyo than in London, and then sell the yen for dollars in London, she can make money on the transaction (with minimal risk). Currency traders also use sophisticated devices, such as futures contracts, to minimize their risk and make money.

The International Monetary Fund plays a key role in operations that help a nation manage the value of its currency.

The International Monetary Fund

The International Monetary Fund (www.imf.org) is like a central bank for the world's central banks. It is headquartered in Washington, D.C., has 186 member nations, and is an agency of the World Bank, which we discuss in Chapter 19. The IMF has a board of governors consisting of one representative from each member nation. The board of governors elects a 24-member executive board to conduct regular operations.

The goals of the IMF are to promote world trade, stable exchange rates, and orderly correction of balance of payments problems. One important part of this is preventing situations in which a nation devalues its currency purely to promote its exports. That kind of devaluation is often considered unfairly competitive if underlying issues, such as poor fiscal and monetary policies, are not addressed by the nation.

Member nations maintain funds in the form of currency reserve units called Special Drawing Rights (SDRs) on deposit with the IMF. (This is a bit like the federal funds that U.S. commercial banks keep on deposit with the Federal Reserve.) From 1974 to 1980, the value of SDRs was based on the currencies of 16 leading trading nations. From 1980 to 2000, it was based on the currencies of the five largest exporting nations, which were the United States, Japan, Great Britain, Germany, and France. From 2001 to the present, to account for the introduction of the euro on January 1, 1999, it has been based on the dollar, euro, yen, and pound sterling.

SDRs are held in the accounts of IMF nations in proportion to their contribution to the fund, with the United States being the largest contributor. Participating nations agree to accept SDRs in exchange for reserve currencies—that is, foreign exchange currencies—in settling international accounts. All IMF accounting is done in SDRs, and commercial banks accept SDR-denominated deposits. By using SDRs as the unit of value, the IMF simplifies its own and its member nations' payment and accounting procedures.

In addition to maintaining the system of SDRs and promoting international liquidity, the IMF monitors worldwide economic developments, and provides policy advice, loans, and technical assistance in situations like the following:

- After the collapse of the Soviet Union, the IMF helped Russia, the Baltic states, and other former Soviet countries set up treasury systems to assist them in moving from planned to market-based economies.

- During the Asian financial crisis of 1997 and 1998, the IMF helped South Korea to bolster its reserves. The IMF pledged $21 billion to help South Korea reform its economy, restructure its financial and corporate sectors, and recover from recession.

- In October 2000, the IMF approved a $52 million loan for Kenya to help it deal with severe drought. This was part of a three-year $193 million loan under an IMF lending program for low-income nations.

- During the late 2000s financial crisis, the IMF served as lender of last resort, providing funds to Iceland, Hungary, and other nations and working with central bankers to calm the financial markets.

Most economists judge the current international monetary system a success. It permits market forces and national economic performance to determine the value of foreign currencies, yet enables nations to maintain orderly foreign exchange markets by cooperating through the IMF.

The Dollar and the U.S. Economy

A strong dollar—one that can purchase more foreign currency relative to a weak dollar—means that U.S. consumers pay less for imports. It also means that foreign consumers must pay more for U.S. exports.

A weak dollar—one that can purchase less foreign currency relative to a strong dollar—means that U.S. consumers must pay more for imports from foreign nations. However, foreign consumers will pay less for U.S. goods and services, which will help increase production and employment in America.

So the strong dollar and the weak dollar each have positive and negative effects. Think about it: a strong dollar helps U.S. consumers because it makes foreign goods cheaper, yet it hurts U.S. exports and, therefore, U.S. production and employment. It also makes the United States a less-affordable travel destination for foreign visitors.

Meanwhile, a weak dollar makes U.S. exports and travel in the United States more affordable for foreigners. That helps U.S. production and employment. However, it also raises the price of imports for Americans. This, in a sense, limits U.S. consumers' choices (and can contribute to inflation), but it shifts buying behavior in favor of U.S. products, which also helps U.S. employment.

The best dollar policy is, therefore, one that balances the pros and cons of a strong and weak dollar, and that takes the economies of our trading partners into account. That last point can be important: a dollar that is strong against the euro, for example, will weaken the euro. EU products will become more affordable to Americans, and Americans will be encouraged to travel to Europe. That can help EU nations struggling with recession and unemployment.

Indeed, much of Europe and Asia correctly view the United States as the engine of growth for the global economy. The U.S. market is so large, strong, driven by consumption, and partial to imports that it can boost production in European and Asian nations. That's a large responsibility and one that Americans, by virtue of their free-spending ways, unwittingly but willingly took on for much of the past 30 years. Likewise, when the U.S. business cycle turns down and demand decreases, no one in Europe or Asia is happy about it. Of course, economic policies and behavior in Europe and Asia are larger determinants of their economic fate. So it would be going too far to say, "When the United States sneezes, Europe catches cold," but there is a grain of truth in it.

The Least You Need to Know

- Fixed exchange rates are set by the nation's central bank or international agreement. Floating exchange rates are determined by market forces. Managed exchange rates are influenced by central banks but are not targeted to a fixed exchange rate. The managed float that we have today mixes elements of floating and managed rates.

- The balance of payments summarizes all the international transactions of a nation.

- Some people worry about their nation having a negative balance of trade, yet most economists believe that a trade deficit or a trade surplus can be good or bad, depending on the situation.

- The International Monetary Fund, an agency of the World Bank, aims to promote international monetary cooperation, financial stability, global trade, orderly exchange rates, high employment, economic growth, and reduced poverty.

- A strong dollar and a weak dollar each have their positive and negative effects.

The Global Economy

In This Chapter

- The international distribution of income
- Key developments in the global economy
- The perils of high global debt
- The role of multinational corporations

The term *global economy* covers a lot of ground. It includes the mansions of Beverly Hills and the favelas (shantytowns) in the hills of Rio de Janeiro. Its inhabitants range from billionaire oil sheiks to people so poor that they eat rats in order to survive. Its markets operate with all the sophistication of a trading floor in Hong Kong and all the simplicity of the barter society of the Huli tribe in Papau New Guinea.

It's not going too far to say that it's impossible to understand the world we live in without understanding its economics. In this chapter, we take a tour of the world economy and get to know some of the key players on a national level. We also look at major economic developments going on in the world today and the stakes in these issues for various parties.

A Three-Part World?

In the past, people classified nations into three different worlds: the first world of nations aligned with the United States and capitalism, the second world of nations aligned with the now-defunct Soviet Union and communism, and the third world of nonaligned (and generally poor) nations. People now use the term *third world* to refer to poor nations in general, but many people are not certain of its origin. (Some think that it means that one third of the world is poor.) In any event, the classifications of nations according to their wealth and poverty and stage of economic development has become more sophisticated over the past 20 years or so.

This is just as well and not just because more precise language is generally better. With the end of the Soviet Union in 1989, the three-world scheme became obsolete. The United States, standard-bearer of capitalism, and the Soviet Union, at the time the star of socialism, served as polar opposites and organizing principles for the world economy. However, the Soviet economy collapsed due to its inefficiency and its attempts to compete with the U.S. defense industry.

Without the countervailing force of the Soviet Union and the alternative economic system of socialism—as ineffectual as that force ultimately proved to be—the United States stands out as an economic superpower even more, for better and worse. On the one hand, it stands as a shining example of the standard of living industrious people can achieve in a free market economy. On the other hand, it stands as a symbol of acquisitiveness, consumption, and even economic and cultural imperialism. It is easy and comfortable for many Americans to ignore or dismiss the negative characterization, but that doesn't make it any less real for people around the world who agree with it.

Let's take a look at that world, with the goal of understanding it.

The World's Economies

Rather than take the three-world view, economists usually classify the world's economies as developed or developing. Other ways of saying *developed* include *advanced* and *industrialized*. Alternatives to *developing* include *emerging* or, in cases of the more developed among them, *newly industrialized*, and in cases of the less developed, *underdeveloped* or *less developed* countries.

The term *newly industrialized countries* (NICs) is not used quite as widely as it was in the 1980s and 1990s, when the Four Tigers (Hong Kong, Singapore, South Korea, and Taiwan) set out on their courses of rapid development. These nations, particularly Hong Kong and Singapore, are now considered advanced by many criteria. Less developed countries (LDCs) are nations with severe, intractable impediments to advancement, including lack of political, educational, and basic productive infrastructure. The latter includes general access to electricity, sanitation, clean water, and basic health care.

Each of these types of countries has specific characteristics that we examine in this section. However, most classification schemes have components of judgment, rather than strict thresholds (say for GDP, household income, or exports) that result in a given classification. For instance, the IMF assesses per capita income, export diversification, and level of integration into the global financial system, but it will also consider an event such as admission to the European Union as a factor in classifying a country as advanced (which occurred when Malta was admitted). Each of these types of countries also has certain economic issues, which we examine in this chapter.

By the way, a number of organizations—the IMF, the United Nations, and the Central Intelligence Agency (CIA)—issue these classifications, which are often available at their websites.

ECONOTIP

For the most up-to-date information on country classifications and data, see the United Nations site (www.un.org), the IMF site (www.imf.org), and (www.cia.gov) and click on the appropriate menu items.

Industrialized Economies: Growing and Growing Old

In this discussion, I am using the term *industrialized economy* to distinguish the established economies of the United States, Canada, Japan, and Western Europe from those that may be classified as advanced (such as Malta, classified as advanced by the IMF) or that are rapidly advancing (such as China) but lack those nations' productive infrastructure.

An industrialized economy has a large base of productive capital, sophisticated banking systems and financial markets, a variety of industries producing a broad range of products, and vigorous and varied international trade. Industrialized nations also have well-established systems of government and law and provide educational opportunities for their people.

The countries in the Group of Seven (G-7) have the most industrialized economies. The G-7 are the United States, Canada, Japan, Germany, France, the United Kingdom, and Italy (with Germany, France, the United Kingdom, and Italy comprising Europe's Big Four). Incidentally, the G-7 and G-8 (which includes the G-7 plus Russia) are not government bodies and have no legal jurisdiction. Rather, the terms designate groups composed of the chief finance ministers (such as the U.S. Secretary of the Treasury) of each of the member nations.

However, the entire EU—which also includes Austria, Belgium, Finland, Greece, Ireland, Luxembourg, the Netherlands, Portugal, and Spain—is industrialized, although economic performance and levels of poverty vary wildly within the EU. Some European nations outside the EU, such as Switzerland, Sweden, and Denmark, are also industrialized, as are Australia and New Zealand.

Toward the end of the last century, less than 20 percent of the world's population lived in industrialized nations, and they accounted for about 70 percent of world output. That fact—and the income inequality that it generates—creates some of the questions these countries face, such as: What is the realistic and responsible role for developed nations to play in the economies of less developed countries? What are the moral and ecological implications of using such a large share of the earth's resources (relative to the share other nations use) to sustain the levels of production and growth that industrialized nations have achieved? What, in fact, constitutes *sustainable growth*, and is it achievable? (We take up that question in Part 6.)

ECONOTALK

The term **sustainable growth** refers to economic growth based on renewable resources (and efforts to renew them) and minimal environmental degradation. You will often hear about efforts to achieve sustainable growth in an economy or in the global economy.

However, the calculus has changed a bit with the phenomenal growth of China's economy in the 1990s and 2000s. China is now the world's second-largest economy. In 2009, more cars were sold in China than in the United States, the first year that has happened in any nation. This raises the question of how much—if anything—a nation like China (or India, another large, rapidly developing economy) should do to restrain its growth, its use of energy, or its amount of air and water pollution to meet new standards.

THE REAL WORLD

Economic arguments, and even trade-offs, are changing rapidly. The standard argument and trade-off has been between higher growth and smaller footprint, the term for total environmental impact, including total energy and resource usage and pollution in all its forms.

However, China is investing heavily in green and clean-energy industries to position itself for the future, which clearly will include diminishing use of fossil fuels. Indeed, very strong cases have been made (for instance, by Tom Friedman of *The New York Times*) that investment in clean energy and green technologies will almost guarantee economic growth for nations that succeed in those industries.

Industrialized economies and some developing economies face the problems of maintaining low unemployment and inflation, choosing the optimal mix of public and private goods, and coping with domestic poverty, crime, and disease. Also, the United States, Japan, and Western Europe are experiencing record-low birth rates coupled with longer life expectancies. This translates to a graying of the population, in which older people will come to outnumber younger people. This holds serious implications for funding their retirement and health care.

This is especially the case given the levels of debt that the U.S. and EU economies have taken on over the past several years.

High Sovereign Debt

Debt issued by national governments (as opposed to state, provincial, and local governments) is called sovereign debt. Because those debt instruments, usually called notes and bonds, are backed by the taxing power of the national government, they are generally viewed as safe investments. However, some economies (and governments) are safer investments than others. U.S. securities are generally viewed as risk-free, at least in terms of default (usually defined as missed payments or nonpayment). Inflation risk is a reality, but that is a risk of investing in almost any security.

The United States and a number of EU governments took on huge amounts of debt to stimulate their economies during and after the 2008–2009 recession. (This was a case of applying the fiscal stimulus you learned about in Part 3.) At the end of 2009, those efforts were qualified successes in that economic depression had been avoided and a recovery appeared to be underway. But the debt overhang remained significant. These levels of debt have prompted concern among some parties, including the rating agencies that judge the creditworthiness of governments, companies, and banks.

Greece was the most urgent EU case, potentially putting the EU in the position of either bailing out the country or allowing a debt crisis. In the latter case, the debt would have to be restructured and Greece's future borrowing potential would be undermined. In addition, potential problems related to sovereign debt loomed in Spain, Portugal, and Ireland.

Given this, in spring 2010, the European Union provided debt guarantees of €750 (or $1 trillion) for *eurozone* governments in danger of defaulting on their debt.

The prospect of a sovereign default, or even a restructuring of sovereign debt, means that the nation issuing the debt suffers impaired future ability to borrow. That can undermine that nation's development and its fiscal policy flexibility. In the past, the failure of a single financial institution, such as Bear Stearns or Lehman Brothers, has had widespread effects due to the interconnectedness of financial institutions and the markets. Also, the failure of a major bank, let alone default by a nation, can spread panic throughout the financial markets over the possibility of another, more devastating failure. That panic can become a self-fulfilling expectation as massive sell-offs of securities and indiscriminate runs on banks occur.

Of course, other sovereign governments can step in to assist a troubled nation, and that is essentially what happened when the EU issued its loan guarantees in 2010. However, that can strain the finances of other governments, causing more budget deficits and increasing the competition for funds and the risks to those governments—and perhaps to the financial system.

For all these reasons, many governments (and many households and banks) must bring their debt down to more manageable levels and get their expenses under much tighter control while promoting economic growth. This is far easier said than done, of course, and very difficult without serious political discussions and a certain amount of short-term sacrifice—both of which have been in short supply in both Europe and the United States.

All of that said, the problems of industrialized economies are at times the envy of much of the world.

Newly Industrialized Countries: Getting Going

Newly industrialized countries (NICs) have a rapidly growing base of productive capital and rising incomes. Most of these nations have sound governments and banking and financial systems, although they may occasionally be subject to financial or political dislocation. As noted, newly industrialized countries include Hong Kong, Singapore, South Korea, and Taiwan—which were known as Asia's Four Tigers—and Pakistan, Malaysia, Indonesia, Thailand, Mexico, Chile, Venezuela, Israel, South Africa, and Hungary.

The Four Tigers followed a strategy of export-oriented industrialization, in which they moved from the status of developing country to that of NIC in the 1970s and 1980s. These nations ambitiously took Japan as a role model but concentrated on light manufacturing. The Tigers have been held up by the World Bank and the International Monetary Fund as models for other developing and underdeveloped nations. However, export-oriented growth isn't possible for every nation, especially when other nations engage in protectionism.

In the 2000s much attention and investment shifted to the BRIC (pronounced *brick*) nations: Brazil, Russia, India, and China. In a sense, the BRICs are the new NICs. The attention and investment are warranted because of the geographic size, populations, and resources of these nations. They are fairly stable politically (albeit under communism in China), and their general economic performance, particularly in the case of China, has been very good. Indeed, the IMF projects that, in 2015, China's economy (at about $9 trillion) will be about half the size of the U.S. economy (at about $18 trillion), up from about one third of the U.S. economy in 2009.

NICs face a variety of problems, depending on their specific situations. One common issue is financing growth. How much can and should they rely on foreign borrowing? How much money for capital investment can they reasonably expect to generate themselves? A number of newly industrialized countries need more sophisticated banking and financial systems and might benefit from more integration into the global financial system.

THE REAL WORLD

A tremendous amount of capital has flowed into the BRIC nations and other emerging markets (as they are known) over the past decade. These investments typically offer relatively high returns but, of course, at higher risk than investments in securities of companies and nations in the developed world.

A number of investment analysts are bullish on the long-term economic and financial prospects of the BRIC nations and see economic growth in North America and the EU as relatively limited.

NICs essentially move from economies based on producing and exporting natural resources to producing and exporting manufactured goods. Diversity of exports is the mark of an industrial economy and a stabilizer of any economy. But this transition can be difficult, especially for nations such as Venezuela and Mexico, which export oil and have come to depend on the large revenues that oil exports produce.

Developing Nations

Developing nations range from the poorest in the world to those that have begun to build an industrial base but have yet to achieve stable growth in production and income and widespread distribution of income. A number of these nations have large, growing urban populations and serious difficulties with unemployment, crime, and poverty in the cities.

The Organization for Economic Cooperation and Development (OECD) includes the following nations in its official list of developing countries used by its Development Assistance Committee:

- All countries of Africa except the Republic of South Africa

- All countries of Asia except Hong Kong, Japan, Singapore, South Korea, and Taiwan

- All countries in Latin America

- All countries in the Middle East, except Israel

This list literally covers a lot of ground and includes some nations that some economists would classify elsewhere. For example, China, the world's second largest economy, is included as developing while the Four Tigers are not. That is due to China's uneven income distribution and generally low levels of economic development given its massive population. Saudi Arabia is also characterized by wide disparity in income.

Indeed, most economists place the oil-producing nations of the Middle East in a separate category. OPEC nations suffer serious internal income inequality and have not diversified their industrial base significantly beyond oil production. But it's difficult to think of Saudi Arabia, with per capita income of over $20,000 as being in the same category as Zimbabwe, with per capita income of about $500.

Many less developed countries experience intense periodic political upheaval, including war, as well as natural disasters, such as drought and hurricanes. Most of them depend on small-scale commercial farming, which produces exports such as coffee, bananas, and timber, and on subsistence farming, in which people grow their own food.

The staggering array of economic problems in truly less developed countries includes lack of skills, productive capital, organized financial markets, commercial diversification, transportation and communication infrastructure, technological infrastructure, capital formation, stable currency, and stable government. The poverty in many of these nations results in lack of food, clothing, housing, health care, education, and even drinkable water and basic sanitation.

Virtually all less developed countries receive some forms of economic aid and assistance. Yet in many cases the extent and persistence of their internal economic and political problems render this help almost symbolic.

Production and Income Classifications

Another quantitative method of classifying national economies is by per capita GDP or per capita income. The World Bank classifies countries into high-income, upper-middle income, lower-middle income, and low-income groups. The range of incomes for each group, in dollars, and examples of nations in each group are as follows:

Table 19.1   World Bank Income Classifications

World Bank Classification	Average Income
High income	$11,906 or more (United States, Western Europe, Japan)
Upper-middle income	3,856–11,905 (Argentina, Mexico, Poland)
Lower-middle income	976–3,855 (China, Pakistan, Philippines)
Low income	975 or less (Sub-Saharan Africa, North Korea)

Here are the numbers and percentages of the world's population in each of these groups, based on aggregate data from 2002, the most recent I could locate:

Table 19.2   Population and Percentage of World's Population in World Bank Income Classifications

	Population (thousands)	Percentage
High income	955,000	15.6
Upper-middle income	503,700	8.2
Lower-middle income	2,163,500	35.3
Low income	2,511,400	40.9
Total	6,133,600	100.0

Here are selected characteristics I've chosen from those compiled by the World Bank on the four groups of economies.

Table 19.3 Characteristics of World Bank Classifications

	High Income	Upper Middle	Lower Middle	Low Income
Average per capita income	22,818	5,175	1,808	388
Percent of world pop.	15.6	8.2	35.3	40.9
Life expectancy (years at birth)	76.8	70.1	68.1	54.6
Manufactured exports as % of total exports	73.8	52.6	43.2	28.0
Phone lines per 1,000 people	487	180	113	17
Waiting time for phone line (years)	0.03	1.85	4.51	5.31
Televisions per 1,000 people	490	293	205	65.1
Personal computers per 1,000 people	170	35	11	2
Literacy rate (percent of adult pop.)	97	86	81	54
Scientists & technicians per 1,000 people	3.3	1.0	1.3	0.4
Patent applications	76,507	18,801	10,008	336

These data speak for themselves. They show the correlation between technological and communications infrastructure (telephones and so on) and economic success. They also show the importance of investment in human capital in terms of literacy and scientific and technical education. The low life expectancy in low-income countries indicates the lack of adequate nutrition and health care and a high infant mortality rate.

A Worldwide Market?

The degree and extent of poverty in the world holds many implications. In 2005, the World Bank revised the manner in which it calculates the extreme poverty threshold. Rather than the old $1 a day (which was actually $1.08 a day), it revised it to $1.25 a day. Further, the World Bank estimated that about 1.4 billion people were living in this extreme poverty.

When 1.4 billion people are living on $1.25 a day, and one-fifth of the world garners 80 percent of its income, the situation can only be described as income inequality. The degree and extent of poverty in the world holds many implications. But rather than dwell on the moral aspects, which are as controversial as they are obvious, I want to point out the implications for the global market.

Quite bluntly, the industrialized nations of the world cannot sell goods and services to people who are living on less than $2 a day (closer to $3 a day in 2010)—those in the lowest and second-lowest global income quintiles. (These statements are based on global income quintiles from 2002, but are still valid relative to what people can afford.) Many of these people go through their entire lives without riding in a car or using a telephone. How do you mass market merchandise to a population that has only 65 televisions per 1,000 people? How do you sell goods to people who don't have a home? How do you sell to people who spend all day trying to get enough food to live on? You cannot. The only goods that can be sold to people in the lowest two quintiles are those that can be distributed through relief agencies.

Even in the third quintile, where income takes a big jump over the lowest two, many people are doing without a refrigerator, let alone a car. Their average annual income of $3,000 is about $8.20 a day (or about $3,500 annually and $9.50 a day in 2010), which is what most working people in the highest quintile spend on commuting and lunch each day.

So the three lowest quintiles, by definition, account for about 4.1 billion people. That is an immense potential market (on goods and services)—if they had a decent level of income.

The fourth quintile is the first one where people normally have decent housing, refrigerators, and maybe even a car. They earn about $19 per day per person (or about $25 a day in 2010), so they have disposable income beyond that needed for the bare necessities. Yet they possess less than one-third the purchasing power of people in the top quintile.

By virtue of the fact that you're reading this book, you are probably in the top income quintile. Most marketing efforts, as companies in industrialized nations normally define them, are directed to this segment of the world's population. This means that when people talk about the global market, they are generally omitting 60 to 80 percent of the world's population from their definition of global.

Indeed, the goal of a multinational corporation dealing with an LDC may not be developing the local market but rather developing an inexpensive production site. You might think that would lead to the LDC becoming a viable market—after all, production means jobs, jobs mean income, and income means consumption—but sometimes that isn't the case.

Multinational Corporations and Globalization

First, let's define these two terms. A multinational corporation (MNC) is a large company engaged in international production and, usually, sales. The largest MNCs—also known as MNEs, or multinational enterprises—have production sites in several or even dozens of nations. An MNC typically scans the whole world, or at least substantial regions of the world, for markets, production sites, and sources of raw materials.

Globalization essentially means free movement of goods, services, people, and capital across national borders. This creates global markets for goods, services, labor, and capital. However, the term *globalization* has also come to mean something more: economic and cultural hegemony on the part of industrial enterprises, such as MNCs, and industrialized nations, particularly the United States. Those who oppose globalization use the term to describe these negative phenomena and to raise the specter of a world controlled by a handful of MNCs.

I'm discussing MNCs and globalization together because they are related. An MNC benefits from free movement of goods, services, people, and capital across national borders, just as U.S. companies have benefited from that situation in North America. As a corporation, an MNC has one main objective—to make a profit—and the free movement of goods, services, workers, and capital enhances profitability. It does that by giving management freer access to the factors of production and the ability to make decisions based more purely on cost and revenue considerations.

Also, MNCs promote globalization by their very existence and business practices. When McDonald's introduces its customer experience and its menu, even in modified form, to another culture, it begins to change that culture. When Ford sets up an assembly plant in Brazil, it attracts workers from the countryside and changes their economic aspirations, for better or worse. Similarly, the agenda of the World Bank and the IMF generally favor freer trade—a force for globalization—but many developing nations find free trade to be a mixed blessing.

The key problem in talking about MNCs and globalization, aside from the emotions they stir up, is that they are both creatures of the industrialized world. That is an undeniable fact, whether you oppose or support MNCs and globalization. The poorest nations in the world are not launching MNCs. Given that economically powerful entities rarely aim to benefit the poor, those who oppose MNCs and globalization—regardless of how emotionally they state their case—do have a point.

THE REAL WORLD

Various nongovernmental organizations (NGOs) organize protests against globalization. NGOs typically state that they represent the interests of poor, working, oppressed, and economically disadvantaged people. Critics view them as uninformed elitists, while supporters see them as fighting exploitation and economic injustice. In truth, some NGOs, such as Amnesty International, Oxfam, and the Red Cross, do much to alleviate misery and aid the suffering. Others indeed amount to radical fringe groups.

People from each type of NGO, as well as unaffiliated protesters, have targeted globalization as evil. They have mounted protests in Washington (against the International Monetary Fund and the World Bank); Seattle (against the World Trade Organization); Barcelona (against the European Union); Genoa (against the G-7); and Davos, Switzerland (against the World Economic Forum, which is sponsored by some 1,000 major corporations from across the industrialized world), to name a few.

The major points in the case against MNCs are:

- They don't alleviate local poverty.
- They give economic and political power to external, commercial interests.
- They create economic instability when they become a major employer and then cut production or shut down operations.
- They substitute local customs, values, and traditions with Western-style materialism, and consumer customs, values, and traditions.
- They extract more economic benefit from local economies than they contribute.

On the other hand, supporters of MNCs argue that:

- They provide employment that usually pays better than other available opportunities.
- They stabilize and stimulate local economies and raise standards of living. (Remember the multiplier effect?)

- They promote positive values, such as nonviolent conflict resolution, diversity, and equality for women.

- They promote efficient production and bring a broader range of products to a wider market.

- They create an environment of nonviolence and international peace and economic cooperation.

As usual, each side has valid points. Moreover, each side can cite statistical and anecdotal evidence to support its case.

In any event, globalization has been a fact of international business life. However, the United States is now one of the world's superpowers—and its major producer and consumer of goods and services. America draws criticism (and sometimes violent responses) for its real and perceived economic and cultural power. From France's complaints about Euro Disney to radical Islam's characterization of the United States as the Great Satan, from lack of U.S. cooperation on international environmental agreements to its role in often negatively perceived, pro-growth institutions like the World Bank and the IMF, there are forces working against the United States and globalization.

Thus, the story of globalization and the role of MNCs in the world are still being written. MNCs and globalization can be forces for good or ill. Both could clearly help the world economy produce the greatest good for the greatest number of people. However, in practice, MNCs may have to go about their business a bit differently and globalization may need to be less imperialistic for that to occur.

Overcoming Barriers to Development

Regardless of how it happens or what form it takes, economic development—and only economic development—will alleviate poverty and raise standards of living. But there are many barriers to development that must be overcome. The success of the United States, Canada, Western Europe, Japan, and Australia has been difficult for other nations to duplicate. (I'm leaving aside for the moment the idea of whether such success is possible from the standpoint of resource and environmental sustainability, a matter taken up in Part 6.)

Many observers in these democracies argue that establishing democratic governments and reducing corruption would set the LDCs on the path to economic achievement.

Others believe that the right kind of foreign aid would do the trick. Still others believe that if these nations engaged in free trade and took a seat at the table with industrialized nations, they would prosper. While some of these measures would help, none of them alone would generate development.

Democracy and reduced corruption might help in some cases, but movement to democratically elected governments (for instance, in South America) has not eliminated serious economic difficulties. Western democracy means more than free elections. It means a free press to ensure greater governmental accountability and sound fiscal and monetary policies. A sound central bank is as important as an elected government. However, the examples of the Four Tigers and China hold important lessons. Much appears to depend on a nation's ability to truly focus on achieving economic growth. This, of course, depends on the ability of the government to focus on economic growth and to institute policies that support it. For all its faults as a communist dictatorship, China, for example, has, if not embraced, at least permitted capitalist-style modifications to its economic system. Although the government still practices censorship and political repression, it did permit financial incentives for farmers. The nation has also purchased large amounts of U.S. debt, at least partly to spur U.S. purchases of its products and thus encourage growth in its productive capacity. Moreover, China has achieved its gains largely based on its internal resources and without foreign aid.

However, foreign aid has in the past done wonders. It was the *Marshall Plan*, one of the largest foreign aid programs in history, that rebuilt Europe after World War II and helped Germany become an economic giant. Many people who denounce foreign aid forget this, yet it is often difficult to assess the benefits of foreign aid in LDCs. Some of the money certainly finds its way into the wrong pockets. That said, many economists believe that the wealthy creditor nations that have lent billions to developing nations should forgive much or even all of that debt in order to give these nations a fresh start.

ECONOTALK

The **Marshall Plan,** named for Secretary of State George C. Marshall, who proposed it in 1947, provided up to $20 billion in aid (in late-1940s dollars) for relief and rebuilding. The condition was that European nations had to act together and cooperate economically. By 1953, the United States had contributed $13 billion and Europe was on its way to recovery.

The U.S. economy also benefited from the plan, because the money was used to buy productive capital and other goods from America. These were to be shipped to Europe on American merchant vessels. Without a doubt, the Marshall Plan was a success for all parties involved.

Free trade doesn't necessarily help a country join the ranks of developed nations. Yet most economists believe that developed nations should end protectionist practices that limit imports from developing nations. Textiles, as noted, are one area, and farm products are another.

Thus a mix of economic and political measures—ideally, tailored to the specific nation—is the recipe for economic development.

What Does the Future Hold?

Economic trends and forecasts bear out the old saying, "The rich get richer and the poor get poorer." Well, not exactly. The poor are slowly earning more money in real terms. However, as is the case in the United States, the rich are earning even more. So in relative terms the gap between the wealthy—meaning the developed nations— and the poor—meaning the less developed countries—is widening, and it is expected to continue to widen unless international policies change in significant ways.

The Least You Need to Know

- Economists classify the world's economies as industrialized or developed countries, newly industrialized countries, and developing or less developed countries.
- The top 20 percent of the world's population earns about 80 percent of its income.
- Multinational corporations have production sites in several or even dozens of nations. An MNC typically scans the whole world, or at least substantial regions of the world, for markets, production sites, and sources of raw materials.
- Globalization means free movement of goods, services, people, and capital across national borders, which creates global markets for goods, services, labor, and capital.
- Barriers to economic development include lack of sound financial markets and central banking systems, lack of education and skills, and lack of stable, account-able government.
- China has grown its economy by adopting some features of a capitalist, market economy. However, China has not moved toward democracy and has kept many aspects of its totalitarian government in place.

Situational Economics

Does economics have any practical application to those of us who are not trading currencies or attempting to influence the money supply? Can this stuff help you make money, save money, or manage your business or career? Equally—if not more—important, can it help you become a more informed voter and a better citizen and neighbor?

Yes! But first you have to spend a little time learning about policy basics, especially regarding key areas such as health care and environmental economics, and about monitoring the economy. Regarding policies, there's a lot of emotional argument and political theater that barely passes for discussion or analysis. If you understand the competing interests and the economics of the situation, you will understand the arguments more clearly. As for monitoring the economy, if you glance at the business pages of your newspaper, listen with one ear to the business news on the radio or TV, and, once or twice a month, check in at three or four websites, you will be watching closely enough to know the general condition and direction of the economy.

So in the first two chapters in this final part of the book, I'll discuss the two largest long-term issues in the U.S. (and global) economy: health care and environmental sustainability. The chapter after that will show you how to monitor the economy so you know where you are in relation to it. Then, in the last chapter, I'll cover some everyday decisions and situations in which knowledge of economics may help you.

U.S. Health Care—On Life Support?

In This Chapter

- The debate on health care and health insurance
- How the U.S. health-care system compares with others
- Past efforts to promote the health of U.S. citizens
- Policy options for health-care reform

Few topics in U.S. economic policy are as complex, emotionally charged, and vital to the nation's global competitiveness as health care. Yet many Americans are misinformed about health-care policy and economics. This chapter sheds some light on the topic, while recognizing that there are no easy or inexpensive solutions to the U.S. health-care problem.

In this chapter we examine economic issues in health care, beginning with the question of whether it is a public or a private good, and we examine the U.S. approach to funding it. We then turn to health-care costs and what is driving them and to U.S. government efforts to improve health care. Finally, the chapter closes with a look at options for health-care reform.

This chapter recognizes the U.S. health-care reform passed by Congress in 2010 and that the law preserves the current U.S. system of private insurance. Moreover, it does not take full effect until 2014, does little to solve underlying cost problems, and is likely to be contested in the Supreme Court by some states and, perhaps, modified by future legislation.

Public Good or Private Good?

A lot of your beliefs about health-care policy will depend on whether you see health care as a public good or a private good. Economists define a public good as one that everyone benefits from but that no one has a market incentive to pay for individually. National defense may be the best example, but others include the highway system, judicial system, and clean air and water. In contrast, a private good is one that primarily benefits individuals and that they will pay for. Private goods include virtually everything one purchases and consumes in the marketplace.

> **THE REAL WORLD**
>
> In the United States, health care has come to resemble many other areas of economic life in that people are either winners or losers, and the winners win big while the losers lose badly. If you have good health insurance, you receive good care at a fraction of what it would cost you out of pocket. If you don't have health insurance, you'll get only emergency care and you will not be followed by the same doctor nor receive medications at reasonable cost. If you suffer something chronic or catastrophic, you could be financially ruined.

Gray areas abound. Education is a public good because we all benefit when our fellow voters can understand the issues and our workers can compete internationally. Yet education is also a private good because it benefits the individual and people will pay for it. Also, education depends on things one can directly control, such as homework and test preparation.

Yet while health care has characteristics of a private good *and* a public good, there are six reasons to consider it a public good from a policy standpoint:

- First, the costs of health care are borne by everyone, given that we provide, on moral grounds, emergency care to those who cannot afford it. The higher costs of that kind of care are passed on to us all through higher insurance and hospital fees and increased taxes.

- Second, healthy people spend less money on health care, which frees resources for other uses. In any economy, money spent on avoidable illnesses or injuries has been diverted from other public and private expenditures that would be more productive, profitable, or enjoyable than, say, chemotherapy or intensive care.

- Third, health care reduces human suffering, and most of us would prefer that our fellow citizens be free from suffering.

- Fourth, physically healthy people transmit fewer (if any) communicable diseases, and the mentally healthy resort less frequently to violence. This leaves us all healthier and safer and frees resources for more productive and enjoyable purposes.

- Fifth, healthy people are more productive and miss fewer workdays. The entire economy bears the cost of productivity lost due to missed workdays or years of disability.

- Sixth, a good health-care system, like a good police, legal, and penal system (another public good) is associated with high levels of economic development and political stability.

Health care is also a private good in that we can control many determinants of our health, benefit as individuals, and spend our own money on care. Reasons to consider it a private good from a policy standpoint include controlling public expenditures, keeping taxes low, and minimizing moral hazard. In practice, the United States tends to treat health care as a private good, even more so than education.

In general, the more you view health care as a private good, the more you'll tend to favor market solutions; the more you view it as a public good, the more you'll tend to favor public-policy solutions. But, however you view health care, its funding (like that of education) represents an important policy decision. By several measures, it's a decision the United States has made badly.

THE REAL WORLD

Many Americans are driven to declare bankruptcy due to hospital bills. A February 2, 2005, press release from Harvard Medical School stated that 50 percent of personal bankruptcies involved medical bills and that, "Surprisingly, most of those bankrupted by medical problems had health insurance."

Hospitals cannot deny emergency care to anyone, but they do expect to be paid. They also expect to be paid if a person with a lengthy illness is underinsured and not covered for the procedures, dropped by his insurer, loses her insurance in a job change, or when the insurer won't pay the claim.

The U.S. Approach

The United States employs a far more market-based approach to funding health care than any other developed economy. Its two major public programs are Medicare, the federal program for people 65 and over or disabled under Social Security guidelines, and Medicaid, the state-run (but largely federally funded) program for people under 65 who qualify due to family circumstances or disability. A third, smaller initiative is the Children's Health Insurance Program (CHIP), which helps states insure low-income children who are ineligible for Medicaid but cannot afford private insurance.

Medicare is an entitlement program, meaning that the contributions people make to the insurance fund through payroll taxes entitle them to benefits when they reach the age of eligibility (65). In contrast, Medicaid is a means-tested program, meaning that recipients must show they need the assistance to pay for care; however, more poor people *do not* qualify than qualify.

Aside from those programs, the main mechanism for funding health care is private health insurance purchased by people individually or through group plans administered by their employers. Anyone can buy health insurance directly without an employer, but relatively few people can afford to do so.

Linking health insurance mainly to employment or to being 65 or over or disabled has generated about 46 million uninsured Americans. Leaving 46 million people uninsured might be economically rational if the system delivered results that were superior to other systems, but it doesn't. By most aggregate measures, U.S. health care is inferior to that in other developed economies—and even some poorer ones—although it consumes a much larger percentage of the U.S. gross domestic product (GDP). Actually, that's due more to the U.S. system of health insurance than to its system of health care.

What Is Health Insurance?

What we call health insurance has characteristics of insurance, but differs from it in certain ways. Health insurance resembles life insurance in that at some point most people suffer injury or illness, just as everyone dies. Yet death is universal and its result is uniform. Because everyone dies and the benefit payout is known beforehand, it's easy to set premiums actuarially that will fund the payouts. That's not the case with health insurance.

Health insurance resembles car and fire insurance because it pays benefits intended to make you whole when an insurable event occurs. But not everyone has a serious car accident, and most houses don't burn down. For that matter, not everyone drives a car. If your auto insurance becomes too expensive, you can stop driving and move to a city with good public transportation, work from home, walk, or ride a bicycle. However, if your health insurance becomes unaffordable, you can't simply decide not to get sick or hurt. It can happen to anyone at any time.

In a sense, health insurance is not traditional insurance, but a payment mechanism. Of course, all insurance is a payment mechanism. It pays an amount that aims, in the case of life insurance, to pay specific compensation for the loss of a significant other or a key person in a business, and in the case of fire and car insurance, to return you to your situation before the fire or fender bender. But health insurance exposes the insured and the insurer to expenses that appear impossible for profit-making companies to build into premiums that average families can afford on their own. Hence the need for the employer-based system, which even many employers cannot afford—and the costs keep climbing.

Health-Care Reform or Insurance Reform?

No one has seriously proposed overhauling the U.S. *health-care* system but rather the *health-insurance* system. In the United States, health-care reform is actually health-insurance reform, although reducing the health-care costs is part of it. Many people seeking health-insurance reform want to reduce the role of the private insurers in the U.S. system, mainly for the following reasons:

- They want to de-link health insurance (and thus health care) from income.

- They want to de-link health insurance from employment.

- They feel the health-insurance industry doesn't add enough value.

- They want to improve cost controls and care.

- They want to improve U.S. companies' global competitiveness.

Private health insurance means that people pay for their insurance or health care out of their own pockets rather than through taxes. Thus, people with more money receive better health care. Supporters of health-insurance reform argue that health care is a public right, so it isn't fair that more money equals better health care.

Many people feel the for-profit health-insurance industry does only administrative work that the government could do more efficiently. This is arguably true and, in fact, insurers have an incentive—the profit motive—*not* to pay for care. Private insurers account for about 15 percent of total health-care costs in the United States, but they deliver no actual care and provide mainly billing and administrative functions. You might think that would control costs, but it hasn't. In fact, Medicare has lower administrative costs than private health insurers (who have selling expenses), *and* Medicare does not have to turn a profit.

Every other major industrial economy has a national health or health-insurance program funded by taxes. That means that companies in those nations do not have that expense. That expense has helped to erode the competitiveness of the U.S. auto industry and made health insurance a major bargaining point in the federal rescue of GM and Chrysler in early 2009. Of course, nations with national health insurance may devote more tax money to health insurance, but their bottom-line health-care costs are still lower. Having to pay for health insurance has made U.S. industry less competitive and has cost the economy manufacturing jobs.

Yet *nobody* in Congress or the Obama administration has proposed closing down the health-insurance industry or doing away with the right to pay for health care or health-care insurance privately. Even in Britain, which has true, nationalized health care, an individual or family can purchase private insurance or pay their hospitals or caregivers directly. That said, an affordable U.S. national health-insurance program would certainly reduce the market share of health-insurance companies and drive some out of business. People who want national health insurance are okay with that, although even many of them would favor gradual introduction of national health insurance.

People who oppose universal government coverage often do so on the grounds that the government is inefficient compared with private industry. Yet they also claim that even offering everyone the option of a national health-insurance program would drive private insurers out of business. This argument isn't logical: a less-efficient operation cannot drive out a more-efficient operation in a market economy. If government subsidies make it more efficient—well, that's the point, isn't it?

In any event, private colleges and universities thrive along with state colleges and universities. Private transportation operates alongside public transportation. Private investment and savings programs exist despite the presence of the Social Security program. Even private security firms thrive despite public police forces. A public health-insurance program in and of itself won't drive private insurers out of a market.

Why the U.S. System Is So Hard to Change

Despite skyrocketing costs, 46 million uninsured, and Medicare's financial problems, the U.S. system is hard to change for three main reasons.

1. Most People Are Happy

About 83 percent of the U.S. population of 300 million has private health-care insurance or Medicare, and they are happy with it. They may not be happy with the cost of the insurance, and there are horror stories (many true) about people being denied coverage or having their coverage pulled when they became ill.

But most people are happy, or at least prefer the status quo over the fear that their private or Medicare coverage will change if the tens of millions of uninsured became insured. In other words, most of the 250 million insured Americans see little reason to change the system.

2. People Feel Insulated from the Costs

The current insurance system encourages caregivers, institutions, and patients to use more rather than fewer services. In many diagnosis and treatment situations, there is very little incentive to limit the use of services. That's because the caregivers, institutions, and patients all see themselves as not paying for the services. All of the costs *appear to be* borne by the insurer.

Yet for-profit insurers must pass the costs onto the insured and their employers. Another factor boosting costs is *defensive medicine*, the procedures that caregivers recommend because they want to cover all their bases in the event of a malpractice suit.

ECONOTALK

Defensive medicine is the practice of doctors and other caregivers ordering every test that might be applicable and overtreating patients in order to avoid potential malpractice lawsuits based on lack of thoroughness.

3. The Insurance Industry Influences Congress

The insurance industry, like scores of others, uses contributions to buy influence over lawmakers. They also often provide employment in the industry or a lobbying firm after a friendly legislator leaves office. U.S. campaign-finance law and the revolving door between elected office and private industry enables industry to influence the laws legislators propose and pass. Indeed, parts of some bills are written by industry representatives.

Thus many politicians of both parties represent industries' financial interests rather than those of the average voter. This amounts to a system of legal graft. Media reports of the "powerful health-insurance industry" refer to this system. With billions of dollars at stake, the industry spends huge amounts to influence legislators to do their bidding. Thus most Republican and some Democratic elected officials oppose essential reform of the U.S. health-care system.

THE REAL WORLD

Health-care reform, of a sort, was passed in 2010 after a bruising battle in which both Democrats and Republicans essentially fought for measures that preserved the current system of private insurance—and mandated coverage of about 85 percent of those not covered. The law, which doesn't go completely into effect until 2014, provides subsidies for people to purchase health insurance. However, a few states are challenging the constitutionality of the law, and although it is an important step toward universal coverage, it does not represent a solution to the problems of health-care or health-insurance costs.

Why the Current System Is Unsustainable

Although the current U.S. system of health care and health insurance is difficult to change, it is economically unsustainable. The following forces are working against it, and the 2010 legislation often derisively called Obamacare won't do away with them.

Growth of Costs

Health-care and health-insurance costs have greatly outpaced inflation in most of the past 20 years. Health-insurance premiums more than doubled for the average U.S. worker from 2001 to 2007 and have continued to grow at comparable (or greater) rates, while insurance coverage has become increasingly stingy. This makes it harder for people to afford health care and health insurance and causes some to forego those expenses. If people forego health care, they can become sick and suffer, can infect others, and can develop more serious and costly conditions. If people forego insurance and obtain care through emergency rooms, that simply passes their costs on to the rest of us.

Health Care's Disproportionate Claim on U.S. Productive Capacity

According to the U.S. Department of Health and Human Services, national health expenditures were expected to total 17.6 percent of GDP in 2009 and to reach 18.5 percent in 2014 and 20.3 percent in 2018. The United States devotes a larger share of its productive resources to health care than any other United Nations member except East Timor. Thus the United States spends disproportionately on one area of the economy—an area in which one-third of spending on patients occurs in the last year of life.

Worse, compared with nations that spend far less on health care, all this expenditure produces demonstrably inferior outcomes by many measures, including life expectancy and infant mortality.

ECONOTIP

Visit the site of the U.S. Department of Health and Human Services at www.hhs.gov for information from the administration on health care and health-care insurance.

Medicare Is in Trouble

Medicare is potentially in even worse financial straits than Social Security. Congressional Budget Office projections state that Medicare (and Medicaid) equaled 4 percent of GDP in 2007, but that that figure will rise to 9 percent in 2032 and to 19 percent in 2082.

Although 2082 is a long way off, the trend is for health-care costs to chew up an ever-larger portion of the federal budget. There is a Medicare Trust Fund, but it is much like the Social Security Trust Fund. Both funds hold U.S. Treasury bonds but these are merely claims on future tax revenues. Those claims are rising fast as the U.S. population ages. Worse, while Social Security can be limited to a defined payout, that's not the case with medical expenses, which are more open-ended.

The U.S. Population Is Aging

The 76 million baby boomers (born from 1946 through 1965) start to turn 65 in 2011. By 2030 they will all have turned 65 and all will, under current law, be eligible for Medicare. Aging baby boomers will fuel rapid growth in the 65-and-over cohort, boosting it from 12 percent of the population in 2010 to 19.3 percent in 2030 according to U.S. Census Bureau projections. Of course, older people require more health care.

This aging population is a chief reason for Congressional Budget Office projections that say that health care will consume more than 20 percent of GDP by 2018, and 29 percent by 2030.

Current Cost Controls Aren't Working

Insurance companies assemble networks of providers and negotiate schedules for fees. After that, insurers tend to do one or more of the following:

1. Write a more or less blank check for a patient's care.

2. Set limits on the procedures that a caregiver can provide to a patient.

3. Deny or attempt to deny coverage of a patient's illness.

None of these patient-level measures have proven to be effective cost controls. In the first case, the patient has little incentive to refuse a recommended procedure, and doctors have little incentive not to recommend a potentially helpful one. In the second case, the insurer may override the doctor's judgment, which can be dangerous to the patient's health and to the insurer's relationship with the doctor, and it may generate patient lawsuits. In the third case, the insurer may be weaseling out of the contract or taking advantage of a patient's confusion.

The Current System Just Shifts Costs Around

Medicare or private insurers may limit the reimbursement for a certain procedure, but the doctor and hospital must still be paid for their true costs. They thus try to charge insurance companies more. Insurers resist that and try to get the institutions and caregivers to absorb the costs. Or they pass them on to employers, who may switch to cheaper insurance, charge employees more for the premium, or hire fewer employees. Some employees lose their jobs. Others forego coverage until their condition worsens, then go to hospital emergency rooms for treatment that is more expensive—and may ultimately be paid for by the taxpayers.

You might argue that costs are always being shifted in various markets. That's true, but most markets do not deal in a necessity like health care, most do not involve an insurance system, and most do not have laws requiring an institution to deliver its product even if it might not be paid, like hospital emergency rooms.

U.S. Global Competitiveness Is Being Undermined

There's a reason that every other industrial nation has a national program: it is a sound, sustainable economic and industrial policy. It's difficult to obtain solid data on this, but even in the early 1990s, U.S. automakers were complaining that about

$1,500 of the cost of every vehicle was health-insurance costs. When U.S. companies and workers must compete with those in nations with national health-insurance systems—and with nations that devote few resources to health care—they are at a disadvantage.

So for all these reasons, it's inevitable that the current U.S. system will change in more fundamental ways than those brought about by the 2010 health-care reform. That reform aimed mainly to extend coverage to the uninsured while preserving the current U.S. system of private insurance. It also aimed to control costs, but that presumes that the nation can do so under the current system.

The Private Insurance Dilemma

The current U.S. system of relying so heavily on private insurance represents a huge problem. About 15 percent of total health-care expenditures go to private insurers. In addition to hefty payrolls, they have huge administrative, office, technology, and marketing expenses—and must make a profit. All those dollars are not going to providers, hospitals, or other institutions delivering care.

Private insurers have been experimenting with different models of care for more than 30 years, most of which somehow limit consumer choice. Insurers have de-emphasized indemnity coverage (the original Blue Cross/Blue Shield) in favor of the health-maintenance organization (HMO) or preferred provider organization (PPO). Indemnity plans provide greater choice but fewer cost controls. HMOs and PPOs limit choice of providers to those within the organization. The point is that private insurers limit choice—and ration care—just as government solutions would, and they do so on ability to pay as well as on need.

Insurers have put up barriers to obtaining care. Some discourage referrals to specialists, even providing financial incentives for doctors to act as gatekeepers. A few unscrupulous companies work hard to deny claims, usually by combing patients' files for any symptom that could conceivably indicate that the condition was pre-existing and thus one they don't have to pay for treating. The 2010 reform immediately outlawed most of these practices; however, that is not going to control the growth of either health-care or insurance costs.

The health-insurance industry came into being when health care, like everything else, was simpler, less costly, and more personal. Now it appears that the industry is adding complexity, costs, and impersonality. If the industry is not creating a broad risk-pool of insured people who pay their costs through affordable premiums, and cannot control costs other than by rationing care (which the government could do more cheaply), then what purpose is it serving?

There are answers to that. They include the cost-control/rationing function and a market-making (as opposed to monopoly) function, two areas in which the government has not proven particularly adept. For those with good private insurance, the system works. The industry also has a huge infrastructure in place and provides tens of thousands of jobs that the nation can ill afford to lose. The government could absorb some of those workers, but not nearly all of them, which would defeat the purpose of reducing costs anyway.

However, the uninsured are real, as are the effects on global competitiveness, and the insurance industry obstructs universal coverage. Despite arguments against government involvement in health care, that involvement is real and will probably expand, as it has in the past.

Options for Reform of the U.S. Health-Care System

This section summarizes the major options for reforming the U.S. health-care system and explains the terminology. No option calls for banning private insurance or for forbidding anyone from paying for his own insurance or health care.

Universal Health Care

Universal health care refers to any system that covers or aims to cover every citizen in a nation, state, or other jurisdiction. Ideally, it covers medical, dental, and mental health care, but the latter two are often slighted and sometimes only a basic level of care may be provided. Universal care usually occurs through single-payer or state-owned facilities staffed by government employees. In the United States, universal health care generally means universal insurance coverage with care delivered by the private sector.

National Health Insurance or National Health Care

These are means by which universal health care can be achieved. National *health insurance* leaves the delivery of health care largely to the private sector, but not necessarily completely. (Hospitals for veterans may continue, along with some publicly owned hospitals.) True national *health care* amounts to socialized medicine, with government employees as providers working in government-owned hospitals.

Canada has a system of national health *insurance* in which tax revenues fund a single-payer system called Medicare, which is similar to the U.S. Medicare system except that it covers all Canadians. Care is delivered mainly through doctors in private practice and privately owned hospitals. Dental care is not covered, nor are non-Western providers, such as acupuncturists. The system has been criticized on those grounds and for excessive waiting times for certain procedures.

The United Kingdom has national health *care* in that most (but not all) doctors and caregivers are employees of the National Health Service (NHS) and most hospitals are publicly owned. NHS has four divisions—for England, Wales, Scotland, and Northern Ireland—and is funded through taxes. The UK system has been criticized for long waits, decreasing access to dental care, and limited access to drugs that the NHS sees as cost-ineffective.

Single Payer

The term *single payer* refers to a single, usually government-owned, funding source or payment mechanism for health-care services. It is usually funded through taxes from general revenues or specific health-insurance taxes on individuals, employers, or both (like U.S. FICA). U.S. supporters of "Medicare for all" want a government-funded, single-payer system, extending Medicare coverage to everyone or, at least initially, to the uninsured.

Supporters of a single-payer system note that Medicare is in place and working reasonably well and that it would preserve patient choice while saving money. Savings would derive from setting standards and reducing the role of for-profit health-insurance companies.

Opponents note that Medicare is subject to fraud and inefficiencies, that private insurers would be put out of business, and that the nation cannot afford the plan. They also note that Medicare under-reimburses caregivers and hospitals.

Supporters favor government funding of health care as a public good. Opponents favor market mechanisms and decry socialized medicine. Some, perhaps most, private insurers would indeed see their role and their profits decrease, but that's actually a goal of a single-payer system.

Socialized Health Care

In socialized systems (such as Cuba's, China's, and the United Kingdom's), the care-givers are government employees and the health-care institutions are owned by the government. No prominent, serious policymaker has advocated for such a system in the United States.

Hybrid Approaches

When U.S. reformers talk about a hybrid approach to universal coverage, they usually mean leaving private insurers in place and providing tax credits or other subsidies for individuals to purchase policies directly from them. This is expensive and opponents see it as a half measure meant to protect private insurers. Yet that's also the reason such a solution was passed in 2010. Ultimately, however, a single-payer system will probably evolve in the United States, due to the aging population and the towering costs of the current system.

Given U.S. economic and political realities, it is quite likely that health care will remain a problem for some years to come as the population ages, costs mount, and economic issues continue to accumulate.

The Least You Need to Know

- Health care has characteristics of a private good and a public good and is treated as having elements of both in the United States.

- The United States is alone among developed economies in the extent to which it relies on market forces to allocate health care. This leaves some U.S. companies at a disadvantage against many global competitors.

- In 2009, health care consumed about 17 percent of U.S. GDP—a figure expected to rise to 20 percent by 2018. Key drivers of costs include rising demand, heavy end-of-life spending, high technology, liability suits, and malpractice insurance costs.

- Skilled practitioners and sophisticated technology enable the U.S. system to deliver high-quality care to those with access to the system. But some 46 million Americans lack the private or public insurance that provides access to regular, nonemergency care.

- Given the financial pressures on Medicare and Medicaid, the number of uninsured Americans, and the aging of the baby boomers, pressure is building for the United States to enact massive health-care reform in the next several years.

The Economics of Sustainable Growth

In This Chapter

- The determinants of sustainable economic growth
- Oil and sustainable energy sources
- Education and innovation as drivers of growth
- Problems of sustainability in the U.S. economy

Back in the 1960s and 1970s, when most people became aware that ecosystems can be fragile and fossil fuels generate pollution, one popular bumper sticker said, "Ecology: The Last Fad."

Since then, concerns about ecology have morphed from fad status into serious concerns about which practices of businesses and households are sustainable and which are not. Even setting aside concerns about the long- and short-term effects of pollution, reliance on fossil fuels is clearly not sustainable given that there is only so much oil and coal in the ground. So the search for renewable energy sources has intensified.

In addition, concerns in this arena have broadened beyond issues of fuel and pollution to include more general policies related to innovation and education. This reflects a concern with the true roots of sustainable, long-term economic growth, particularly in a world that is becoming increasingly competitive.

This chapter introduces and examines these concerns and provides a way of thinking about and evaluating certain practices on the basis of their sustainability. This has become an increasing concern not only in our personal lives but for many organizations that now are considering ways of reducing not only fuel and electricity usage but also their use of packaging, storage space, and materials that can pose health and safety dangers. We begin the chapter by defining our terms and examining the big picture.

Sustainability, Politics, and Policies

Let's start with the term *sustainability* itself. Sustainability, in an economic context, refers to the fact that certain practices of consumers, businesses, and governments can generate or at least contribute to long-term economic growth and others cannot. Practices that can generate long-term growth are sustainable and those that cannot are unsustainable. (Long term generally means 10 or more years into the future, but usually less than 100.)

ECONOTALK

In an economic context, **sustainability** refers to a set of practices by consumers, businesses, and governments that are consistent with long-term economic growth and prosperity. They generally have to do with conservation of natural resources, stewardship of the environment, support of public goods, development of non-fossil fuels, and, often, international economic cooperation.

In some cases, the practices themselves are not sustainable. For example, when a species of sea life is fished to extinction, it is no longer available. The practice itself caused the extinction. Similarly, when the earth's oil reserves are completely depleted, then oil will no longer be available.

In other cases, the practices either are creating or may create more costs than benefits over the long term. The current, mainly market-driven, system of U.S. health insurance is a good example. By some measures, such as infant mortality and life expectancy, this system is already generating results that are inferior to those of the public systems in other developed nations. This system has also put U.S. businesses (and workers) at a disadvantage in global markets, and it has not curbed growth in health-care costs. Thus a practice that could theoretically go on indefinitely can become unsustainable on the basis of its costs.

This chapter examines various dimensions of sustainability. Although people often focus only on the important topics of sustainable energy or environmental sustainability, those are just aspects of the issue. Other aspects include practices of consumers, businesses, and governments unrelated to the environment and energy, such as investing, borrowing, education, and innovation.

That's a lot, and I cannot in this chapter cover every aspect of sustainability in depth. I can give you a good overview of the topic and show how the U.S. economy might move to more sustainable practices; I won't, however, go deeply into the politics of sustainability, because the arguments around energy, education, and environmental issues are well known and typically follow party lines. In general, people on the political right take a pro-growth approach and tend to oppose environmental and other government regulations. People on the left take a pro-environment or green approach to the environment and other aspects of sustainability and tend to favor regulation to achieve those ends.

Despite this divide, pro-growth and green are not mutually exclusive. *New York Times* op-ed columnist Tom Friedman, author of the best-seller *The World Is Flat*, has argued persuasively that green technologies and industries will probably become growth industries in the next couple of decades. He has also marveled at the fact that the world's largest solar panel factory is located in China and not in the United States. There are various reasons, but one is that there is relatively little U.S. government support for alternative energy sources and other policies that favor sustainable growth.

ECONOTIP

If you're not concerned about sustainability, consider the fact that certain practices are economically doomed in the long term. Not all resources are unlimited or renewable, and the long-term costs of unsustainable practices are almost never fully loaded into prices. Also, the nations that discover the renewable fuels and clean and green technologies of the future will secure a huge economic advantage over others.

The general economic argument for sustainable practices is that the long-term benefits will outweigh the costs. One of those benefits is that we pass on to future generations the advantages that we enjoyed, such as national parks, clean oceans, educated voters, and freedom from debt. Why would anyone oppose sustainable growth? In general, the economic argument against sustainable practices is that they increase current costs and thus reduce current profits and future growth (which is financed through profits).

Either of these basic arguments can be correct when it is applied to a specific practice. In general, sustainable practices do increase near-term costs, but they do so in anticipation of longer-term benefits. The choice for any society is whether the costs are outweighed by the benefits. Arguments that belittle environmentalists as tree huggers or portray pro-growth people as whale killers obscure this choice. There *are* costs associated with investing in environmental protection, alternative energy sources, education, innovation, and infrastructure. The question is whether those investments are worth making. That question should be answered analytically and rationally. Therefore, when you hear people making emotional appeals in this area, look at what's in it for them from the logical (and financial) standpoints.

Long-term investments tend to pay off in very tangible ways. Consider the U.S. system of interstate highways and then imagine life without it. Then try that exercise with the sewer system, power grid, Internet, telephone system, and public school system. They all came about as a result of public and private investment geared to the long term. That kind of investment, which supports sustainable growth, is desperately needed in the United States today.

Aspects of Sustainability

By narrow definitions, sustainability measures the ability of the earth to support the human population. That measure is the *carrying capacity* of the planet. That concept poses the question: can the earth—which now supports some 6.8 billion people—support 15 billion, 20 billion, or 30 billion people? If it had to support that many, what steps must be taken to provide those people with a reasonable standard of living? What changes in diet, work, transportation, and other practices might be necessary?

ECONOTALK

The **carrying capacity** of the planet is the number of people the planet could support at a baseline lifestyle and level of consumption. In other contexts, carrying capacity can refer to that of a transportation or communication system.

One of the most interesting things I've read on this subject was a *New York Times* op-ed piece a few years ago in which the authors stated that if every one of the 6.8 billion people currently living on Earth were to achieve the lifestyle of the average North American or Western European, their usage of food, water, fuel, and other resources would equate to that of more than *70 billion* people. The authors pointed out that some experts believe the earth could support 15 or 20 billion people, but no one believes it could support 70 billion people with the lifestyle of the average North American or Western European.

However, I use sustainability here to indicate more than only carrying capacity. I define sustainability to mean *sustainable economic growth* and the factors related to it. This definition includes sustainable dietary, energy usage, and housing practices, and sustainable education, investment, and public financial policies.

For our purposes, sustainability relates to five broad areas of the economy:

- Environmental impact and natural resources
- Population and nutrition
- Energy availability and usage
- Infrastructure
- Innovation and education

Much of this has to do with the use of Earth's resources, particularly by the U.S. economy. As you may know, U.S. residents consume far more resources and produce more pollution (and produce far more goods and services) than people elsewhere. Americans constitute 5 percent of the world's population. That 5 percent consumes 25 percent of the world's energy, and produces and consumes 22 percent of world GDP. The U.S. economic model is based on high consumption and high production. How sustainable is this economic model? Examining these five areas will help us answer that question.

Environmental Impact and Natural Resources

The environmental impact of U.S. consumption and production practices far outweighs that of other nations—particularly developing nations—especially when viewed in per capita terms. According to Vic Cox in his article, "U.S. Consumption Deserves Reappraisal," U.S. "CO_2 emissions rate 18 times greater than [those of] the low-income countries with 41 percent of the world's population."

According to www.mindfully.org, the average American generates 52 tons of garbage by age 75, and the United States throws out about 200,000 tons of edible food every day. Also, "50 percent of the wetlands, 90 percent of the northwestern old-growth forests, and 99 percent of the tall-grass prairie have been destroyed in the last 200 years." Oil production in the lower 48 states peaked back in the 1970s. In other words, although non–Native Americans arrived in the United States only about 200 years ago, they have used up most of a number of natural resources.

The Department of Energy's Energy Information Administration (EIA) reports that in 2005, U.S. energy-related carbon dioxide emissions amounted to about 21 percent of the world total. (Again, the United States has about 5 percent of the world's population.) U.S. carbon dioxide emissions are expected to decrease as a percentage of the world total in the next two decades, from 19.3 percent in 2010 to 16.2 percent in 2030. However, those emissions will still be increasing in volume. They will decrease as a percentage of world volume partly because China's share of world volume is projected to increase from 22.2 percent in 2010 to 28.4 percent in 2030. China does, of course, have a population of about 1.3 billion people, or roughly four times the U.S. population, but emissions growth in China is among the world's major environmental concerns.

The problem of emissions and air quality has been the subject of clean air legislation in the United States and in other nations. The American Clean Energy and Security Act of 2009 passed the House in the summer but faced an uphill battle in the Senate in the autumn. This bill included *cap-and-trade provisions*, which are among the more practical and politically acceptable methods of controlling general air pollution. In a cap-and-trade arrangement, an overall air-quality or emissions target is set and various sources of emissions are identified. Then various entities, such as factories, businesses, and power plants are permitted to emit a certain amount of pollutants. If they emit a lower-than-allowed level of pollutants (for instance, because they adopted better emission controls) then they can sell their right to pollute, the allowances, to other entities. This has the virtue of targeting levels of air quality and then having the private sector sort out how that target will be reached. However, cap-and-trade can leave specific regions overly polluted even though overall targets are being met.

ECONOTALK

Cap-and-trade provisions set an overall target for air quality in a geographic area and then issue permits that allow each industrial entity in the area to emit a certain level of pollutants (that's the *cap* part). The entities are then allowed to buy and sell part of their emissions permits (that's the *trade* part). This rewards companies that get below their caps and enables those that cannot to make the transition at a pace they can afford.

International efforts to control air and water pollutants, over-fishing of the sea, logging in the rainforests, and killing of whales, seals, and dolphins meet with varying degrees of success. Individual nations generally resist international efforts to control their practices, and the United States has been no exception in recent years. One significant example of this was the U.S. refusal to ratify and participate in the Kyoto Protocol, an international, United Nations–related agreement regarding emissions and global warming that has been ratified by more than 180 countries.

Population and Nutrition Issues

The American diet is high in protein—particularly animal protein as opposed to plant protein. This diet requires huge amounts of grain and water to produce the same amount of nutrition that could be had by eating smaller amounts of meat and larger amounts of beans, seeds, nuts, tofu, oatmeal, and spinach. The issue is not that eating meat is bad (although overconsumption of red meat is associated with higher cholesterol and heart disease—and, of course, the animals may be mistreated and *are* being killed). The issue—or at least the economic issue—is that meat requires far more resources to produce a given amount of nutrition and provides more protein than people require.

According to www.mindfully.org, 80 percent of U.S. corn and 95 percent of U.S. oat production is fed to livestock, and 56 percent of available farmland is used for beef production. It takes seven pounds of grain to produce one pound of beef. Grazing and cropland may appear to be a renewable resource, but that's not so. According to a 1997 Cornell University report, "about 90 percent of U.S. cropland is losing soil—to wind and water erosion—at 13 times above the sustainable rate."

In addition, factory farms and animal feedlots have become a major source of water pollution and are serious threats to human (and animal) health. For example, runoff from chicken farms and accidents at hog waste lagoons have killed millions of fish and contaminated air and groundwater.

Although factory farming has made nutritious food readily available and affordable in the United States, the U.S. diet demands many land, water, fuel, transportation, and human resources to deliver levels of nutrition that could be had by consuming less animal protein and more plant protein. We may be approaching the upper limits of the farming system when outbreaks of E. coli and salmonella and pollution of groundwater from hog waste have become problematic. However, sustainable farming would call for a U.S. diet far lower in animal protein.

Efforts to achieve sustainable farming have received little attention from legislators, but the market has spoken in many areas—or at least in affluent areas. The United

States long ago ceased to support the family farm as an economic unit. The success of Whole Foods Markets and of organic and natural food products over the past 10 to 15 years shows there are alternatives to factory farming and heavily processed foods. Also, instances of food-borne infections have raised people's awareness of conditions that compromise food purity.

The farming, ranching, and processed-foods industries—and the population's dependence on them—guarantee slow progress on this front. Yet people who can afford alternatives to highly processed foods (Whole Foods Markets are found only in affluent neighborhoods) and who are educated enough to be aware of the dangers of high fat, sodium, and animal protein often make changes along the lines of a "diet for a small planet." That phrase is from the title of a 1979 best-seller written by Frances Moore Lappé, the first popular book on the manmade causes of world hunger.

The issue of sustainability extends to the sea. Major fishing areas of the North Atlantic, such as Georges Bank, have become far less productive than in past decades. This has sparked battles between those favoring long-term planning and restricted fishing and those who resist regulation and restrictions. But nature will take its course. In his book, *The Big Oyster,* author Mark Kurlansky cites accounts from colonial times when the floor of New York Harbor was literally covered with oysters. Those days are long past, replaced now by efforts to bring native oysters back to those waters.

The current U.S. diet is unsustainable for a worldwide population and perhaps for the United States as well. Even if sustainable for Americans, it is clearly less economical and, in certain ways, less healthy than a diet based less on animal protein.

ECONOTIP

To get some perspective on food and nutrition issues, you might read *Hope's Edge: The Next Diet for a Small Planet,* by Frances Moore Lappé and Anne Lappé; *Fast Food Nation,* by Eric Schlosser; and *The Omnivore's Dilemma,* by Michael Pollan.

Energy Availability and Usage

U.S. energy policy has been to allow markets and short-term considerations to determine energy usage. U.S. energy policy has not, however, been completely market driven. The nation has subsidized the petroleum industry (and the auto industry) by building highways, roads, bridges, and tunnels paid for at the local, state, and federal levels with tax dollars (including gasoline taxes and tolls). Moreover, oil has long been a major U.S. foreign policy consideration, as evidenced by support of Iranian dictator Shah Reza Palavi from the 1950s through the 1970s, U.S. protection of Kuwait from the 1990 invasion by Iraq, and U.S. invasion of Iraq after 9/11.

Combustion in engines for transportation and production and to produce electricity and heat generates huge amounts of greenhouse gases and other pollutants. The fossil fuels that drive combustion—oil, gasoline, coal, and natural gas—are nonrenewable resources. When they are gone, they are gone, and we are using them at increasing rates globally. The extractive industries have contributed greatly to the growth of the U.S. and other economies, but a move toward *renewable sources of energy* appears to be called for at this time.

ECONOTALK

Renewable sources of energy are those powered by natural resources that are not forever used up in the production of energy. These include solar, wind, hydro (waterfalls and rivers), wave and tidal, and geothermal (heat from the earth itself) sources. Although some people consider biomass fuels, such as ethanol made from corn, to be renewable, they are not in the same sense that solar, wind, and tidal sources are. It actually requires a lot of oil to produce and transport the corn to make ethanol.

The growing economies of China and India are expected to ratchet up global demand for oil. Current world demand runs at about 85 million barrels per day, and known reserves of recoverable oil total about 1 trillion barrels. That's a bit over 30 years worth of oil, although new reserves are often discovered and new technology keeps redefining recoverable oil. Optimistic estimates put global peak oil—the point at which oil production starts falling—at about 20 to 30 years from now. Pessimistic estimates say that the peak is here or just behind us.

The Hirsch Report

A February 2005 report prepared for the U.S. Department of Energy (DOE) titled *Peaking of World Oil Production: Impacts, Mitigation, and Risk Management,* examined the issue of peak oil and its consequences in some depth. Known as the Hirsch Report after its author, energy expert and agency official Robert L. Hirsch, the document is summarized in "The Inevitable Peaking of World Oil Production" in the October 2005 bulletin of the Atlantic Council of the United States.

This summary makes five key points:

- World oil demand is forecast to grow by 50 percent by 2025 according to the DOE.

- Some experts are warning that world oil supply will not satisfy world demand in 10 to 15 years.

- Oil production is in decline in 33 of the world's 48 largest oil-producing countries.

- U.S. oil production peaked in 1970 despite sharp price hikes in the 1970s and technology advances in the 1980s and 1990s. (This peak was predicted.)

- Analysis of regions that have passed peak oil production, including Texas, North America, the United Kingdom, and Norway, shows that peaks can be sharp and unexpected.

With 90 percent of U.S. transportation depending on oil, Hirsch urges the nation (and world) to reduce dependence on oil, mainly for economic sustainability. Substitutes that he sites as promising in the near term include fuel-efficient transportation, heavy oil (which requires more resources to recover than conventional oil), coal liquefaction, enhanced oil recovery, and gas-to-liquids technologies. Although these all depend on fossil fuels, developing them would still require an accelerated program of development.

Hirsch defines the overall problem as a liquid fuels problem rather than an energy crisis. His concern is that vehicles, planes, trains, and ships have no ready alternative to liquid fuels. He states that waiting until peaking occurs would leave the world with a significant liquid fuel deficit for two decades. Acting 10 years in advance of peak oil would create a 10-year deficit, and acting 20 years in advance—meaning now—would mitigate the deficit.

An even larger energy crisis also looms. Although still relatively cheap, coal—which is used heavily in electricity generation—is the worst producer of greenhouse gases. Coal is neither a renewable nor a sustainable source of energy. Fortunately, early stage projects in the United States and elsewhere are underway in technologies such as solar power and wind power. Also, while nuclear power generation has been controversial in the United States, it has an excellent overall safety record and is more commonly used in Europe, particularly France.

So there are steps the U.S. economy and other economies can take and alternatives to current sources of fuel. However, they must be invested in, researched, developed, and commercialized in the near future if those economies are to sustain their historic growth trajectories.

ECONOTIP

See the Hirsch Report for yourself at www.netl.doe.gov/publications/others/pdf/Oil_Peaking_NETL.pdf.

Infrastructure

The term *infrastructure* means various things. Broadly, the term refers to the social infrastructure of government agencies, such as police, courts, corrections, tax collection, and education, and to the laws and legal system that enable people to make contracts, extend credit, and settle disputes. That social infrastructure extends to the banking system and financial markets. This infrastructure is still sound and reliable in advanced nations, but creating these institutions is a key challenge in war-torn third-world nations and dictatorships. Infrastructure also includes the military and defense capabilities.

Of more concern to people worried about U.S. economic sustainability is the infrastructure of power generation, air travel, telecommunications, ground transportation, and so on. Also known as critical infrastructure, this includes the power grid, roads, bridges, tunnels, railways, subway and bus systems, hospitals and health care, wired and wireless telecommunication systems, the Internet, water supplies, sewage and sanitation, and fuel production and distribution.

These systems are potential targets of terrorist attack. Moreover, the United States in recent decades has also invested less in some of these systems than it has in the past. Of course, it has also invested in important elements of the infrastructure, notably the Internet, wireless communications, and health-care technology. However, the nation has underinvested in roadways, bridges, tunnels, railways, and power distribution. It has also arguably overinvested in defense and underinvested in education (a separate issue, covered shortly). A developed nation must maintain and continue to develop its infrastructure in order to sustain economic growth.

The United States has a costly health-care system, a highly politicized defense establishment (in which even outdated weapons programs are very difficult to end), substandard roadways, suboptimal power generation and distribution, and interstate railways that fall far short of European and Japanese rail systems. The United States must actively attend to this driver of economic well-being.

Innovation and Education

The United States has a long history of innovation that extends to this day, with the Internet among the most successful and revolutionary examples. In fact, the Internet represents an excellent, recent example of the three ways in which many major innovations have occurred in the United States:

- It was a public/private effort.

- It delivered true economic advantages.

- It has been a disruptive technology.

Many people don't realize that the Internet grew directly out of research and development (R&D) in a unit of the U.S. Department of Defense (the Defense Advance Research Projects Agency, or DARPA). Further R&D was funded by the U.S. government and conducted by academics in university labs. This work began in the 1960s, about two decades before commercialization even began and almost three decades before the launch of the World Wide Web.

The Internet made information access, communication, bill paying, shopping, advertising, workplace collaboration, and many other daily activities far more efficient and effective, unlike so many innovations that are mere product-line extensions (Cool Ranch Doritos, Coke Zero) or that generate little actual value (cosmetic changes to cars). Hundreds of billions of dollars of value—in money saved and earned and in stock valuations of companies—have been generated by the Internet.

Disruptive technologies significantly change the playing field in one or more industries. Like the automobile, telephone, and television, they almost immediately outdate previous ways of doing things. This can change ways in which people do business and conduct their lives and can disrupt existing industries. Fear of disruption is why people in established industries often resist innovation, as is the case with energy and auto industries resisting development of alternative fuel technologies. But the fear often simply stifles innovation and hinders progress.

Innovation occurs most often and most effectively when it is supported by investment and education. Investment is needed to fund innovation and to pay for R&D

personnel, facilities, equipment, and activities. It can take decades to develop a new technology and years for a new technology to lead to profitable products. That's why public funding of basic R&D, for instance in university research laboratories, is so necessary. Education is equally important to sustained economic growth.

THE REAL WORLD

In the United States, Europe, and other countries, major companies are taking corporate responsibility and sustainability (CR&S) seriously. Many are actively seeking to reduce waste, packaging, energy and water usage, and emissions. Many are also investing in developing sustainable products and practices. A number of companies have a senior executive tasked with CR&S responsibilities and issue CR&S reports to investors.

Issues in U.S. Education and Investment

Scientific and technical knowledge is always advancing, and educated people—often highly educated people—advance it. Scientific and technical education (for instance, in various branches of engineering) is important to innovation in medicine, electronics, materials, information technology, telecommunications, defense, production technology, and infrastructure improvement. Education in the humanities is important to innovation in music, art, literature, and cinema, as well as in management, health care, and education itself.

The United States has underinvested in education relative to other nations. This has become clear in international comparisons of student performance in areas such as days spent in school, test scores, and number of science and engineering graduates. The U.S. system of funding K–12 education mainly through local property taxes perpetuates separate pockets of affluence and poverty, a situation in which the rich get richer and the poor have babies (literally). This creates a huge waste of brainpower and an economic burden on society in terms of poverty, unemployment, and crime with resulting impacts on health care, police, court, and corrections systems.

To sustain economic growth and quality of life, the United States must invest more in education and in R&D. The U.S. economy does not lack for investment funds, but rather for effective use of those funds. The short-term nature of corporate goals—and high rewards for short-term performance rather than long-term results—have undercut economic growth. So has the financial (and tax) system that rewards speculation (even with borrowed funds) and financial engineering, a term that often means moving money around.

Private and public innovation is essential to sustained economic growth because markets constantly pressure companies to meet new needs and to meet old needs in better ways. Some people and companies are going to find ways to meet those demands. Economies with those people and companies will be the most prosperous over the long term, and continued long-term prosperity is an excellent definition of sustainability.

Factors Working For and Against U.S. Sustainability

The United States and other economies engage in a number of practices that undermine sustainable economic growth. If, with the support of the populace, the U.S. government were to take steps to curb, replace, or end these practices, the economy would be better able to generate sustainable growth.

There has been evidence that the United States can change in ways that support sustainability, including these events and trends of the relatively recent past:

- U.S. legislative efforts on air quality include the Air Pollution Control Act of 1955; the Clean Air Acts of 1963, 1970, and 1977; and 1990 amendments to the Clean Air Act of 1970.

- The Clean Water Act of 1972 did much to eliminate and control industrial pollution of U.S. lakes and rivers; the Comprehensive Environmental Response, Compensation, and Liability Act of 1980 (Superfund legislation) led to the cleanup of 14,000 toxic waste sites.

- Efforts in the United States and elsewhere to develop alternative energy sources, such as wind and solar power, and to develop hybrid and electric cars appear quite promising.

- U.S. conservation, recycling, and pollution-control efforts have generally found support among consumers, particularly when upheld by the law.

- The United States continues to be a magnet for global investment due to its size, productivity, affluence, financial markets, and legal system.

In addition, reform of the U.S. health-insurance system has begun. Education became more of a focus at the federal level in the 2000s with No Child Left Behind enacted (if feebly funded) and other legislation in the works. Infrastructure projects were part of the Obama stimulus program to counter the Great Recession, but that area has received far less funding than it requires. For instance, a number of other nations surpass the number of Internet connections in the United States—the nation that invented it.

Meanwhile, Around the World

The high-production, high-consumption U.S. economy may have become a victim of its own success. Americans developed and projected to the world an economic system in which individuals are free to follow their interests, impulses, and dreams. It's a system in which people can start businesses, create careers, and invest in themselves relatively free of government regulation, religious law, and family obligations. Largely as a result, Americans have—and expect to have—more, faster, and better products and services than most of the world. They have the largest homes and cars, the widest variety of products and services, the fastest pace of life, and the greatest consumption of resources.

Americans also have the largest waistlines, longest workweeks, fewest days off, flimsiest family ties, highest incarceration rates, highest medical bills, and very high debt. Vic Cox, in "U.S. Consumption Deserves Reappraisal," points out that the richest 10 percent of Americans (25 million people, at the time he wrote the book) have an income greater than the poorest 43 percent of the world's people (2 billion). Though they sacrifice for their material success, Americans face serious questions about their way of life, levels of public and private debt, and questions of economic sustainability. For instance, in deciding to reduce taxes in the 2000s while increasing government expenditures—including two wars—the United States took on trillions of dollars in debt. Most of this debt was not used to build infrastructure or to launch R&D projects, but to fund wars and current expenses.

Such decisions, along with other factors, threaten U.S. economic sustainability. The world will not continue to purchase U.S. debt indefinitely, particularly if the value of the dollar falls. Oil-producing nations will not sell to their best customer but to the highest bidder. Emerging middle classes in China, India, and elsewhere will want the products that go with a middle-class lifestyle—few of which are produced in the United States. Water pollution, factory farming, and relentless overfishing cannot continue without increasing health hazards and economic costs.

A persistent focus on narrow, short-term interests—whether the next quarter's earnings for an executive or the next election for a politician—is not compatible with economic sustainability. Sustainability demands a focus on broad, long-term interests and that focus remains elusive.

The Least You Need to Know

- Broadly, sustainability refers to the carrying capacity of the planet—the number of people the earth could support. More specifically, economic sustainability refers to practices that contribute to continued economic growth.

- Five key aspects of sustainability are environmental issues and natural resources, population and nutrition, energy availability and usage, infrastructure, and innovation and education.

- The basic argument against sustainable practices is that they increase current costs and thus reduce current profits and future growth. The basic economic argument for sustainable practices is that the long-term benefits will outweigh the costs.

- Although arguments about sustainability are often couched in emotional or politically charged terms, the best policies come about through scientific and economic analysis and rational argument.

- The United States and other nations engage in various unsustainable practices, but there has also been encouraging progress in such areas as antipollution legislation, recycling, energy efficiency, alternative energy sources, and organic and natural farming.

Learning to "Read" the Economy

In This Chapter

- Avoid getting fooled by economic doublespeak
- Solid sources for economic information
- Interpreting key economic indicators
- Understanding interest rates

People working in business and finance used to operate in their own worlds, served by their own media. They read the *Wall Street Journal* and *Fortune*, *Forbes*, and *BusinessWeek* magazines. Television news programs reported major business developments and some new products (brought to their attention by public relations firms). Local print and broadcast media focused on local businesses, often for helping a worthy cause.

But, except in cases of tough economic times or major business frauds, most media devoted little coverage to business and economic news. There were no business TV or radio channels, no money shows, and few business best-sellers. People who didn't work in business tended not to think much about it.

That has changed, and generally, the expansion in coverage has been a good thing. More information is available and people can more easily understand why businesses make the decisions they make. Yet, many people are still badly misinformed about basic economic and business realities. Part of this is because economic data are not gathered, analyzed, and released as quickly as most of us would like, nor are the data always precisely comparable over the years. However, the data are timely and comparable enough to provide a good gauge of economic performance.

This chapter will show you how to track key economic indicators. I have discussed several of these indicators in this book, including gross domestic product (GDP) growth, unemployment, inflation, and the fed funds rate. Others I have not discussed. Recall, too, that in Part 4, I touched upon how to become a Fed watcher so you can understand what the U.S. central bank is up to.

Reading this chapter will not make you an economist. But you will be better able to understand economic news, data, and trends. You will also be better able to judge the effectiveness of economic policies and what they really mean to your wallet and well-being.

Words of Caution

Whenever you read or hear any economic information, evaluate it critically. Always remember that economics is a social science. Degrees of accuracy, certainty, and predictability are generally lower than those in the physical sciences. People often have business or political agendas when they quote economic data. Sometimes they cite only data that supports their opinions, but honest confusion can occur simply because of the complexity of the data or of the forces that produce it.

Here are some useful guidelines to assist you.

Understand the Terms

Most economic data are defined in technical ways. For example, the unemployment rate counts only people who have looked for work in the past four weeks. That leaves out a lot of unemployed people. Also, if the Bureau of Labor Statistics (BLS) were to change the way it calculates inflation, the rate may appear lower or higher than it otherwise would. In fact, in the 1980s, the BLS started counting home ownership costs as rental equivalents rather than as actual costs of owning a home. That is, they looked at what owners would receive if they rented their houses out rather than at what they actually paid to own them. If rental costs lagged ownership costs, which they often do, it would understate inflation, which it did.

Technical definitions of terms can require detailed study if you are to understand them fully. If you are curious, you can find the definitions at the sources, but the main thing is to understand that people can calculate data in various ways.

Always Consider Trends

Economic data can be inaccurate and numbers can bounce around from period to period. Often a single factor, such as a major layoff at a large company or a leap in home prices in a single region, can alter a value. Data from one month or quarter doesn't equal a trend. It's generally best to compare data from *at least* three periods (months, quarters, or years) to establish an upward or downward trend.

Distinguish Causality from Correlation

Just because two measures move in the same or in opposite directions at the same time and pace doesn't mean that one is causing the other. Causal links in economics can be hard to prove. For instance, interest rates and economic growth are well correlated but causality is not guaranteed.

Understand Data Expressed as Rates

Economic data, such as unemployment, growth, and inflation, are often presented as rates. Three important issues arise in understanding rates.

The first is method of calculation. As noted, there are many ways to calculate who is employed, various prices to use for tracking for inflation, and so on. Be sure to understand the definition of the rate and its basic method of calculation.

Next is the type of rate and base of comparison. A rate can be reported as a monthly, quarterly, or annual rate and compared either year-over-year or change from the previous period. So you may hear, "Auto sales rose 15 percent in June compared with June of last year" or "compared with May." Such a rate would usually not be annualized, although rates of GDP growth and inflation usually are. You annualize a quarterly rate by multiplying it by 4, and you annualize a monthly rate by multiplying it by 12.

Finally, reporting of rates. If the fed funds rate decreases from 2.5 percent to 2 percent, there are various ways to report that. The report might say the rate "decreased by one half of 1 percent," "decreased by 50 basis points" (a basis point is one hundredth of a percent or .01 percent and applies only to interest rates), or "decreased by 20 percent" (because 50 basis points is 20 percent of 250 basis points or 2.5 percent).

Reports of changes in growth rates can also be confusing. If GDP growth falls from 3.5 percent in the first quarter to 3 percent in the second quarter, the economy is still ex-panding but at a decreasing rate. This could be a sign of slowing economic growth, but it is not contraction or recession. The term "negative growth" means actual contraction, as in "the economy contracted at an annual rate of 3 percent in the second quarter," which means that the economy is not growing, but becoming smaller.

Ask "*Qui bono*?"

You should consider this Latin phrase, "Who benefits?", whenever you hear economic statistics. When people from a group quote data or express opinions in the media, they are representing the interests of their group. (One exception is, or is supposed to be, academics, who are not speaking for their universities but who can be influenced by their political biases—or, when they exist, their consulting clients.) If a housing-industry spokesperson says interest rates should be lower, he's probably saying they're not low enough to boost housing starts and home sales. It may or may not be good overall policy to lower rates, but it would help his industry.

Be especially skeptical of advertising for or against an economic policy. Check out the website and understand their politics before you buy their argument. Also, never be influenced by the name of a legislative act or an organization. Something like The Committee for Fairness for American Workers could be anything from a socialist organization to an industry group bent on exporting U.S. jobs to other nations.

THE REAL WORLD

Economic exploitation is real, but the idea of government-led economic conspiracies is, at best, fanciful. The idea that someone somewhere controls the national or world economy appeals to some people, but the fact is that most economic exploitation goes on in plain sight (think campaign contributions), and the U.S. and world economies are too large to control. Also competition and human greed are too pervasive for anyone to keep such a conspiracy an actual secret for long.

Go Directly to the Sources

Economic news is useful, but it can be better to consult the original sources of the data. Reports mainly just repackage facts from press releases from the sources, so why not go to the original?

The most reliable sources of financial market indicators and data are the entities that compile and report the data, usually as media news releases. These entities' websites will generally be the most reliable and current sources of that data.

At many sites, getting the precise data you want can take some digging. Recent press releases are usually readily available, but obtaining the exact historical data you need in order to identify a trend can be a challenge. Comparing different indicators from separate sources usually means making your own calculations, unless you can locate a research paper or article in which an author has already made the comparison. Even then, it may not be the comparison or the time frame you actually want.

Going to various sites for various data can be time consuming. So the best general sources for market indexes and general economic and business news are usually the *New York Times* and the *Wall Street Journal*. The mainstream media and the web offer a huge array of views and opinions ranging from recognized experts who develop reasoned analyses to uninformed, anonymous crazies. Serious publications and news sources edit their journalists and rely on journalistic standards and (usually) named sources for a reason: everyone has opinions and everyone has a right to them, but opinion and facts are often two very different things.

All of that said, here are sources you can go to for economic data and information:

Government Agencies

Bureau of Economic Analysis
1441 L Street, NW
Washington, DC 20230
Phone: 202-606-6900
www.bea.gov

Bureau of Labor Statistics
Postal Square Building, 2 Massachusetts Avenue, NE
Washington, DC 20212-0001
Phone: 202-691-5200
www.bls.gov

Federal Reserve System
20th Street and Constitution Avenue, NW
Washington, DC 20551
Phone: 202-452-3000
www.federalreserve.gov

U.S. Agency for International Development (Information Center)
Ronald Reagan Building
Washington, DC 20523-1000
Phone: 202-712-4810
Fax: 202-216-3524
www.usaid.gov

U.S. Census Bureau
Postal address:
U.S. Census Bureau
Washington, DC 20233
Street address:
U.S. Census Bureau
4700 Silver Hill Road
Suitland, MD 20746
Phone: 301-495-4700
www.census.gov

U.S. Department of Commerce
1401 Constitution Avenue, NW
Washington, DC 20230
Phone: 202-482-2000
www.commerce.gov

U.S. Department of Labor
Frances Perkins Building
200 Constitution Avenue, NW
Washington, DC 20210
Phone: 1-866-487-2365 (1-866-4-USA-DOL)
www.dol.gov

United States Department of the Treasury
1500 Pennsylvania Avenue, NW
Washington, DC 20220
Phone: 202-622-2000
www.ustreas.gov

European Union
Delegation of the European Commission to the United States
2300 M Street, NW
Washington, DC 20037
Phone: 202-862-9500
Fax: 202-429-1766

World Bank
1818 H Street, NW
Washington, DC 20433
Phone: 202-473-1000
Fax: 202-477-6391
www.worldbank.org

World Trade Organization
Centre William Rappard
Rue de Lausanne 154
CH-1211 Geneva 21
Switzerland
Phone: 41 (0)22 739 51 11
Fax: 41 (0)22 731 42 06
www.wto.org

Nonprofit

National Bureau of Economic Research, Inc.
1050 Massachusetts Avenue
Cambridge, MA 02138-5398
Phone: 617-868-3900
Fax: 617-868-2742
www.nber.org

Commercial and Investment Banks

A number of private, for-profit companies specialize in economic information and forecasting, notably IHS Global Insight and Moody's Economy.com. Also, major banks have one or more economists on staff to interpret economic data and develop forecasts for management and for the bank's lenders, traders, investment managers, and customers.

Among the best of the bank websites is that of JPMorgan Chase, at www.jpmorgan.com/pages/jpmorgan/investbk/research/global_economic_research. If that URL changes, enter "JPMorgan Chase economic research" into your favorite search engine. Other banks also have excellent economic research, but JPMorgan makes a good amount—including a daily economic briefing—available to the public for free. The bank, like most others, also sells research reports on specialized topics.

Do-It-Yourself Economic Watch

The Bureau of Economic Analysis (BEA) releases key economic data, including GDP growth, two or three months after the quarter. The BEA releases an advance estimate of GDP growth for a quarter about a month after the quarter ends, a second estimate about two months after it ends, and a third estimate three months after it ends. These estimates are all subject to revision—and revisions can be significant. Without going into the technicalities, I can say that the delays and estimated nature of these measures reflect the difficulty of measuring something as huge and varied as the U.S. economy.

In this section I provide brief explanations of the indicators and the primary source for the data. Most of these data are widely reported in the media soon after—usually the same day—they are released. Newspaper and media reports will usually provide analysis regarding the causes and trends of the indicator.

- GDP growth: Bureau of Economic Analysis (www.bea.com)

- Unemployment and employment data: Bureau of Labor Statistics (www.bls.com)

- Inflation: Bureau of Labor Statistics (www.bls.com)

- Fed funds rate: Federal Reserve System (www.federalreserve.gov)

- Consumer and business confidence: Conference Board (www.conference-board.org) and University of Michigan (www.sca.isr.umich.edu/main.php)

- Housing starts and home sales: National Association of Homebuilders (www.nahb.org)

- Retail sales: Department of Commerce, Census Bureau (www.census.gov)

- Auto sales: Motor Intelligence (www.motorintelligence.com)

- Stock market indicators: Dow Jones (www.dowjones.com) and Bloomberg News (www.bloomberg.com)

- Gold prices: Dow Jones (www.dowjones.com) and Bloomberg News (www.bloomberg.com)

- Oil prices: Bloomberg News (www.bloomberg.com/energy)

- The Composite Index of Leading Indicators: Conference Board (www. conference-board.org)

Let's look at these indicators in depth.

Economic Indicators

GDP growth measures the rate of expansion or contraction in the economy, that is in output and demand. It is reported on a monthly basis, but the quarterly releases are more accurate and the annual numbers still more accurate. As noted above, these data are subject to revision. The long-term trend for U.S. GDP growth—and the rate traditionally targeted by the Federal Reserve and the federal government—is 3 percent annually, according to the BEA.

The unemployment rate is widely reported, as is the number of jobs gained or lost. The target unemployment rate is about 4 percent, which basically accounts for people between jobs and laid-off workers who will soon find jobs. A U.S. unemployment rate above 6 percent causes concern; at the end of 2008 it stood at 7.5 percent, and in October 2009 it reached 10.2 percent. Also, the rate understates the number of unemployed because it omits people deemed to have stopped seeking employment.

Inflation has been under control—meaning under 3 percent—over the past two decades. However rising inflation may be among the dangers of the fiscal and monetary stimulus programs and lower tax receipts during the Great Recession, and of deficits piled up in the past. That said, a number of economists and other observers are concerned about deflation, which would also be evident in the same economic indicator. Inflation (and deflation) are measured by the consumer price index (CPI)—the usual reported inflation rate—and the producer price index (PPI)—which can be an indicator of inflation that will hit consumers later.

Changes in interest rates indicate conditions in the credit markets and the direction of Fed policy. The most widely reported is the fed funds rate, which is set by the Fed periodically. With reductions to interest rates, the Fed tries to stimulate lending, increase the money supply, and ignite or sustain growth. With increases, the Fed tries to do the opposite. If the Fed leaves rates unchanged, then it wants economic activity to continue on the current trajectory.

The two main indicators of consumer confidence are the Conference Board's Consumer Confidence Index and the University of Michigan Consumer Confidence

Index. These are somewhat soft indicators of consumer sentiment—that is, consumers' optimism or pessimism about the future of the economy and their finances. These are not based on market activity or dollars allocated but on responses to survey questions. Each of these indicators is an index, in which the responses were compiled for a base year and then compared to that base year from month to month. Thus, it is important to watch for *sustained* increases or decreases in the indexes.

Housing starts measure economic growth and the potential for future growth, and so do new and existing home sales. They also measure the consumer's mood. Rising housing starts and sales generally indicate that expansion is underway. The national numbers on housing starts and sales can be misleading because home building and sales activity can be very local phenomena. Thus the data for your state will probably tell you more than those for the nation. Look for a rising (or falling) trend over three or more months. Total starts—the reported number—includes single-family homes and multifamily dwellings, but you can find both at the source, along with discussions of regional patterns and forecasts.

The Census Bureau (part of the U.S. Department of Commerce) issues a report on monthly sales for retail and food services. Look at the month-to-month trends and year-over-year comparisons. This report breaks spending out into major categories, including motor vehicles, furniture, electronics, building materials, clothing, and other key areas so you can track spending on specific goods.

Vehicle sales are an excellent gauge of consumers' willingness to spend—and they tanked in 2008 and much of 2009. At their peak in the 2002–2007 expansion, auto sales topped 16 million, but then they fell to an annual rate of under 10 million in 2008. Annual U.S. sales of 13 to 14 million vehicles would be a sign of recovery in the industry.

The daily market averages—the Dow Jones Industrial Average, S&P 500, and NASDAQ (National Association of Securities Dealers Automatic Quotations)—indicate the mood of investors. Stock prices rise during expansions and fall during contractions, but by the time a true change in the market trend is established, the new economic growth trend is already in place.

Gold has long been viewed as a hedge against inflation and as the ultimate safe investment. The price of gold has trended upward after 9/11, and with the war in Iraq, the housing bubble, and the disorder in the financial markets in the late 2000s. In general, a rising trend in the price of gold indicates economic concerns and a flight from securities; a falling trend indicates economic optimism and movement of money into securities.

U.S. dependence on foreign oil, unrest in the Middle East, and rising demand in China and India have focused attention on oil prices. Early in the 2000s, economists forecasted disaster for the U.S. economy if oil prices hit $50 per barrel, and then again if they hit $80, but they peaked at over $100 per barrel and the U.S. economy survived. Rising gasoline prices may spark conservation and development of alternative fuels, but they can also spark inflation. They definitely hit lower- and middle-income groups hard.

The Composite Index of Leading Indicators is generated by the Conference Board and released around the twentieth of each month. It is widely reported in the media and is available at the Conference Board's website (www.conference-board.org). The website's monthly press release discusses the index and which of the individual indicators increased or decreased. As is the case for most indexes, this one is tied to a base year (1996 in this case) in which the value of the index is pegged at 100.

These are called leading indicators because movement in them—and in the index itself—occurs *before* movement in the economy as measured by GDP growth. The composite index is calculated on the basis of 10 indicators, which are assigned statistical standardization factors. These factors indicate the weight of each indicator in the index and are periodically adjusted to achieve greater accuracy. The indicators and the factors are the following:

Factor

1. Average weekly hours worked, manufacturing	.2549
2. Average weekly initial claims for unemployment insurance	.0307
3. Manufacturers' new orders, consumer goods and materials	.0774
4. Index of supplier deliveries—vendor performance	.0677
5. Manufacturers' new orders, nondefense capital goods	.0180
6. Building permits, new private housing units	.0270
7. Stock prices, 500 common stocks	.0390
8. Money supply, M-2	.3580
9. Interest rate spread, 10-year Treasury bonds less federal funds rate	.0991
10. Index of consumer expectations	.0282

These 10 indicators are those that the Conference Board has determined, by means of statistical analysis, best indicate the future direction of the economy. The factor assigned to the indicator represents the weight that the indicator has in the index. The higher the factor, the greater that indicator's weight in the index. In other words, the higher the factor, the higher the predictive value of the indicator. (The 10 factors add up to 1.)

> **ECONOTIP**
>
> The Composite Index of Leading Indicators is not foolproof; indeed, there are no foolproof indicators of future economic performance. Even professional economic forecasters armed with sophisticated economic models have a very mixed record of success.

According to this analysis, the two indicators with the greatest weight are the money supply (with a weight of 0.3580) and average weekly hours worked in manufacturing (with a weight of 0.2549). In fact, these two indicators account for about 60 percent of the predictive value of the composite index (because .3580 + .2549 = .6129, or 61 percent).

The other eight indicators account for about 40 percent of the composite's predictive value. Note that stock prices as measured by the S&P 500 have a relatively low weight in the index and that the index uses the broader measures of stock prices—the S&P 500—rather than the much narrower Dow Jones Industrial Average, which is based on only 30 stocks.

Again, changes in the index are more important than its actual value.

Why Interest Rates Are of Interest

If you look to the financial markets for indicators of the future of the economy, interest rates will usually tell you more than the stock market will. Interest rates are the price of money. The price of money depends on the money supply and on the demand for money (in the form of credit) by businesses, consumers, and the government.

Apart from supply and demand, the lengths of time over which borrowers want to borrow and lenders want to lend will affect rates. Usually, the longer the borrowing period, the higher the rate. Another factor is lenders' views of the likelihood of repayment, but each lender makes that decision case by case.

These forces work together in the credit markets to generate short-term, intermediate, and long-term rates. The credit markets are the parts of the financial markets where companies, banks, and governments lend and borrow funds. Short-term borrowings occur through commercial paper (for companies and banks), reserves held with the Fed (for banks), and Treasury bills (for the U.S. government). Long-term borrowing occurs through bonds issued by all types of entities.

Debt securities are traded in the public credit markets, and you can learn about investors' expectations of future economic conditions by examining the yield curve. The yield curve is a graph that shows the interest rates of debt instruments of the same quality but different maturities, arranged from shortest to longest maturity.

The yield curve most commonly referred to is that defined by U.S. Treasury securities. Because U.S. Treasuries are considered risk-free, they provide a "pure" reading of interest rates as "the time value of money," because there is no credit risk (the risk of not being repaid). Generally, maturities are shown for 1-, 3-, and 6-month Treasury bills; for 1-, 2-, 3-, 5-, 7-, 10-, and 20-year Treasury notes; and for the 30-year Treasury bond.

What the Yield Curve Means

The yield curve can be positive (pointing upward from left to right), flat, or negative. The slope of the yield curve results from investors' behavior in the bond markets, and the three potential curves—positive, flat, or negative—hold different implications.

The yield curve is positive when long-term rates are higher than short-term rates. That is the normal state of affairs given that the longer the maturity of a bond, the more risk is involved because repayment is further in the future.

The yield curve is flat when there is minimal difference between short-term and long-term rates in the *interest-rate spread*. The curve flattens (from a positive position) when investors shift from short-term to long-term securities. Their increased demand for long-term securities bids up the price of long-term securities, drives down the yield, and brings long-term rates down closer to short-term rates.

 ECONOTALK

Here, the **interest-rate spread** is the difference between short-term and long-term rates on securities of similar quality. People in the financial markets will talk about the narrowing or widening spread between short-term and long-term rates. The word spread has other meanings in finance as well. For instance, the spread is also the difference between the rate a bank pays on deposits and earns on loans. The spread is also the difference in the exchange rate of a currency in two different markets. In the context of the yield curve, however, it means the difference between short- and long-term rates.

The yield curve is negative when long-term rates are lower than short-term rates. This inverted yield curve usually means that a recession is ahead. This reflects investors' pessimism about the future. They want to be in a secure investment for the long term. When money moves from short-term paper to long-term paper, short-term yields rise to attract more investors to those instruments. That actually results in short-term rates being higher than long-term rates.

The following table shows the yields for selected Treasuries at the end of each year from 1999 through 2009. (We won't plot the curves here, but they result when you graph the interest rates for the various maturities on a given date. Thus the curve for the rates dated 12/31/99 in the table would be plotted from 5.33 percent to 6.83 percent and would be upward-sloping.)

U.S. Treasury Yield Curve Rates (percent)

Date	3-mo.	1-year	5-year	10-year	20-year
12/31/99	5.33	5.98	6.36	6.45	6.83
12/29/00	5.89	5.32	4.99	5.12	5.59
12/31/01	1.74	2.17	4.38	5.07	5.74
12/31/02	1.22	1.32	2.78	3.83	4.83
12/31/03	0.95	1.26	3.25	4.27	5.10
12/31/04	2.22	2.75	3.63	4.24	4.85
12/30/05	4.08	4.38	4.35	4.39	4.61
12/29/06	5.02	5.00	4.74	4.71	4.91
12/31/07	3.36	3.34	3.45	4.04	4.50
12/31/08	0.11	0.37	1.55	2.25	3.05
12/31/09	0.06	0.47	2.47	3.85	4.58

Source: U.S. Treasury

The table shows a positive yield curve at the end of 1999. Then during 2000, the yield curve turned slightly negative—the 3-month T-bill yield (5.89 percent) was higher than that on the 20-year note (5.59 percent). This accurately foretold the brief, mild recession of 2001. One reason it was brief is that the Fed ratcheted down rates in 2001. By the end of that year, as the table shows, the yield curve had returned to normal, with the 3-month T-bill rate at 1.74 percent and the 20-year note at 5.74 percent.

A positive yield curve prevailed until 2005. By the end of that year, the curve had flattened to the point at which the 3-month rate of 4.08 percent was only about one half of 1 percent lower than the 20-year rate of 4.61 percent.

By the end of 2006, the 3-month rate of 5.02 percent slightly exceeded the 20-year rate of 4.91 percent. Like the inverted curve of 2000, this interest rate picture foretold a recession—the Great Recession of 2008–2009. Seeing economic conditions deteriorate in 2007, the Fed reduced rates throughout that year and throughout the recession.

The good news is that, at the end of 2009, the yield curve was sharply positive. The 3-month T-bill stood at 0.06 percent and the 20-year rate at 4.58 percent. That curve points to a recovery, which indeed was underway in the second half of 2009.

You can gauge credit-market conditions by monitoring the spread between the 3-month rate and the 20-year rate. A narrowing spread means the yield curve is flattening and investors expect slower growth. If the short-term rate exceeds the long-term rate, they probably expect a recession. If the spread is widening, then the yield curve is becoming more positive. That means investors expect growth to commence or to continue.

Heads Up

Even economic forecasters have a fairly poor track record of forecasting turning points in the business cycle. However, economic indicators do provide a good picture of what's going on in the economy. Even if the data are imperfect, they are by and large reliably and rigorously compiled by economists and analysts who are attempting to understand the economy in a scientific manner—that is, by examining data and seeking correlations and causal relationships.

In the Great Recession, the data clearly reflected the severity of job losses and unemployment, difficulties in the housing and credit markets, and sluggish retail and auto sales. Similarly, before the recession, the data clearly reflected the frothy heights reached during the expansion of 2002–2007, the low unemployment, unsustainably high home prices (particularly in relation to incomes and rental rates), and loose monetary and fiscal policies.

So the data don't lie, although you must track them consistently and in the context of other data. You also have to grasp the policy implications of loose or tight money and high or low taxes and government spending. Politicians of both parties enjoy promising voters something for nothing, or a lot for a little, whether it is lower taxes with the same government services or consistently high budget deficits and continued prosperity. Meanwhile, the numbers will tell the truth.

The Least You Need to Know

- Economic data are compiled and released by a number of sources, including the Federal Reserve, Bureau of Economic Analysis, and Bureau of Labor Statistics. The Conference Board, economic forecasting companies, and major banks also provide economic analysis and forecasts.

- The growth of real GDP is the key economic indicator. The growth rate will rise and fall with the business cycle, but over the long term, GDP growth will average about 3 percent.

- Economic growth should be viewed in light of the unemployment rate, rate of inflation, and interest rates. Several measures of consumption—particularly housing starts, retail sales, and auto sales—can be useful economic indicators.

- The Composite Index of Leading Indicators is worth checking out, particularly if an expansion or recession has been going on for a while. It may help you anticipate the next turning point.

- The interest rate yield curve, which is set by interactions in the credit and bond markets, is usually a better indicator of future economic performance than the stock market.

Everyday Economics

In This Chapter

- The effects of the business cycle
- Applying principles of economics in your business
- Economics and investing

You are now positioned to nod knowingly when someone starts moaning about the inverted yield curve. You can argue intelligently for a tax cut or a tax increase—or both, if you really want to confuse people. To confuse them further, you can lecture on the need to spend money to boost consumption *and* to save money to build the nation's pool of investable funds. You can hold forth on trade policy and can explain why the Social Security system will be a mess within 10 years.

As an anonymous economist once said, "That and 15¢ will get you on the subway." (He said it in 1957, when the subway fare was 15¢.) What about applying economics to your everyday life? Let's find out.

All Economics Is Local

Speaker of the House Tip O'Neil used to remind his colleagues that, "All politics is local." Well, all economics is local, too. By that, I mean that the broad economic policies and indicators that we've discussed have an impact on your region, state, city, industry, profession, and organization.

For instance, the 2008–2009 recession affected virtually everyone in the U.S. economy and in most other economies. Many people, including many investment and real estate professionals, were shocked to discover that *deep recessions can occur!* Many homeowners were dismayed to find that the prices of their dwellings would not rise indefinitely. People in a huge range of jobs found themselves without work.

What is odd is that many people failed—and still fail—to see any connection between the economic policies of the past two or three decades and these recent (or current) economic events. Had they been unaware that deficit spending had been going on at the federal level for virtually all of that period? Do they believe that the government can cut taxes and still finance two expensive wars and a major drug prescription program? Do they not realize that relatively well-paying manufacturing jobs have essentially been shipped overseas? Do they not understand that the top 20 percent of U.S. households have experienced virtually all of the gains in real income over the past 30 years?

Well, many of them do not. But many of them also fail to realize that broad economic policies—even at the federal level, let alone the state and local levels—actually will have an effect on *them*.

ECONOTIP

Please understand that policies have consequences, but not always the ones that politicians say that they will have. Try to discern the likely economic effects of policies—for example on employment, prices, taxes, and population—and how those effects might impact you and your loved ones.

For instance, a number of states reduce spending on higher education when times get tough. Courses may be cut, departments and even entire schools may be shut down. Classes become larger, services are reduced, and salaries are frozen. Under these circumstances, might it make more sense for a college student to work for a year or two, amass some savings, and start school after the budget crisis is over? If the quality of state schools will suffer, should the savings (along with some borrowings) be put into a private university education instead?

Or suppose you were heavily invested in stocks when the market tanked in 2008 and hit bottom in March 2009. Suppose you planned to retire or reduce your working hours soon. Can you still do that? Should you instead invest some or all of your money in, say, an apartment building in a growing city, so you can reduce your working hours and still collect some income? Or must you wait until the stock market returns to a new high before you retire? If so, when might that high arrive?

Economic events impact everyone. They aren't just the stuff of magazine articles and presidential speeches. This means that everyone must understand how the national, and even international, economy affects his or her local and personal situations.

Rules of Thumb

The following sections introduce a few guidelines to help you think productively about economic trends and their effect on you.

The Laws of Economics Cannot Be Repealed

During the 1990s tech-stock boom, we were told that a new economy had emerged, fueled by digital technologies. In this new economy, people worked with their brains instead of their hands, innovation trumped mass production, and concepts were more important than productive capital. Some people who believed this valued the stock of dot-com companies over those of industrial giants.

In the 2000s real estate boom, we were told that real estate was a foolproof investment and that home prices would rise forever. Cheap money, strong population growth, and newfangled mortgages and mortgage-backed securities would see to that. Some people who believed this borrowed against their paper gains in equity on one property to finance another one.

I am not dismissing the value of innovation and the long-term prospects of the real estate market. But in any business, the economic realities—supply and demand, cyclicality, and the need to make and sell something profitably and to finance investments in sensible ways—inevitably assert themselves.

Expansions and Recessions Always End

The business cycle persists primarily because human behavior in a market economy generates mismatches between supply and demand and savings and investment. Technological developments, financial innovation, population trends, and social phenomena can affect business cycles for better or worse, but they cannot eliminate them. The business cycle is embedded in the structure of market economies.

Fortunately, expansions generally last far longer than recessions. In the past century, there were only two periods of extended economic malaise in the United States: the Great Depression of the 1930s and the Great Inflation of the 1970s. From 1929 through 2002, there were 12 recessions. The longest, by far, was the one that started in August 1929 and lasted through March 1933. This 43-month whopper kicked off the Great Depression, which included another severe 13-month contraction in 1937 and 1938. The rest of the 1930s featured periods of lackluster growth.

The other 10 recessions between 1929 and 2002 ranged from a mere 6 months to 16 months and averaged 11 months. That leaves a lot of room for expansion. In fact, in the years from 1939 through 2002, after the United States absorbed the lessons of the Great Depression, the nation experienced economic growth 86 percent of the time. Granted, some recoveries were stronger than others, but some of the recessions were mild as well.

THE REAL WORLD

The Great Depression was so devastating that people, including those in government, actually learned from the experience. The major lessons were that the banking system and the financial markets cannot be left to themselves and that the government should work to keep the economy stable and growing.

New regulation of the financial services industry and agencies such as the Securities and Exchange Commission helped to ensure more orderly securities markets. Federally insured bank deposits ended the periodic runs on banks that had often disrupted the economy. The government's use of fiscal and monetary policy to cushion the effects of the business cycle greatly improved the economic health of the nation in the past century—and the data prove it.

The mildness of recessions since the 1970s was one reason that the Great Recession of the 2000s came as such a shock. Measured in quarters of economic contraction, that recession lasted about six quarters—essentially all of 2008 and the first half of 2009—or about 18 months. It also generated high unemployment, plummeting real estate prices, and battered financial markets. Sadly, very few economists forecasted this recession, which means that it would have been difficult for most of the rest of us to predict.

So what does this pattern of business cycles mean to your wallet, purse, or piggy bank? First, it means that recessions and expansions are inevitable. No one can forecast when either will come about, but we do know that they will. Second, it means that if you understand the cyclical nature of economic growth, and you believe the economic fundamentals are sound enough to support a renewed growth cycle (or not), you can make moves that benefit you.

I'm not talking about trying to time the business cycle or the stock market's peaks and troughs—that is a fool's labor. I am saying that if the average recession lasts one to one and a half years, when we are in one, you can perhaps wait until the cycle progresses before making your move rather than trying to time it—but you shouldn't wait too long.

For example, if you buy a house two quarters into an economic recession, you will do pretty well on appreciation even over a horizon of a few years. You'll certainly do better than you would by waiting two or more years to make sure that the expansion was underway. Similarly, if you understand that expansions—and increases in asset prices—don't go on forever, you can plan more realistically than if you believe that good times, and asset price bubbles, never end.

Many Industries Have a Cyclical Element

Some businesses—financial services, advertising, real estate, construction, retail, restaurants, travel, and magazine publishing—are sensitive to recessions. Yet these businesses tend to do quite well in expansions, particularly in vigorous expansions. Industries less affected by recessions, such as consumer packaged goods; food; beverages; and gas, electric, and other utilities are also less affected by expansions.

It is essential that you understand the relationship between your industry and the business cycle.

Separate Emotions from Economics

As you know, issues of economics can become emotionally charged. This often occurs by design. For instance, by playing on voters' emotions, politicians with economic agendas—on the right and the left—manipulate people who don't understand the economics of a situation. This lack of understanding extends to the voters' own stake in many issues, and politicians know it. So they appeal to voters' emotions when the economics don't argue for their policies.

THE REAL WORLD

The people who emphasize the emotional aspects of a business arrangement— the people who say, "Trust me," instead of signing a contract—are usually the people who have the upper hand economically. In such situations, always insist on securing your economic interests and on conducting business in a business-like manner.

This happens in business situations as well. We sometimes allow ourselves to be fooled—or fool ourselves—into ignoring economic realities in favor of emotions such as hope, pride, or trust. For example, when losses start to mount, many investors cannot admit they invested incorrectly and simply sell the stock. Worse, many employees fail to understand that the employer/employee relationship is ruled by economics. It's easy for some employees to become emotionally attached to employers. These people find themselves shocked when they are permanently laid off or have their health-insurance benefits reduced after years of loyal service. I realize that some companies protect their employees, but they are in the minority.

Impact of Economics on Business Decisions

In general, consider the following moves, particularly when your industry has a cyclical element:

- Expand your business during an economic expansion, but avoid buying or building based on the assumption that the recovery will last forever. Ask yourself, "What if a recession arrives in 12 months?" If you can finance the expansion through a downturn, proceed (with caution). If not, pull back a bit on your plans. Many companies could have avoided bankruptcy by basing their plans on conservative, rather than optimistic, assumptions.

- When a recession hits, don't wait too long before cutting your costs. Trying to keep people on board when you can't afford them may endanger the entire business.

- Borrow when interest rates are low, and, unless it's short-term, try to lock in the rate for the life of the loan.

- If you're an employee, realize that you may be vulnerable to layoffs and carefully manage your personal finances. Most people in advertising, for instance, understand the cyclical nature of the industry. They try to make themselves as valuable as they can so they minimize the chance of being laid off, but if it occurs, they don't take it (too) personally and they are prepared financially.

- If you want to enter a cyclical industry as an entrepreneur or employee, don't let its cyclical nature keep you out, even if you are trying to enter during a downturn. If the industry or company is a solid one, it will be around when the next expansion arrives.

ECONOTIP

Smart business people carefully monitor their customers' sales, changes in expenses, issues with employees, and areas such as debt levels and age of plant and equipment. Really smart business people also monitor their customers' customers in the same way. That's because if your customers are serving growing, financially sound customers, then you probably are, too. If they aren't, watch out.

Personal Business and Economics

Several concepts central to economics can enrich your life if you apply them to major personal decisions. I am not saying that every decision should be ruled by economic considerations. In fact, often the best way to generate a great financial outcome is to make the decision based on nonfinancial considerations. Choice of career is a good example. But often, economic considerations don't receive the weight they deserve in a decision.

Education and Skills Training

Education is often called an investment in yourself, and two concepts from economics clearly bear this out. The first is the concept of human capital. Human capital enables an economy—or an individual—to produce more goods and services and higher-value goods and services. People increase their own human capital—their ability to produce more and higher-value goods and services—by increasing their knowledge and skills through education and training.

The second concept is returns to education. As we discussed in Chapter 10, the returns to education are extremely high and, over an entire career, they really add up. In general, high school graduates can expect to earn an average of $1.2 million over their working lives, but graduates of a four-year college will earn 75 percent more, an average of $2.1 million. That $900,000 difference represents a healthy return on the four years and $80,000 to $160,000 spent on tuition, books, room, and board.

Training also enables a person to make more money. The technical skills provided by training enable high school graduates to add more value and earn more income. They also give college graduates greater flexibility in the job market, particularly as emerging technologies demand new skills even of established workers.

Starting a Business

The option of starting a business as a career move appeals to more people than ever. This is partly a result of the demise of the social contract that existed between large companies and their employees from the 1940s through the 1970s. That contract stated that if an employee did his or her job well, the company would keep them on board and provide retirement benefits. That state of affairs unraveled in the 1980s and 1990s. The high unemployment of the 2000s recession also reminded people how vulnerable they can be when they rely on employers for their incomes.

Therefore, many people have set up shop for themselves. From the economic standpoint, the individual starting a business must understand that being an entrepreneur differs from being an employee. Remember the role of the entrepreneur? It is to organize the factors of production, to take risks and develop new products and services to serve new needs (or old needs in new ways), and to make a profit. An entrepreneur needs a business plan and needs to think like an owner, not an employee. This is true even for an entrepreneur in a one-person business.

Think in terms of supply and demand. Think about the market dynamics that affect your product or service. Think about ways of adding value to inputs, pricing of outputs, fixed versus variable costs, costs per unit, marginal cost per unit, and sources of profits above and beyond your salary. Few entrepreneurs think deeply about the economics of going into business, which is one reason that 90 percent of all businesses fail within 5 years.

ECONOTIP

If you consider going into business for yourself, be sure you have the motivation and self-discipline it requires. Then be sure you have a business model—a way of actually selling and delivering a product or a service that people will pay for—that you can successfully implement. Plan carefully, particularly the financial aspects, and get all the advice that you can.

One good starting point would be *The Complete Idiot's Guide to Starting Your Own Business, Fifth Edition,* by Ed Paulson.

Home Buying

The housing price bubble of 2002–2007, and the subsequent subprime mortgage crisis, showed that people can even botch up an investment as surefire as real estate. Actually, it was the notion that a home is not just an investment but a potential jackpot that got so many people into trouble. Much of the bubble was actually driven by speculative purchases, financed with cheap money, that were made in anticipation of flipping the house in a year or two (or even less).

When mortgage professionals are making loans with no income verification, and when they have the ability to resell bad loans along with good loans, then the greediest mortgage professionals and homebuyers will take advantage of the situation. But, as we saw, the situation could not continue.

Given that the bubble burst and the U.S. housing market is, as I write this, still in recovery, we can assume that the fundamentals of the residential (and commercial) real estate markets will reassert themselves. Those fundamentals, of course, rest upon supply and demand and the pricing mechanism. In the 2000s, demand became distorted, artificially inflated by cheap money and by the recruitment of new, previously unqualified buyers. That led to overbuilding and oversupply and, ultimately, to the housing bust, particularly in highly desirable areas or rapidly growing areas, such as Miami, California, and Las Vegas.

With the return to fundamentals, your home-buying decisions should rest upon the most basic consideration—where you would like to live—but should also, to some extent, factor in other economic considerations. For example, I personally wouldn't move to an area just because it was growing rapidly or had good economic prospects, but I would avoid one with poor long-term economic prospects. A home is an investment, and a home in an area with poor long-term economic prospects will generally appreciate at a lower rate than one in a growing area.

Infrastructure is another key consideration in home buying. For instance, a home in a community known for superior schools is almost always a good investment. Other factors worth considering include job opportunities, accessible transportation, nearby universities, cultural and recreational opportunities, and the socioeconomic profile of the population. Regarding the latter, a comparable house in a desirable community will almost always hold its value better and appreciate more than a similar one in a less-desirable community.

That said, it's important not to overpay. As we saw in the housing price bubble, it's quite possible that home prices are becoming inflated when the price of homes in an area are outstripping rental prices. The sales price of housing reflects the value of the building as shelter and as an investment. The rental prices more accurately reflect the pure shelter value.

One way to judge this relationship is to look at the ratio of home prices to annual rents. You can calculate this nationwide or for a local area. Over the past 60 years, this ratio has risen substantially, from about 9 in the 1940s to 17 in 2000 to 20 in 2005 at about the height of the housing bubble, according to U.S. Census data reported by MSN SmartMoney. In general, the ratio should be approximately 16. That means, for instance, that a home with a sales price of $500,000 and an annual rent of $30,000 ($2,500 a month) is priced about right (because 500,000 ÷ 30,000 = 16.7). At a sales price of $600,000, the ratio would be 20 and the house could be considered overpriced.

In general, American families tend to prefer owning rather than renting. However, it is not always the best deal from the economic standpoint, particularly when you factor in time and money expended on maintenance and all of your carrying costs, including interest on the mortgage. Of course, that mortgage interest is tax deductible, and in that way home ownership is subsidized by the U.S. government.

THE REAL WORLD

The decision to buy or own your home is a major one, but many people make it on autopilot. That's because the advantages of ownership, particularly tax deductibility of mortgage interest and the prospect of long-term price appreciation, appear so strong. But you are paying that interest, which might not be the case if your landlord owns the building outright, and the price appreciation does not always equal that of stocks and mutual funds, which require no maintenance and are far easier to sell.

I am not a real estate professional, so I am not dispensing professional advice here. But I am saying that before going to open houses and making an offer on a condo or house, consider the larger economic aspects of the decision.

Borrowing and Investing

The United States truly is a culture of debt. I say this not just because consumers and the government are carrying so much debt relative to their incomes and revenues, but also because of what the debt is financing. In general, businesses use debt more wisely than consumers and the government.

What is debt financing in the United States? Mortgage debt is financing the purchase of homes. That's a good use of debt. A home is a long-term asset, and thus it should be financed with long-term debt. Even an auto loan makes sense because the loan is paid off over the life of the car. You use the home or the car as you pay it off.

Consider the difference when you finance a vacation, a lavish restaurant meal, or tickets to a Broadway play on a credit card. If you pay the total amount of the debt off when the credit card statement arrives, that's wonderful. Your interest expense will be minimal, even zero on some cards. But if you take months or years to pay off that vacation, meal, or play, you are not matching the term of the debt to the life of the asset being financed. You are paying for an asset (to use the term loosely) that you have long since consumed.

Here's the worst part: you're paying an interest rate of two to three times the rate for a mortgage or auto loan. Consider the cruel irony of paying a higher rate for what is supposed to be a short-term loan. The economics are so unfavorable that credit card debt is to consumers' financial health as cigarette smoking is to their physical health—it's deadly.

THE REAL WORLD

It is possible that the U.S. culture of debt may be changing in the wake of the Great Recession. For one thing, many people found their debt harder to repay when their incomes dropped due to job loss or reduced opportunities. For another, the lost value on investments and real estate reduces people's wealth, which encourages them to pay down their debts. Finally, consumption of luxury goods, large vehicles and homes, and expensive vacations and restaurant meals has fallen. Many people are bound to realize these are not necessities and not worth going into debt over.

So rule number one is to match the term of a loan to the life of the asset being financed—and understand that a restaurant meal is not an asset. Pay for services with cash and checks (or pay off your monthly credit card balance), and borrow only to finance long-term assets. These include houses and autos, and items such as major appliances and computers.

Rule number two is to obtain the best interest rate possible. The interest a household pays on a loan is often largely unrelated to its creditworthiness. In other words, if you qualify for a loan at a given lender, you will usually pay a rate very similar to that which other borrowers pay that lender, even if you have a better credit record. Consumer credit is a numbers game, and the lenders have limited time and operational resources for considering differences among their borrowers—particularly if they'll earn a lower interest rate on the loan as a result.

I'm not saying that a good credit score doesn't help. I'm saying that timing and type of loan are generally more important in securing a low rate. Timing means making major purchases when interest rates are low or sellers are hungry. If you buy and borrow at the height of the market for *anything*, you will pay more than you will if you buy when demand is low. This is most dramatically evident when it comes to investing in financial assets.

Investing Economically

In a world where many investors barely examine the financial statements of the companies they invest in, it may seem quixotic to suggest that investors consider economics. Yet an awareness of economic fundamentals and of the business cycle can help you avoid problems and, perhaps, to capitalize on certain situations.

I've already discussed this as it relates to housing. When it comes to investments, knowledge of the business cycle and of how households, businesses, governments, and investors behave can help you—particularly when it comes to timing your entry into or exit from an investment.

For instance, there were (a few) fund managers who realized in the mid-2000s that stocks had reached a cyclical peak and got their clients out of the market. Others (and in some cases, the same ones) realized that a move into gold would be smart. Of course, the savviest real estate investors got out of the housing market when they saw that it had indeed become a bubble.

ECONOTIP

If you're investing long-term in a stock, examine the fundamentals of the company. Check out their financial statements, specifically the annual report issued by the company, which is usually available on their website. The 10-k report, filed with the SEC by publicly traded companies, provides similar information but in greater depth.

Although I am not an investment advisor and am not dispensing investment advice, as a fellow investor I do have a few suggestions that may guide you when investing in stocks.

First, watch out for companies with heavy debt loads, especially if the debt was used to finance speculative assets or assets (such as acquisitions) that have not proven to be profitable. If the debt payments are not being financed by the assets—with some left over for profits—then the company's profits may erode. (I say *may* because other corporate divisions may be profitable enough to offset the effects of the bad acquisition.)

Second, if you invest in bonds, you *must* understand the yield curve (explained in Chapter 22) and the workings of the bond markets in relation to both the stock market and the interest rate environment. In general, bond prices fall as stock prices rise, and vice versa. This occurs because money moves out of stocks and into bonds, or out of bonds and into stocks, depending on the relative strength of each market.

Also, when bond prices rise, interest rates fall, and when bond prices fall, interest rates rise. In that way, the selling price of the bond is adjusted by the market to reflect the yield that the bond should be earning in the prevailing interest-rate environment. For instance, if a $10,000 bond pays interest at 5 percent, that means that the holder of the bond is paid $500 a year. If the price of the bond rises to $11,000, the yield falls to about 4.5 percent, which equals $500 divided by $11,000. Similarly, if the price of the bond falls to $9,000, then the yield rises to about 5.6 percent, which equals $500 divided by $9,000. The company that issued the bond always pays the same amount. The yield that the amount represents, however, depends on the price the holder paid for the bond.

Third, for any investment, you must understand your investment horizon and the risks to the economy and to the financial markets over that horizon. For example, recessions will occasionally come, and a severe one could hobble stock prices for several years. Will you want (or need) to withdraw funds during such a period? If so, how do you plan to deal with that situation?

Finally, although it's good to understand where you are in the business cycle and to buy during stock market troughs and economic recessions, I emphasize that trying to time the peaks and troughs is generally judged to be a waste of time, or worse. Even professional money managers have a very poor record at it.

ECONOTIP

Dollar-cost averaging is a sensible alternative to trying to time stock market peaks and troughs. Dollar-cost averaging calls for picking several stocks or mutual funds that you believe in as long-term investments and investing a fixed amount of money in them regularly (say every month or every quarter), regardless of where the market or the securities are in their cycle.

This way, you buy more shares when the price of the stock or fund is low than when it is high. The average cost of the stock or fund will be lower than if you purchased a fixed number of shares every month or quarter. This technique is also called the constant dollar plan.

The best long-term investment strategy is to understand the amount of risk that you can accept, and then to choose securities or mutual funds that reflect that risk and that will perform at least as well as the economy as it continues its long-term growth trajectory. (This doesn't mean that you can't set 10 percent of your portfolio aside for flyers on riskier investments.)

Economics and Citizenship: Understanding the Issues

Economics may come in handiest when trying to understand what politicians are saying—and not saying. The awful truth, which almost no politician will utter, is that goods, services, or transfer payments from the government must be paid for with tax revenues and that individual taxpayers are the major source of those revenues.

So when a candidate or an official says that he can improve education without increasing taxes or reducing other government services, you will know that it can't be done. When he says he can reduce taxes but doesn't mention all the debt that will pile up as a result, you'll know he's leaving things out.

THE REAL WORLD

Tens of millions of middle-class U.S. voters have supported policies that have actually hurt them economically. Many policies, supported by both parties, moved the share of national income from the lower 80 percent of the population to the top 20 percent (or top 5 or 1 percent!).

Politicians never discuss this. Instead they discuss emotionally charged social or moral issues, which is quite cynical considering their personal lives, and promise tax cuts with no reduction in government services, which is dishonest. Yet voters continually reward these behaviors.

Most issues in government today revolve around economic realities, and the more in touch with those realities we are, the better we can decide where we want to go as a nation and what we are willing to pay to get there.

The Least You Need to Know

- The business cycle is a permanent fixture of a market economy because people are free to make their own production and purchasing decisions. Sooner or later those decisions create a mismatch between supply and demand and savings and investment.

- Attempting to time the peak or trough of the business cycle or the stock market consistently is impossible. Sophisticated economists in government and the investment community, armed with the best analytical tools, cannot do it.

- Education and training builds human capital for individuals as well as for nations. They also yield high returns in dollars and in the quality of life for an individual or a nation.

- When borrowing money, match the term of the loan to the life of the asset being purchased and obtain the best possible interest rate. This means not using credit cards (unless you pay the full balance each month) and always paying for services with cash or a check.

- Bond prices fall as stock prices rise, and vice versa, because money moves out of stocks and into bonds, or out of bonds and into stocks, depending on the relative strength of each market.

- When you hear a politician talking about taxes, spending, or other economic policies, listen for what he or she is leaving out—and then fill in the blanks.

Additional Resources

Associations

Agricultural & Applied Economics Association
555 East Wells Street, Suite 1100
Milwaukee, WI 53202
Phone: 414-918-3190
Fax: 414-276-3349
www.aaea.org

American Economic Association
2014 Broadway Suite 305
Nashville, TN 37203
Phone: 615-322-2595
Fax: 615-343-7590
www.vanderbilt.edu/AEA

The American Real Estate & Urban Economics Association
PO Box 9958
Richmond, VA 23228
Phone: 1-866-273-8321
Fax: 1-877-273-8323
www.areuea.org

Association of Environmental and Resource Economists
13006 Peaceful Terrace
Silver Spring, MD 20904
Phone: 301-879-4778
www.aere.org

Canadian Association for Business Economics
PO Box 828 Station B
Ottawa, Ontario
K1P 5P9
Phone: 613-238-4831
www.cabe.ca

International Association for Energy Economics
28790 Chagrin Boulevard Suite 350
Cleveland, OH 44122
Phone: 216-464-5365
www.iaee.org

International Health Economics Association
2 White Pine Ridge
Hubley, Nova Scotia
Canada
Phone: 902-461-4432
Fax: 416-352-1395
www.healtheconomics.org

National Association for Business Economics
1233 20th Street, NW #505
Washington, DC 20036
Phone: 202-463-6223
Fax: 202-463-6239
www.nabe.com

Government Agencies

Bureau of Economic Analysis
1441 L Street, NW
Washington, DC 20230
Phone: 202-606-6900
www.bea.gov

Bureau of Labor Statistics
Postal Square Building
2 Massachusetts Avenue, NE
Washington, DC 20212-0001
Phone: 202-691-5200
www.bls.gov

European Union
Delegation of the European Commission to the United States
2175 K Street, NW
Washington, DC 20037
Phone: 202-862-9500
Fax: 202-429-1766
europa.eu/index_en.htm

Federal Reserve System
20th Street and Constitution Avenue, NW
Washington, DC 20551
Phone: 202-452-3000
www.federalreserve.gov

U.S. Agency for International Development
(Information Center)
Ronald Reagan Building
Washington, DC 20523-1000
Phone: 202-712-4810
Fax: 202-216-3524
www.usaid.gov

U.S. Census Bureau
Postal address:
U.S. Census Bureau
Washington, DC 20233
Street address:
U.S. Census Bureau
4600 Silver Hill Road
Suitland, MD 20746
Phone: 301-495-4700
www.census.gov

U.S. Department of Commerce
1401 Constitution Avenue, NW
Washington, DC 20230
202-482-2000
www.commerce.gov

U.S. Department of Labor
Frances Perkins Building
200 Constitution Avenue, NW
Washington, DC 20210
Phone: 1-866-487-2365 (1-866-4-USA-DOL)
www.dol.gov

United States Department of the Treasury
1500 Pennsylvania Avenue, NW
Washington, DC 20220
Phone: 202-622-2000
www.ustreas.gov

World Bank
1818 H Street, NW
Washington, DC 20433
Phone: 202-473-1000
Fax: 202-477-6391
www.worldbank.org

World Trade Organization
Centre William Rappard
Rue de Lausanne 154
CH-1211 Geneva 21
Switzerland
Phone: 41 (0)22 739 51 11
Fax: 41 (0)22 731 42 06
www.wto.org

Economic Information Companies

The Conference Board
845 Third Avenue
New York, NY 10022-6679
Phone: 212-759-0900
Fax: 212-980-7014
www.conference-board.org

IHS Global Insight Inc.
24 Hartwell Avenue
Lexington, MA 02421-3103
Phone: 781-301-9100
www.ihsglobalinsight.com

Moody's Economy.com
121 North Walnut Street Suite 500
West Chester, PA 19380-3166
Phone: 610-235-5299
Fax: 610-235-5302
www.economy.com

Books

- Friedman, Milton. *Capitalism and Freedom, Fortieth Anniversary Edition.* University of Chicago Press, Chicago, IL, 2002.

- Hazlitt, Henry. *Economics in One Lesson, Fiftieth Anniversary Edition.* Laissez Faire Books, Gilbert, AZ, 2008.

- Heilbroner, Robert L. *The Worldly Philosophers: The Lives, Times, and Ideas of the Great Economic Thinkers, Seventh Edition.* Touchstone/Simon & Schuster, New York, NY, 1999.

- Heilbroner, Robert L., and Lester C. Thurow. *Economics Explained.* Touchstone Books/Simon & Schuster, New York, NY, 1998.

- Leavitt, Stephen D., and Stephen J. Dubner. *Freakonomics: A Rogue Economist Explores the Hidden Side of Everything.* Harper Perennial, New York, NY, 2009.

- Parkin, Michael. *Economics, Eighth Edition.* Addison-Wesley, Reading, MA, 1999.

- Samuelson, Paul A., and William D. Nordhaus. *Economics, Nineteenth Edition.* McGraw-Hill, New York, NY, 2009.

- Slavin, Stephen L. *Economics: A Self-Teaching Guide.* Wiley & Sons, New York, NY, 1988.

- Sowell, Thomas. *Basic Economics: A Common Sense Guide to the Economy, Third Edition.* Basic Books, New York, NY, 2007.

- Staff of *The Economist* magazine. *The Economist Guide to Economic Indicators, Sixth Edition.* Bloomberg Press, New York, NY, 2007.

- Wheelan, Charles J. *Naked Economics: Undressing the Dismal Science.* W.W. Norton & Company, New York, NY, 2010.

Index

Numbers

E

G

J

N